Language Learning Environments

SECOND LANGUAGE ACQUISITION

Series Editors: **Professor David Singleton**, *University of Pannonia, Hungary* and Fellow Emeritus, *Trinity College, Dublin, Ireland* and **Associate Professor Simone E. Pfenninger**, *University of Salzburg, Austria*

This series brings together titles dealing with a variety of aspects of language acquisition and processing in situations where a language or languages other than the native language is involved. Second language is thus interpreted in its broadest possible sense. The volumes included in the series all offer in their different ways, on the one hand, exposition and discussion of empirical findings and, on the other, some degree of theoretical reflection. In this latter connection, no particular theoretical stance is privileged in the series; nor is any relevant perspective – sociolinguistic, psycholinguistic, neurolinguistic, etc. – deemed out of place. The intended readership of the series includes final-year undergraduates working on second language acquisition projects, postgraduate students involved in second language acquisition research, and researchers, teachers and policymakers in general whose interests include a second language acquisition component.

All books in this series are externally peer-reviewed.

Full details of all the books in this series and of all our other publications can be found on http://www.multilingual-matters.com, or by writing to Multilingual Matters, St Nicholas House, 31-34 High Street, Bristol BS1 2AW, UK.

SECOND LANGUAGE ACQUISITION: 147

Language Learning Environments

Spatial Perspectives on SLA

Phil Benson

MULTILINGUAL MATTERS
Bristol • Blue Ridge Summit

DOI https://doi.org/10.21832/BENSON4900
Library of Congress Cataloging in Publication Data
A catalog record for this book is available from the Library of Congress.
Names: Benson, Phil - author.
Title: Language Learning Environments: Spatial Perspectives on SLA/Phil Benson.
Description: Bristol, UK; Blue Ridge Summit: Multilingual Matters, 2021. | Series: Second Language Acquisition: 147 | Includes bibliographical references and index. | Summary: "This book is the first in-depth examination of the application of theories of space to issues of second language learning. The author outlines a new conceptual framework for researching SLA that centres on the idea of 'language learning environments' and demonstrates that where people learn languages is equally as important as how they do so"—Provided by publisher.
Identifiers: LCCN 2021004709 (print) | LCCN 2021004710 (ebook) | ISBN 9781788924894 (paperback) | ISBN 9781788924900 (hardback) | ISBN 9781788924917 (pdf) | ISBN 9781788924924 (epub) | ISBN 9781788924931 (kindle edition)
Subjects: LCSH: Second language acquisition. | Language and languages—Study and teaching—Methodology. | School environment.
Classification: LCC P118.2 .B465 2021 (print) | LCC P118.2 (ebook) | DDC 401/.93—dc23 LC record available at https://lccn.loc.gov/2021004709
LC ebook record available at https://lccn.loc.gov/2021004710

British Library Cataloguing in Publication Data
A catalogue entry for this book is available from the British Library.

ISBN-13: 978-1-78892-490-0 (hbk)
ISBN-13: 978-1-78892-489-4 (pbk)

Multilingual Matters
UK: St Nicholas House, 31-34 High Street, Bristol BS1 2AW, UK.
USA: NBN, Blue Ridge Summit, PA, USA.

Website: www.multilingual-matters.com
Twitter: Multi_Ling_Mat
Facebook: https://www.facebook.com/multilingualmatters
Blog: www.channelviewpublications.wordpress.com

Copyright © 2021 Phil Benson.

All rights reserved. No part of this work may be reproduced in any form or by any means without permission in writing from the publisher.

The policy of Multilingual Matters/Channel View Publications is to use papers that are natural, renewable and recyclable products, made from wood grown in sustainable forests. In the manufacturing process of our books, and to further support our policy, preference is given to printers that have FSC and PEFC Chain of Custody certification. The FSC and/or PEFC logos will appear on those books where full certification has been granted to the printer concerned.

Typeset by Deanta Global Publishing Services, Chennai, India.
Printed and bound in the UK by the CPI Books Group Ltd.
Printed and bound in the US by NBN.

Contents

	Figures	vi
	Acknowledgements	vii
1	The *Where* of Second Language Learning	1
2	Theories of Space	11
3	Linguistics and the Spatiality of Language	37
4	Language-Bearing Assemblages	65
5	Language Learning Environments	91
6	Space and SLA Research	119
	References	141
	Index	155

Figures

Figure 2.1	Schiphol Airport, Amsterdam	10
Figure 3.1	Standardisation and spatialisation. The *Vocabolario degli Accademici della Crusca*	36
Figure 4.1	A multilingual language-bearing assemblage in motion, Kennedy Town, Hong Kong	64
Figure 5.1	In the year 2000: At School, by Jean-Marc Côté (1901)	90
Figure 6.1	A heritage language learner's experience of learning Macedonian in Sydney	118

Acknowledgements

This book was conceived and partly written during a six-month overseas study programme in 2018, which was funded by the Faculty of Human Sciences at Macquarie University. I am grateful to Macquarie University for providing me with the opportunity to get the book started. I am also grateful to my colleagues in the Linguistics Department and the Multilingualism Research Centre at Macquarie for helping provide an environment in which new ideas can flourish. Special thanks go to co-researchers Alice Chik, Jim Forrest, Phil Chappell and Lynda Yates, who have contributed more than they may imagine to the ideas in this book. Special thanks also to Mayumi Kashima, whose masters and doctoral work prompted me to explore the idea of language learning environments in more depth.

I would like to acknowledge several academics with whom I had stimulating conversations during my overseas studies programme visit to the United Kingdom: especially, Terry Lamb, Yaron Matras, Anna Pauwels and Li Wei, as well as Steven Thorne, Diane Larsen-Freeman and Sarah Mercer whose comments on conference presentations have been critical but extremely valuable. I also want to acknowledge an enormous academic debt to the late Leo van Lier with whom I was privileged to spend a good deal of time during 2010 and 2011. Although this book is critical of some of Leo's ideas on the ecology of language learning, I hope that I am carrying them in directions he would have found interesting. Lastly, many thanks to Anna Roderick, Laura Longworth and the Multilingual Matters team for taking on this project and seeing it through to its conclusion.

1 The *Where* of Second Language Learning

> Being Italian, for me, begins and ends with the fact that I speak and write in the Italian language.... I am therefore Italian, completely and with pride. But if I could, I would descend into all languages and let myself be permeated by them all. Even the terrible Google Translate consoles me. We can be much more than we happen to be.
>
> Ferrante, 2019: 23–24

In the 1970s, second language acquisition (SLA) researchers turned the spotlight of second language learning research away from the forms and structures of language and pointed it at the language learning process. As a consequence, we now know a great deal about both *what* second language learners learn and *how* they learn it. For some, who emphasised the importance of investigating the learning process in its social contexts, SLA did not go far enough. Following the 'social turn' of the 1990s and 2000s (Block, 2003), we now know much more about the *who* and *why* of language learning. However, the social context of language learning is now very often reduced to a context of person-to-person interaction. As a result, much that is of interest to SLA researchers in the space of the human and non-human world is left out of account. Using the concept of language learning environments to capture the full range of interactions between language learners and the worlds in which they lead their lives, this book aims to ground the idea of context in space in order to shine the spotlight on the *where* of language learning.

Grounding Context in Space

Why is it important to ground context in space? The most compelling reasons, I believe, are connected to globalisation and mobility, the range and variety of settings in which language learning now takes place and the globalisation of SLA research itself. Globalisation and second language learning now go hand in hand (Kramsch, 2014). This is most evident in the influence of population movements on second language learning since the early 1960s. International migration, education and tourism, all of which have grown exponentially over this period, have generated demands for second language learning that have been met by a rapidly growing second language teaching and learning industry in the public and private sectors. Social mobility, often associated with internal migration from rural to urban areas, is contributing much to this demand. In many parts of the world, second language learning 'at home' is seen as holding the potential for future mobility overseas. There are also the stretched circuits of commodity production and distribution, in which products and processes cross language barriers and take on an increasingly global character. Lastly, the globalisation of information technologies and communication media contributes to the fluidity with which knowledge and ideas circulate around the world, adding to demand for second language learning. The effects of globalisation on second language learning are thus mediated by the accelerated mobilities of people, things and information. Everyone and everything, including language itself, seem to be on the move. One of the challenges for SLA research is to understand how second language learning practices and processes intersect with these mobilities in an increasingly globalised world.

One of the effects of globalisation is a growing awareness that it is multilingualism, rather than monolingualism, that is the norm for language knowledge and use (May, 2014). The majority of the world's population is multilingual and the major cities of the world are increasingly 'multilingual cities' (King & Carson, 2016). The languages spoken in multilingual cities are now counted in the hundreds, with the effect that the few 'world languages' of the past are now joined by a multiplicity of languages that are global in the sense that they are dispersed across the major cities of the world. The new focus on multilingualism in SLA research is leading us to look at second language learning in new ways, notably as a matter of 'becoming multilingual' (Ortega, 2014). It also raises questions about the boundaries between languages and the spatial dimensions of translanguaging (Canagarajah, 2018; Li, 2018). Multilingualism and translanguaging tend to be associated with spatial mobility, while monolingualism is associated with immobility. But the globalisation of second language learning also has uneven local effects, with important implications for the question of who gets to learn which languages where.

The uneven effects of globalisation on language learning are well documented, although more so in the field of sociolinguistics than in SLA (Block, 2010; Blommaert, 2010; Pennycook, 2007). The effects of second language learning on globalisation are less well understood. If second language learners around the world were to 'down tools', globalisation would grind to a halt. However improbable it may seem, the idea of a language learners' 'strike' highlights the sense in which globalisation and second language learning are mutually dependent. Perhaps it is wrong to think of this mutual dependence in terms of influences and effects. If globalisation is a multilayered construct of relatively independent economic, political, cultural, biological and geological flows (Appadurai, 1996; Bauman, 1998; Beck, 2000), the flow of languages through second language learning could be seen as one of the less examined layers of globalisation. No matter where it takes place, second language learning is now woven into the multiple flows of globalisation and the myriad uses of space that they entail.

Along with the globalisation of the practice of second language learning comes a heightened diversity in the spaces in which language learning takes place. Interest in these spaces first focused on the language classroom (Allwright & Bailey, 1991; van Lier, 1988). Defining the classroom as 'the gathering, for a given period of time, of two or more persons (one of whom generally assumes the role of instructor) for the purpose of language learning', van Lier (1988: 47) highlighted the diversity within the classroom setting. Bailey (2006: 8) argued that 'the classroom is the setting for and the object of investigation in language classroom research'. Yet, although classroom research succeeded in moving SLA out of the laboratory and into settings where language learning actually takes place, it was less successful in establishing the variety of these settings as an object of investigation. Language learning beyond the classroom has proved a more fruitful field for investigation of the spaces of language learning, evolving over the years from studies of institutional settings such as language laboratories, self-access centres and computer laboratories (Egbert & Hanson-Smith, 1999; Gardner & Miller, 1999; Little, 2015) to studies of wider offline and online worlds of second language learning and use (Benson & Reinders, 2011; Hellermann *et al.*, 2019; Lai, 2017; Nunan & Richards, 2015; Reinders & Benson, 2017; Sockett, 2014; Toffoli, 2020). But in this area, also, more attention has been given to language learning processes than to the spaces in which they take place (Benson, 2011a).

People who achieve high degrees of second language proficiency typically learn and use languages in multiple settings over a prolonged period of time. They learn both in language classrooms and in a variety of institutional and non-institutional settings beyond the classroom. The distribution of their time and effort across these settings also changes over time. We are, thus, coming to appreciate the complexity of the *where* of language learning at both global and local levels, and in relation to time. In addition, because people rarely learn second languages in a single space, we need to attend to the configurations of spaces in which they learn, or the ways in which learners assemble the *where* of language learning in space and over time. Globally, the *where* of second language learning is about who gets to learn second languages in various parts of the world, which languages they learn, their learning purposes and the competencies they develop. Locally, it is about the ways in which individuals use spatially located resources for purposes of second language learning. Conventionally, individual differences in language learning relate to biography (language background and languages learned, age, gender, educational level, socioeconomic status, purpose, etc.). In the context of globalisation, the *where* of second language learning is now emerging as one the most important factors of difference that influence second language learning outcomes.

The globalisation of second language learning also involves the globalisation of SLA research, which is now, more than ever, an enterprise in which researchers from every corner of the world play a part. There is still a preponderance of work written by researchers from the wealthier English-speaking regions of the world in published research. Nevertheless, research increasingly reflects the diversity within second language learning itself. There is also a corresponding scepticism about the universality of research findings, as the question of where a study was conducted becomes crucial to interpretations of its wider significance. This scepticism involves a heightened sense of the importance of local context, and to speak of *local* context is to begin to ground context in space. There are also uncertainties surrounding this enhanced awareness of the local specificity of research findings and their practical implications. As Kramsch (2014: 296) argues, globalisation has changed the world of language learning 'to such an extent that language teachers are no longer sure of what they are supposed to teach'. Our awareness of the diversity of spatial contexts to which theories must apply if they are to be truly universal means that many SLA researchers are abandoning the certainties of universality for more localised understandings. A reflexive awareness of the local specificity of our own teaching and learning situations contributes to an interest in the *where* of language learning and space as a theoretical and practical concept for SLA research. This book attempts to make sense of the theory that might underpin a better understanding of the spatial dimensions of second language learning and its potential for application in SLA research.

Contents of the Book

Chapter 2 introduces a body of work, under the heading of critical spatial theory, that has had considerable influence in geography and the social sciences since the 1980s (Cresswell, 2015; Hubbard *et al.*, 2004; Low, 2016). This work underpins the concept of language learning environments that lies at the heart of this book. The theory at issue is critical in that it confronts what I will call an 'objects-*in*-space' view of the world; a view in which space is seen as the container of, or background to, things and events. This is a largely taken-for-granted view not only in everyday life but also in the social sciences, where we are accustomed to think of things happening 'in' space. Against this view, critical spatial theory adopts what I will call an 'objects-*as*-space' conception of the world, in which space consists of, rather than contains, the objects that comprise it. One of the key ideas in Chapter 2 is that 'space matters' (Soja, 2009), that *'where* things happen is critical to knowing *how* and *why* they happen' (Wharf & Arias, 2009). There is a play on words in the phrase 'space matters'; space matters not only because it is important, but also because it is material, or physical as I prefer to describe it in this book.

The literature on spatial theory is vast and my treatment of it in Chapter 2 is selective and designed to support arguments I will develop later in the book. The perspective that I adopt is often called the 'production of space' perspective, which views space as the product of the social relations of production of its era. This view is Marxist in origin and involves the argument that capitalism has survived into the 21st century through a series of 'spatial fixes'. These include the production of urban space on a massive scale and the uneven development of the regions of the world (Harvey, 1982; Lefebvre, 1991). My argument adds to this view the idea that the production of language and languages is an integral aspect of the production of space on a global scale. The view of space that I adopt, however, is more postmodern than Marxist and emphasises the fragmentation, fluidity and heterogeneity of 21st-century space (Amin & Thrift, 2002; Massey, 2005). Chapter 2 also considers the alternative, humanistic 'construction of place' perspective, which counters the objects-*in*-space view with an emphasis on the human transformation of empty space into meaningful place (Tuan, 1977). I find the production of space perspective especially helpful in thinking about the relationship of language learning environments around the world to currents in the global circulation of people, goods and information. The construction of place perspective is more helpful in thinking about language learners' construction of individualised environments from the raw materials of these wider environments.

Chapter 3 shifts the focus to the discipline of linguistics and its conception of the spatiality of language. It builds on an insight from the literature on the production of space that, although there is no empty space, space is often produced in the image of empty space. Modern linguistics, from which SLA derives its basic conception of the nature of language, has no explicit theory of the spatiality of language, of how language fits into space. But, I argue, it does work with an implicit conception of language as a self-contained, systemic object-*in*-space. Chapter 3 explores this view through two histories of emergence: first, the emergence of linguistics as an object in the disciplinary space of the social sciences and, second, the emergence of the idea of language and its internal systems, structures and networks. Lastly, I look at how the idea of the language system connects to a history of the physical production of languages as self-contained systems through the semiotic geometries of standardisation, grammars and dictionaries.

Chapter 4 begins the task of developing an alternative 'objects-*as*-space' view of language and SLA, by introducing two additional areas of theory: the new philosophies of object-oriented ontology (OOO) (Harman, 2018) and assemblage theory (DeLanda, 2016) and Urry's (2007) mobilities theory. The first task is to develop what I call a spatial ontology of language, or an understanding of how language exists spatially. In writing this book, OOO and assemblage theory have been helpful in two ways. The idea of a flat ontology, in which everything is an object and exists equally as an object, has helped me think beyond the limitations of a social view of SLA. Crucially, if everything is an object, human beings and language are also objects. We need not be constrained by the idea of an opposition between human and non-human entities, or the idea that language is an exclusively human phenomenon.

Assemblage theory has helped me think through the relation of language to the physicality of space. In assemblage theory, an assemblage is a complex object that has emergent properties that make it more than a simple aggregate of its component parts (think, for example, of the relation of water to its component parts, atoms of hydrogen and oxygen). I find assemblage theory helpful in thinking about how language, a non-physical object, is present in a space that is conceptualised as physical space. My argument is that language interacts with various physical objects to form what I call 'language-bearing assemblages'. These are, at a basic level, thought, speech and writing, and, at more complex levels, they include assemblages such as conversation and meetings, letters and notes, and technologically enhanced assemblages such as printed documents, audio and video recordings, and broadcast audio and speech. From this point of view, language is a non-physical object that can *only* be present in the space of the world as a component of physical language-bearing assemblages. And because the space of the world is now largely shaped by human activity, we live in a language-saturated world that is formed by the social production of space.

Urry (2007) can be given much of the credit for the current perception that we also live in a world of mobilities, of objects and assemblages in motion. The mobility of languages entails the idea that languages spread and come into contact with each other. If this spread and contact is explained at all, it is typically explained by the mobility of people. Chapter 4 draws on the idea of mobilities to explain how the wider circulation of language-bearing assemblages – people, goods and broadcast and digital information – puts language into motion on a global scale. I choose the term language-*bearing* assemblages to capture the sense in which language is already in motion as it takes on a physical form. Linking the circulation of language-bearing assemblages to DeLanda's (2016) understanding of the formation of social assemblages at various levels of scale (community, institution, city, region, nation), I argue that social assemblages and languages are mutually constitutive. The circulation of language-bearing assemblages *within* social assemblages transforms an undifferentiated language-saturated space into the geographically differentiated spaces of languages and language varieties. The circulation of language-bearing assemblages *across* large-scale social assemblages is the fundamental spatial circumstance for second language learning. Moreover, the extraordinarily complex patterns in the circulation of language-bearing assemblages produced by contemporary globalisation produce a corresponding complexity in these spatial circumstances, especially in the fragmented, fluid and heterogeneous spaces of multilingual cities around the world.

Chapter 5 outlines what I see as one possible framework for investigating the spatial circumstances of second language learning on the ground, in the spaces where second languages circulate and are learned. In this chapter, language-bearing assemblages are conceptualised as environmental resources for second language learning. I believe that ecological approaches to learning (Bronfenbrenner, 1979) and language learning (van Lier, 2004) provide a strong basis for understanding the *how* of language learning from an environmental perspective. However, I argue that these approaches are insufficiently explicit on the spatial character of the environment. In particular, the idea that second language learning resources are often *scarce* resources calls for more attention to the ways in which they get into language learning environments and how learners' access to them is shaped by their experiences and uses of space.

The framework that I propose discards the notion of context and, instead, uses the terms environment and setting to ground context in space (on the ways in which I use these terms, see below). It also involves two perspectives on language learning environments – an areal perspective in which the environment is viewed as a geographically demarcated area (e.g. a campus, a city or a region) and an individual perspective in which the environment is viewed as a configuration of settings assembled by an individual learner. Chapter 5 also discusses the multilingual city as a relevant areal unit and the place of online resources in language learning environments. Lastly, I touch on some issues related to inequities in second language learning that I believe can often be explained in terms of differences that arise from uneven patterns in the global distribution of second language learning resources.

For the most part, this book does not refer to the work of other SLA researchers who have addressed space in their work. This is largely for the sake of clarity in the argument that I want to develop. Chapter 6, however, includes summaries of relevant work by SLA researchers, some of which refers to sources on spatial theory that I cite in Chapter 2, and some which explores important issues of space with reference to other sources. Much of this work is closely aligned with the direction I propose. Chapter 6 also summarises some of my own research on language learning beyond the classroom, Hong Kong students studying languages abroad and international students studying English in Sydney, from which the idea of language learning environments emerged. In conclusion, I make suggestions pertinent to a research agenda on the *where* of second language learning, including topics and issues that call for further research and innovative research methodologies.

Some Key Terms

As the summary of its contents suggests, the chapters of this book are probably best read in the order they appear. The book takes the form of an argument in which the ideas in later chapters depend on those introduced in earlier chapters. However, I have also attempted to write each chapter so it is readable independently of the others. Readers who need to refer back to earlier chapters could do so by referring to the chapter summaries in this introductory chapter, which more or less summarises the argument of the book as a whole. The ideas introduced in this chapter may seem somewhat abstract. My task in the chapters that follow is to explain and exemplify these ideas to the extent that space allows. It remains for me to clarify the use of certain terms that may lead the reader astray.

In this book, second language learning refers to the learning of a language after a person has acquired one or more first languages in early childhood. This could be any language at all: English, Spanish, Chinese, Latin, Welsh, Esperanto or High Valyrian. Indeed, it seems important that the language learning environment concept should work for any member of the expanding range of languages that now participate in the world of second language learning and for any part of the world in which they are learned. Accordingly, I do not make a distinction between second language learning and additional or foreign language learning. Additional language learning would, perhaps, be the better term, but I have opted for second language learning in order to make the link to SLA research. SLA refers, here, both to the specialised field of largely experimental research that emerged around the journal *Studies in Second Language Acquisition* in the 1970s, and also to the broader field of second language study that is also known as 'applied linguistics'.

By an 'object' I mean more or less anything at all that can be said to exist: human or non-human, animate or inanimate, physical or non-physical. As the distinction between things, processes and events is really a matter of duration, processes and events are also treated as objects. 'Entities' might be a better term, but I use the word 'objects' in order to maintain a connection to OOO, which discusses the nature of objects in depth (Harman, 2018). An assemblage is a complex object made up of other objects (DeLanda, 2016). Because most objects are made up of other objects, most objects are assemblages. To this extent, the terms object and assemblage are more or less interchangeable. Language is an exception to this. For reasons I will explain in Chapter 4, I do not consider language to be an assemblage. Although one could say that language is made of words, one could also say that words are made of language. It is difficult to say, in fact, what language is 'made of'. Here, I see language as a non-physical object that only exists in the world in the form of physical assemblages such as thought, speech and writing.

I should also mention that I make a strong distinction between language and speech. I find that linguists often stumble over this distinction, treating language as if it were speech or speech as if it were language. Speech is often considered to be both the original and the most important form of language. Both of these claims are disputable, but the main point is that language and speech are two different things. Moreover, if language is too closely identified with speech, we are liable to slip into the highly questionable assumption that speech is the expression of thought, while writing is the transcription of speech. From the perspective I adopt, speech, thought and writing are three different kinds of assemblages. Language is a fourth object that is present in each of these assemblages, but it is also separable from them.

Last, 'environment', 'setting' and 'context' are often used interchangeably in SLA research. Some researchers also use 'context' in a similar sense to that in which I use 'environment' (e.g. Mercer, 2016; Ushioda, 2015). However, I want to discard the word 'context' altogether, because it is too spatially inexplicit to be of use. The context of second language learning could be anything from the language input that the learner reads or hears to the neoliberal world order. I prefer environment and setting as terms that can be made to refer more explicitly to space: hence the goal of 'grounding context in space'. The distinction between environment and setting will be explained in Chapter 5, but, in brief, an environment is an aggregate or configuration of settings. Essentially, a setting is one space, whereas an environment consists of multiple spaces that are related to each other either geographically or in the life of an individual.

Figure 2.1 Schiphol Airport, Amsterdam. 'Over the centuries the land had been regulated, cultivated and built on until the whole region was transformed into a geometrical pattern' (Sebald, 2002: 90) (Source: Google Maps)

2 Theories of Space

> To speak of 'producing' space sounds bizarre, so great is the sway still held by the idea that empty space is prior to whatever ends up filling it.
>
> Lefebvre, 1991: 15

In the 1990s, second language acquisition (SLA) researchers began to engage with a body of theory that has variously been called 'critical', 'social' or 'sociocultural' theory (Block, 1996; Firth & Wagner, 1997; Lantolf, 1996; Rampton, 1997). SLA researchers who had previously sought insight in work on linguistics, psycholinguistics and sociolinguistics were now reading work that was often only tangentially concerned with language. The 'social turn' in SLA (Block, 2003) had two major consequences. First, it introduced the idea that second language learning not only takes place in a social context, but it is also a social process. As a social process, language learning is not only influenced by context but it also contributes to the construction of the contexts in which it takes place. Language learning is part of the life of the world and it has a significant impact on lives, identities and social relations. Second, it established the importance of transdisciplinarity in SLA research. At first, socially oriented researchers had to argue for the introduction of new theories against those who insisted that SLA should be based on linguistics alone. Today, although there may be disagreement on the specific proposals of the Douglas Fir Group's (2016) socially oriented 'transdisciplinary framework' for SLA, few would argue against the principle of transdisciplinarity itself.

The aim of this chapter is to introduce SLA researchers to a body of work on critical spatial theory. This work is critical in the sense that it takes issue with what I will call an 'objects-*in*-space' conception of the world, the largely taken-for-granted view in which we think of space as 'empty' and of things happening 'in' space. Against this view, critical spatial theory largely adopts what I will call an 'objects-*as*-space' conception of the world, in which space consists of, rather than contains, the objects that comprise it. The literature on spatial theory is vast and my treatment of it in this chapter is selective and designed to support arguments I will develop in later chapters. The main themes that I want to explore concern the physicality and social production of space, the fragmentation and heterogeneity of postmodern space and the construction of place.

Some of the work considered in this chapter has been referenced in SLA studies that will be discussed in Chapter 6. But as short papers seldom afford room for in depth discussion of theory, I want to take the opportunity to lay out a more expansive account of the spatial theory that may be relevant to language learning research. Much of this work is written by geographers, but spatial theory is not the same thing as geographical theory. Geography has undergone its own 'spatial turn' as critical geographers have explored work on spatial theory by philosophers, psychologists, anthropologists and social theorists. Critical spatial theory has contributed much to transdisciplinary work on urbanisation, ecology, globalisation and mobility. It has also made significant inroads into the humanities and social sciences, where several interdisciplinary collections on space have been published (Bodenhamer *et al.*, 2010; Dear *et al.*, 2011; Gieseking *et al.*, 2014; Hubbard *et al.*, 2004; Wharf & Arias, 2009). Work on globalisation, mobility and urbanisation has also influenced research on urban sociolinguistics (King & Carson, 2016; Smakman & Heinrich, 2018) and the sociolinguistics of globalisation (Blommaert, 2010). These areas of sociolinguistic research touch on the wider aspects of what I call an environmental approach to SLA research.

Critical Spatial Theory: A Brief History

In this book, I use the term 'critical spatial theory' to refer to a range of approaches to space that have engaged with wider social and postmodernist theory. This distinguishes the body of work that I am interested in from the quantitative approach in geography that was equally theoretical and led to the emergence of positivist 'spatial science' (Johnston, 2009). A brief account of the history of spatial theory will help place this critical work in context.

Historical accounts of spatial theory often begin from the descriptive regional geography of the 1950s in which many critical geographers were trained. Ed Soja and Doreen Massey were two of the leading postmodernist geographers of the late 20th century. For Soja (1989: 38), the 1950s was a decade in which the discipline of geography was 'theoretically asleep', while for Massey (1985: 9–10) it was a period that geography had 'hidden away in embarrassment'. The task of regional geography was to describe the world in encyclopaedic and atheoretical fashion. Theory entered geography through the so-called quantitative revolution of the 1960s, which aimed to give geography a place among the sciences by using statistical data to generate laws of general spatial dynamics. The new 'spatial science' established the concept of space as a central focus of human geography (Cresswell, 2015), but it was quickly superseded by a critical turn in which Marxist theory played a significant role. These two phases are reflected in David Harvey's early career. Harvey's (1969) *Explanation in Geography* was a landmark publication on statistical methods for quantitative geography. Yet, only four years later, Harvey's (1973) *Social Justice in the City* appeared, which critiqued his earlier work and established his more lasting reputation as a Marxist geographer.

The perspective on space adopted in this book is more postmodern than Marxist, but Harvey, Neil Smith (1991) and the iconoclastic French Marxist Henri Lefebvre (1991) are the source of one of the key ideas in critical spatial theory: the social production of space. Up to the 1960s, academic Marxism was constrained by the imperative to remain faithful to the letter of Marx's work. In the 1970s, a generation of intellectuals emerged who proposed, in various ways, to reinterpret Marx's work in the context of 'late capitalism' or 'postmodernity' (Giddens, 1985; Jameson, 1984; Mandel, 1975; Poulantzas, 1978). They were helped in this task by the publication of the *Grundrisse* (Marx, 1973), an extensive set of Marx's notebooks that first appeared in French in 1968. Hitherto, *Capital* (Marx, 1967) had been the main source for Marxist theory. But *Capital* had little to say about the topic of space. The *Grundrisse* proved to be a richer source, and it was from his reading of the *Grundrisse* that Harvey began to develop a Marxist perspective on geography.

At around the same time, Lefebvre was developing a similar perspective in the context of his work on urbanisation. Lefebvre (1991) coined the phrase 'the production of space' in the title of a book published in French in 1974 and in English in 1991. Harvey drew on Marx's work in order to renew geography. As a former member of the French Communist Party, Lefebvre (1991: 343) had the very different aim of renewing Marxism itself, which he maintained would be 'best effected by taking full account of space'. Lefebvre's (1991) work is notable more for the brilliance of its insights than it is for the coherence of its theoretical exposition. It is also wide-ranging in scope, attempting, among other things, a history of social space from its origins in the embodiment of living beings, through antiquity and the Middle Ages up to the late 20th century. Because Lefebvre was prepared to push Marxist thought in directions that Marxist geographers were reluctant to take, his insights were often prescient and have had a more lasting impact. Soja (1989) reviewed a wealth of literature on earlier spatial theory, but reserved a special place for Lefebvre, who helped him free postmodern geography from its Marxist origins.

The Marxist geographers were followed by a generation that Soja (1989) dubbed postmodern. Geographers such as Massey (1985) and

Gregory (1978) retained some of the key ideas of Marxist geography, but had no affiliation to Marxism itself. From their point of view, the main problem with Marxist geography lay in the assumption that capitalism explained everything that needed to be explained about late 20th-century space. They argued both for the agency of space in the social process and more complex explanatory frameworks for empirical data. Massey (1991) (a commentary on Harvey's and Soja's work) and Rose (1993) also developed feminist critiques of both Marxist and postmodern approaches in the male-dominated discipline of geography. More recent critical work has foregrounded the complexity and heterogeneity of postmodern space in the context of work on urbanisation, globalisation and mobility. This work is represented in this book by the later work of Massey (2005) on space and globalisation, Amin and Thrift (2002, 2016) on the city, Urry (2007) on mobilities and Brenner and Schmid (2014, 2015) on 'planetary urbanisation'.

The critical work discussed so far shares a concern with the social production of space. More or less in parallel with this work, a very different humanistic trajectory emerged that emphasised the social construction of place (Golledge, 1999; Hägerstrand, 1973; Kuper, 1972; Richardson, 1982; Rodman, 1992; Tuan, 1977). Both trajectories reject the idea of a geometrically organised empty space that underpins quantitative geography, but instead of contesting the meaning of the concept of space, humanistic geographers focus more on the human experience of the transformation of space into meaningful place. Although the production of space and the construction of place trajectories largely developed independently of each other, they come together in recent overviews of spatial theory by Cresswell (2015) and Low (2016), who both show a preference for place over space. Low (2016) situates spatial theory within environmental psychology, which is probably the most important field beyond geography to have taken an interest in spatial theory.

My thinking on the application of spatial theory to questions of SLA is influenced most by the production of space perspective, which I see as the key to an understanding of the ways in which globalisation shapes language learning environments. From this perspective, the local environments in which languages are learned are outcomes of the production of space under globalisation. I find the humanistic assumptions of the construction of place trajectory problematic. The idea of place is, nevertheless, helpful in thinking about learners' roles in the construction of individual language learning environments. The construction of place perspective is most helpful, perhaps, as a reminder that language learning environments are products not only of impersonal global forces, but also of individual agency. For the present, however, I want to focus on some key ideas in critical spatial theory, and for the sake of clarity I will not encumber the presentation of these ideas with comments on their relevance to second language learning research, which will be discussed in more detail in Chapter 5.

The following discussion is intended to lay the basis for the argument of the chapters that follow and, for this reason, it is selective. I encourage readers who are stimulated by the idea that spatial theory might be relevant to SLA to explore the literature for themselves, beginning, perhaps, with one of the overviews of critical work on space and place provided by Hubbard *et al.* (2004), Cresswell (2015) or Low (2016). The sections that follow discuss three key propositions: 'space matters', 'space is physical' and 'space is socially produced'. The chapter concludes with a brief discussion of work on the social construction of place.

Why Space Matters

'Space matters' is a phrase used by Soja (1989, 2009) to signal the idea that space should be taken more seriously than it is. In fact, philosophers and natural scientists have taken space seriously since ancient times (Casey, 1998). Most of the great thinkers since the time of Aristotle have had something to say about space and many have developed theories of space, although these are often to be found in obscure corners of their work (Shields, 2006). Critical spatial theory is, in part, recovered from the work of modern philosophers, including Bergson, Husserl, Whitehead and Heidegger (Massey, 2005; Soja, 1989; Tuan, 1977). But it took a modern-day philosopher, Edward Casey (1998), to pull together a coherent historical account of the philosophy of space from ancient times to the 20th century. The idea that space matters is, in this sense, a relatively recent one.

Michel Foucault, who was primarily a historian, is Soja's main source on the importance of space. In an interview in the first issue of the French geographical journal *Hérodote* in 1976, Foucault (1980) was asked about his thoughts on geography and the use of spatial concepts in his own work. Foucault (1980: 70) was ambivalent in his responses, but he concluded by speaking of a 'devaluation of space that has prevailed for generations'. At the end of the interview, Foucault (1980: 77) says that he has enjoyed the discussion because it has changed his mind: 'geography must indeed necessarily lie at the heart of my concerns'. Foucault's (1986) strongest statement on space appeared in a paper titled 'Of Other Spaces', which begins with the statement that history was the great obsession of the 19th century. Foucault continues:

> The present epoch will perhaps be above all the epoch of space. We are in the epoch of simultaneity: we are in the epoch of juxtaposition, the epoch of the near and far, of the side-by-side, of the dispersed. We are at a moment I believe when our experience of the world is less that of a long

> life developing through time than that of a network that connects points and intersects with its own skein. (Foucault, 1986: 22)

Foucault then describes three epochs in the history of space: the medieval space of emplacement; the space of extension ushered in by Galileo, in which space became infinitely open and a thing's place became a point in its movement; and the contemporary epoch in which extension is replaced by relations among sites defined by proximity, series, trees, grids and sites. In this epoch, Foucault argues, we are more anxious about space than we are about time.

Pursuing Foucault's idea of the 19th-century's obsession with history, Soja (1989: 15) identified a period from the 1880s to the early 1960s, in which critical thought was characterised by a 'historicism' that 'actively submerges and peripheralizes the geographical or spatial imagination'. Within this historicist view, space appears as a background: 'An already-made geography sets the stage, while the wilful making of history dictates the action and defines the storyline' (Soja, 1989: 14). For Soja, Foucault was a case in point. Like many of the social theorists that he cited for their comments on space, Foucault 'buried his precursory spatial turn in brilliant whirls of historical insight' (Soja, 1989: 16). Citing art critic and novelist John Berger, Soja (1989: 22) described the 1970s as a period in which it is 'space not time that hides consequences for us'. Writing on the modern novel, Berger argued that it was no longer possible to tell a straightforward story, because we are always aware of what is traversing the storyline laterally.

> Such awareness is the result of our constantly having to take into account the simultaneity and extension of events and possibilities. There are so many reasons why this should be so: the range of modern means of communication: the scale of modern power: the degree of personal political responsibility that must be accepted for events all over the world: the fact that the world has become indivisible: the unevenness of economic development within that world: the scale of the exploitation. (Berger, 1974: 40)

The underlying reason for this sense of the simultaneity of geographically dispersed but networked events would now be called a sense of 'globalisation', a word that was not widely used in the 1970s. Yet, the global reach of transportation and communications media, in particular, had already enhanced the perception that events such as wars, political and economic crises, epidemics and threats to the environment were not localised, but happened everywhere at the same time. It was a sense of the need to understand such events spatially, as well historically, that lay behind the urge to theorise space.

Although the spatial theory that I focus on in this book is more postmodern than Marxist, the role of Marxism in its evolution cannot be underestimated. Harvey has consistently adopted a Marxist stance up to the present day, often going directly to Marx in search of spatial interpretations of social and economic phenomena. While Soja (1989) acknowledged Harvey's contributions, his own work drew more on the contemporary post-Marxism of writers such as Jameson (1984), Poulantzas (1978), Mandel (1975) and, above all, Lefebvre (1976). The stakes in this work were high: an explanation of how 'late capitalism' had survived crises that should have brought about its demise that took full account of space. According to Marxist geographers, capitalism had survived and even prospered after a fashion through a series of 'spatial fixes' (Harvey, 1975) or, as Lefebvre (1976: 21) put it, 'by producing a space'. Marxist geography added a much-needed spatial dimension to traditional Marxist theories of the limits of capitalism, while spatially informed Marxist theory explained geographical phenomena such as urbanisation and uneven regional development as spatial solutions to the problems of capitalism (Harvey, 1982; Smith, 1991).

By the late 1970s, postmodernism had emerged as a credible critical alternative to Marxism across the social sciences. Postmodern geographers sought 'a more flexible and dialectical relation between space and society' (Soja, 2009: 56) than the Marxist emphasis on space as a *product* of social structure allowed. Prominent among them was Dick Gregory (1978), who argued,

> The analysis of spatial structure is not derivative and secondary to the analysis of social structure, as the structuralist problematic would suggest: rather, each requires the other. Spatial structure is not, therefore, merely the arena within which class conflicts express themselves, but also the domain within which – and, in part, through which – class relations are constituted. (Gregory, 1978: 120)

Although Marxist in tone, Gregory's geography was more aligned with Giddens' (1985) 'structuration theory', in which both social structure and individual agency contribute to the constitution of society. Structuration theory influenced spatial theory by giving space a certain agency in the constitution of social structure.

The degree to which space 'matters' in social theory remains open for discussion. Critical geographers have tended to position themselves towards the centre of a continuum bounded by two unacceptable risks. At one end of the continuum, there is the risk that space matters only in the orthodox Marxist sense that it is a product of social structure or historical change. At the other end, there is the risk of an environmental determinism in which human behaviour is directly shaped by space. The important point is that space matters, not just as an interesting but neglected dimension of the social world. It matters because there is an 'effectivity of space' (Amin & Thrift, 2002: 39), because 'spatial configuration is... a significant factor in the emergence of the new' (Massey, 2005: 128). Across the social sciences, causality is thought of as something that happens in historical time. Current phenomena are caused by prior processes and events. To take space seriously, then, is to look for a more complex causality, in which *where* things happen is part of the explanation of how and why they happen (Wharf & Arias, 2009). The effectivity of space makes little sense, however, if space is no more than an empty container for processes and events. It only makes sense if space is reconceptualised as something substantial, something that is capable of having effects.

The Physicality of Space

In 1985, Gregory, a geographer, and John Urry, a sociologist, published a collection of papers entitled *Social Relations and Spatial Structures* (Gregory & Urry, 1985). Both Marxist and post-Marxist perspectives were represented in the collection, but most contributors agreed on two points: first, space is *produced*, not given in advance, and second, the space that matters is *social* space. In other words, spatial structures are interwoven with social relations. The social production of space is the topic of the next section of this chapter. First, I want to pause to consider the conception of space that underlies the production of space perspective. Lefebvre (1991: 15) writes: 'To speak of "producing space" sounds bizarre, so great is the sway still held by the idea that empty space is prior to whatever ends up filling it'. We tend to think of space as a void, as *nothing*. If space is socially produced, then we must think of a different kind of space, a space that is *something*. If space is something, what kind of thing is it?

Consider the following passage from D.H. Lawrence's travel journal, *Sea and Sardinia*:

> Ah if one could sail for ever, on a small quiet, lonely ship, from land to land and isle to isle, and saunter through the spaces of this lovely world, always through the spaces of this lovely world. Sweet it would be sometimes to come to the opaque earth, to block oneself against the stiff land, to annul the vibration of one's flight against the inertia of our *terra firma!* but life itself would be in the flight, the tremble of space. Ah the trembling of never-ended space, as one moves in flight! Space, and the frail vibration of space, the glad lonely wringing of the heart. Not to be clogged to the land any more. (Lawrence, 1921: 86)

Lawrence is travelling on an overnight ferry from Palermo to Cagliari. He is irritated by the food, the service, the crew and his fellow passengers, and the journey so far has a claustrophobic feel. But in the early hours of the morning, he finds himself alone on deck. Lawrence's space is an imagined space, empty and never-ending, inspired by a sense of being alone at sea with no land in sight. This is a modernist literary trope that seems to die hard. W.G. Sebald (2002: 67) is more postmodern than modern, yet in the *The Rings of Saturn*, he finds himself on a Suffolk cliff top, gazing at sand martins flying 'at the level that extended from the top of the cliff where I was sitting out into empty space'. For both Lawrence and Sebald, empty space is a romanticised space of freedom, opposed to the inert solidity of 'the opaque earth'.

In everyday usage also 'space' is associated with emptiness. Space is the name given to the imagined void that lies beyond the earth's atmosphere (although we now know that outer space is far from empty). Back on earth, space is equated with air, a medium through which we move almost as if it were a void. Empty spaces also become containers. We might not think of a room full of furniture as a space, but take the furniture away, or imagine that it is taken away, and it becomes a space to be filled with something else. Space can signify distance: not only the infinite extension of Lawrence's and Sebald's imagined space, but also the linear spaces between objects or places. Space can also signify the room we need in order to perform some action, or the distance from something that gets in our way. 'Personal space' is the empty space that we maintain between self and others (Hall, 1966). Personal space is also commodified in the housing of the wealthy, where it signifies both room to spread out and distance from the poor. A house is both an object in space and a container of space, and in both aspects, the more space one has the better (Bachelard, 2014).

Space, thus, has a multiplicity of everyday meanings, at the core of which stands the idea of emptiness. Several other properties cluster around the emptiness of space. Space is flat and smooth, a surface or a medium that permits unfettered movement. Space is the inert background to, or stage on which events unfold. Space is a matrix, framework or grid. Space is given, pre-existing, already 'there'. These everyday ideas of space also have their scientific counterparts. Space is continuous, homogeneous and immobile, geometrical and mathematically measurable. Space is abstract and insubstantial; absolute, universal and infinite. For Lefebvre (1991: 377) it is also 'visual and phallic', and marked by 'the use and overuse of straight lines, right angles, and strict (rectilinear) perspective' (Lefebvre, 1991: 409–410). We also tend to think, both scientifically and as a matter of common sense, of a specific relationship between physical bodies and space: physical bodies move *in* space, but space itself is immobile. Physical objects are *not* space, nor do they *have* space. They occupy or take up space, but space is not something that they hold within them (which we tend to think of as size and dimension).

According to this view, space is not the physical world, it is the container of the physical world in a double sense. First, space is the boundless container of everything that exists in the universe. Scientifically, this is the 'space of extension', which for Foucault (1986) began with Galileo and replaced the medieval 'space of emplacement'. In essence, this was the infinite space of the heavens in which the stars and planets are surrounded and separated from each other by vast expanses of emptiness. Second, objects themselves are containers of the stuff of which they consist, spaces to be filled like boxes or rooms. Massey (2005: 68) describes this as a 'billiard ball view' of space, that we see applied to all kinds of physical and social objects, including the geography of nation states.

> The modernist conception of nation states or cultural isolates resonates with the billiard-ball view of the world proposed by physical mechanics. First the entities exist, in their full identities, and then they come into interaction. There is a distinct inside and outside. (Massey, 2005: 72)

I call this an 'objects-*in*-space' view of the world. In the objects-*in*-space view, space contains objects, and these objects are, in turn, often containers for other objects. The alternative that is proposed by critical spatial theory I will call an objects-*as*-space view.

Casey's (1998) historical account of the European philosophy of space and place tracks modern debates back to a difference between Aristotle and the atomists in ancient Greece. The atomists posited a cosmos formed from 'the interaction of discrete bits of matter within a circumambient empty space' (Casey, 1998: 33), whereas Aristotle asserted the primacy of place, understood as the finite limit of each physical body. For Casey, this difference evolved into a centuries-long struggle between infinite space and finite place from which space emerged victorious in the late 17th century. Crucial to this victory were Christian doctrines of the infinite power of God, which allowed philosophers to explore the idea of unbounded space without fear of persecution. If the power of God was infinite, how could the extent of a divinely created universe be otherwise? The key figure for Casey was Sir Isaac Newton (1642–1727), and the key moment the publication in 1687 of his *Mathematical Principles of Natural Philosophy* (Newton, 1962) (on the importance of Newton, see also Gibson, 1979; Low, 2016; Prigogine & Stengers, 1984; Smith, 1991).

For Newton, 'absolute' and 'relative' space were the key concepts by which he meant to free space from its dependence on matter. 'Absolute' space was a realm of its own kind, real but empty of matter. 'Relative' space, on the other hand, was the space of matter, understood in terms of measurable relations among physical objects in absolute space. These were the spaces of Newton's mechanical laws of motion, which presuppose an empty space in which physical bodies move freely and collide with each other like billiard balls on a frictionless surface. Smith (1991: 16) describes Newton's view as 'the main influence on our common-sense notions of space'. But Newton did not see absolute and relative space as common-sense notions at all, writing: 'I do not define time, space, place, and motion as being well known to all' (cited in Smith, 1991: 94). The common people, Newton wrote, 'concede those quantities under no other notions but from the relation they bear to sensible objects' (Smith, 1991). The idea of an absolute empty space would, however, eventually become the dominant European idea of space: 'fixed and empty, a void waiting to be filled or a grid that can be measured… the container or stage of human activity' (Low, 2016: 15).

Yet, Newton's conception of space did not become the dominant *philosophical* conception of space. As a materialist, Descartes had earlier insisted that 'there can be no completely empty space… There can be no space without body' (cited in Casey, 1998: 152). For Leibniz, described by Low (2016: 15) as 'the founder of the modernist view of space', space was not independent of objects and events, but made up of their relations. In the 18th century, Kant, the most influential philosopher of the Enlightenment, rejected the Newtonian concept of absolute space for the entirely different reason that it was supposedly objective and real. For Kant, space is subjective and ideal and its geometric principles represent only the truth of things as they appear to the senses.

Nor did Newtonian space become the dominant *scientific* conception of space. In their history of the natural sciences, Prigogine and Stengers (1984: 171) observe that modern science was born when 'the homogeneous and isotropic space of Euclid' replaced Aristotelian space. However, they also argue that this conception proved inadequate for the natural sciences, especially chemistry and biology, in the early 19th century. The second law of thermodynamics, formulated by Nicolas Carnot in 1824, which Prigogine and Stengers (1984: 99) describe as the first form of a 'science of complexity', dealt a fatal blow to the idea of free-floating bodies in space. The motion of the industrial age could only be understood in terms of friction and the dissipation of energy. The late 19th century was, for Prigogine and Stengers, as it was for Foucault (1986) and Soja (2009), also the era in which time and history came to the front of stage in, for example, Darwin's theory of evolution and Marx's political economy. It was thus primarily in the social sciences, and in the context of a preference for history as the driving force of social change, that the Newtonian conception of space survived and prospered.

But if space is not empty, in what sense is it physical? One answer might be that space is 'full' of the stuff that comprises it. But while it is true that we always encounter spaces that are *already* full, this line of argument returns to the idea of space as a container to be filled.

In an interesting exercise in tracking the idea of the fullness of space back to its origins, Lefebvre (1991: 13) suggests that matter is no more than energy: 'physical space has no "reality" without the energy that is deployed within it'. Because energy produces physical space, it cannot be compared to the content that fills an empty container. Harvey (2006) attempts to escape the space–matter dualism of Newton's absolute and relative space through Leibniz's 'relational' space. For Harvey (2006: 121), relational space is 'contained in objects in the sense that an object can be said to exist only insofar as it contains and represents within itself relationships to other objects'. The idea that space is contained in objects is very different to the idea that objects are contained in space, and it leads Harvey (2006: 123) to the conclusion that 'processes do not occur *in* space but define their own spatial frame'. Massey (2005: 61) also works with a relational, or interactional, view of space: 'If time unfolds as change then space unfolds as interaction'. This is what I call an 'objects-*as*-space' view of the world.

Gibson's (1979) ecological theory of visual perception is well known as a source for ecological approaches to learning (Barron, 2006; van Lier, 2004). Less well known is the critique of Newtonian space on which Gibson's theory is based, which provides a vital clue to the physical character of language learning environments. It should be noted, first, that Gibson's is not a theory of space as such, but a theory of the physical structure of the environment, for which he found the Newtonian concept of space unhelpful. We tend to assume, he says, that 'we live in a physical world consisting of bodies in space and that what we perceive consists of objects in space' (Gibson, 1979: 12). Gibson (1979: 27) insists, however, that we do not live in 'space', but in environments consisting of 'substances that are more or less substantial; of a medium, the gaseous atmosphere; and of the surfaces that separate the substances from the medium'. Air is so insubstantial that it 'permits unimpeded locomotion from place to place, and... the seeing, smelling, and hearing of the substances at all places' (Gibson, 1979). Although we may perceive air as empty space, air is as much a physical substance as mud or stone. Surfaces separate other substances from the medium in which an animal lives, and, by reflecting and absorbing light, they permit visual perception. It is also at their surfaces that substances are perceived, touch each other, react with each other chemically and vaporise or diffuse into the medium. In sum, Gibson (1979: 93) rejects the Newtonian idea of objects in space entirely: 'Objects do not *fill* space, for there was no such thing as empty space to begin with'. Instead, it is the medium and the persisting surfaces of the environment that provide the framework of reality. Perceptually, then, we live in a medium and a world of surfaces, from which we derive a sense of both space and time.

Two additional points are worth noting on Gibson's view of the environment. First, Gibson emphasises that the environment is always perceived from within, by a mobile organism that is, itself, a part of the environment. Instead of externally observed geometrical points and lines, we have 'points of observation and lines of locomotion' (Gibson, 1979: 13). As the observer moves, the optical, acoustic and chemical information change accordingly, such that each point is a unique point of observation. From repeated observations from multiple vantage points the organism gains a sense of the environment as a whole. Second, Gibson (1979: 30) argues that the motion of bodies is not to be conceived of as 'a change of position along one or more of the dimensions of space', but always as '*a change in the overall surface layout*, a change in the shape of the environment in some sense'. This implies motions that are alien to the geometry of abstract space, including 'stretching, squeezing, bending, twisting, flowing, and the like' (Gibson, 1979: 31). In the Newtonian conception of space, 'human activity does not restructure space; it simply rearranges objects in space' (Smith, 1991: 2). From the objects-*as*-space view, no immobile space remains unaffected by the movement of the objects it contains. Motion always entails a reconfiguration of space itself. And because there are no fixed places 'in' space, independent of the mutual relations of physical objects, physical objects do not move from 'place to place'. There are only the continuous, turbulent mobilities of space itself.

The main idea that I want to carry forward from here is that space matters *because* it is substantial, and by substantial Gibson means physical. This means that, just as there is no empty space, social, ideational or metaphorical spaces only exist in the context of physical space. The social distances of politeness and intimacy, the distances between social classes, the divisions among genres of art, music and literature, the virtual spaces of the internet, the disciplinary fields of knowledge and so on are all grounded in physical space. As Hall (1966) showed, for example, 'personal space' is both social *and* physical, both metaphorically and physically real. Similarly, when Bourdieu (1985: 196) contends that 'the social world can be represented as a space', and that agents are 'defined by their relative positions within that space', he is thinking of an ideological space that is also physically grounded in the spatial relationships among agents and social classes. The problem of moving beyond Gibson's account of the visual perception of the physical environment, to the human perception of social environments is that human environments are both physical and cultural. Human environments are infused with ideology, saturated with ideas and language; however, it is important that we conceive of the cultural and ideological dimensions of environments as being embodied in physical engagement with the physical world (Ingold, 2011).

The Social Production of Space

The idea of the production of space is Marxist in origin. For Marx (1967), production, or the transformation of matter by human labour, is the driving force of human development. Production is social in that it calls for a division of labour, cooperation in the labour process, distribution of products and exchange of surpluses. Each era has its dominant mode of production, involving social relations of production that correspond to the level of development of the productive forces. Beyond subsistence economies in which families or clans produce their own means of life with irregular exchange of surpluses, all modes of production involve some kind of class system in which the many labour in order to provide both their own means of subsistence and surpluses for the few. In the capitalist mode of production, labourers sell their labour power as a commodity and the owners of the means of production take profit from the surplus value that labourers produce over and above the value of their labour power. In addition to being a mode of organising the social relations of production, each mode of production generates its own social and political structures. The family under capitalism, for example, is of a very different kind to the family under feudalism, just as the capitalist state is very different to the feudal state.

What Marxist geography added to this view of the social relations of production was the idea that each mode of production also produces its own space. For Lefebvre (1991: 129), 'the social relations of production have a social existence to the extent that they have a spatial existence; they project themselves into space, becoming inscribed there, and in the process producing that space itself'. Social space consists of the physical space that is produced within the social relations of production of an era, a space that also represents that era. Each mode of production also produces its own spatiality: a certain relationship to space or means of organising the spaces of the world, including the scales on which space is produced (Smith, 1991). In doing so, it inherits and builds upon a space that is already differentiated and patterned by earlier modes of production. Smith (1991) argues that capitalism inherited from feudalism the town, city-state, duchy and kingdom, and a world market. These were transformed into the three main, hierarchically organised scales of capitalist space: the urban, the national and the global. Each of these scales existed before the rise of capitalism, 'but in extent and in substance they are transformed utterly at the hands of capital' (Smith, 1991: 181). Capitalism has thus produced a host of new spaces – factories, storage and waste disposal facilities, industrial zones and housing estates; cities and conurbations; railway lines, docks, airports and transportation networks; nation states, borders, military installations and so on, as well as the spaces of modern education and language learning. And one of the main characteristics of the spatiality of capitalism is the interlocking of all of these spaces into a global multiscalar network of production and consumption.

In some passages of the *Grundrisse*, Marx (1973) discusses space as if it were not merely produced, but also a means of production, alongside labour, machinery and raw materials. For example, the costs of transporting raw materials from their source to the point of production, and of transporting products to the market are factored into their value as commodities. In Marx's time, the steam engine and electricity revolutionised transportation and communications as a global spatial infrastructure of railways, shipping lines and telegraph networks was laid out across the surface of the earth. By reducing the cost of transportation of commodities to measurable quantities of time, this infrastructure brought about 'the annihilation of space by time' (Marx, 1973, cited in Smith, 1991: 127). As the most important spatial product of 19th-century industrial capitalism, global transportation and communication networks also diminished the economic effects of distance on the mobility of capital and, together with the later development of roads, airways and electronic communications networks, they laid the foundations for globalisation in its present forms. They divided the world into an imperialist system of powerful nation states and their colonies, which was transformed into the present-day patchwork of supposedly sovereign member states of the United Nations. They also produced the shape of the modern city – its characteristic centre, periphery and rural hinterland, its zones for industry, housing, commerce, education and leisure, as well as Foucault's (1986) 'heterotopias', or 'other spaces', such as hospitals, gardens, prisons and theatres – that was transformed in the 20th century into the shape of the complex and heterogeneous urban-suburban conglomeration of the present day (Amin & Thrift, 2016; Keil, 2017).

While it would be tedious to go too deeply into the ideas of Marxist geography, two key points are worth highlighting: first, the contention that capitalism must expand spatially in order to survive and, second, the idea that capitalism produces space in the image of Newton's absolute space.

Space and the survival of capitalism

For Marx, capitalism is a profit-driven system and profit is derived from the surplus value produced by labour, or the difference between the time that labourers expend on production and the time needed to reproduce their labour power. Profits are only produced by labour ('variable capital'), but the capitalist must also invest in 'fixed capital' – machinery and other production facilities, much of which turns out to be an investment in space. As the ratio of fixed capital to variable capital increases, the *quantity* of profit increases, but the *rate* of profit on total investment tends to fall, and this falling rate of profit is the main cause of cyclical crises. Crises occur regularly because they are, for Marx, a necessary condition of the growth of capitalism. Capital must accumulate and each phase of accumulation leads to an overproduction of fixed capital and a falling rate of profit. Because investment in fixed capital is investment in space, crises are also, at root, a consequence of the production of space. For Marxists, the solution to crises of overproduction lies in the movement of capital into more labour-intensive sectors where higher rates of profit obtain. The production of space expands across the surface of the earth all the more rapidly because rates of profit tend to be at their highest on the fringes of established capitalist space (Patel & Moore, 2018).

In the 19th century, European capitalism expanded spatially in two ways: industrial cities absorbed rural space, and 'undeveloped' colonial territories were brought into the circuits of production and consumption. This expansion took place on the model of an empty and infinite space waiting to be filled with productive activity. The geographical expansion of capitalism paused with the final partitioning of Africa in the 1880s. Since then, the production of space has been a matter of the internal differentiation and restructuring of spaces that already fall within the sphere of production. After World War II, urbanisation, a relatively labour-intensive process with dramatic effects on space, was identified as one of the most effective spatial solutions to economic crises. Soja (2009: 96) argues that the foundations of capitalist growth are now 'shaped primarily by and through the social production of urbanised space, planned and orchestrated with increasing power by the state, and expanding to encompass more and more of the world's population and resources'. Spatial solutions to crises of overproduction also involve the destruction of previously produced spaces by bulldozers or instruments of war. But for Marxist geographers, 'spatial fixes' always lead to new crises and the need for new spatial solutions. The production of space is seen, rightly or wrongly, as an increasingly desperate survival strategy for a mode of production that threatens to cover the world with a layer of toxic spatial detritus that may never be removed.

The main point that has been carried forward from Marxist geography into present-day critical spatial theory is this idea of the all-encompassing character of the social production of physical space. Smith (1991: 134) argued that in late 20th-century capitalism, geography had become 'more systematically and completely an integral part of the mode of production' than ever before. Boundaries between city and countryside are increasingly blurred (Amin & Thrift, 2002, 2016; Massey, 2005) and almost every corner of the planet is urbanised in one sense or another (Brenner & Schmid, 2014, 2015). Human lives are also increasingly plugged into urbanised modes of production. As Lefebvre (1991: 329) puts it, in urbanised areas *'everything* is produced:

air, light, water – even the land itself'. In this context, Lefebvre also referred to a 'pulverisation' of space: the reduction of space to smaller and smaller volumes and a multiplication of volumes that gives urban space a 'hypercomplex' structure that is not so much geometrical as 'reminiscent of flaky *mille-feuille* pastry' (Lefebvre, 1991: 86). Lefebvre made this comment in the early 1970s when the world was far less urbanised, and space far less fragmented, than it is today. It expresses a view of urban and global space that has now been widely taken up by critical spatial theorists for whom Marxist geography has proved too monocausal in its explanatory approach to accommodate the hyper-complexity and flakiness of 21st-century space.

The production of Newtonian space

If space is physical, what has become of Newton's empty geometrically organised space? Is it purely an ideological construct that has no place in the physical world? Eighteenth-century chemists proposed that combustion was caused by a substance called 'phlogiston'. This theory was later disproved as it turned out that phlogiston did not exist, and did not need to exist. We have seen Gibson (1979: 93) argue that objects do not 'fill' space, because there is 'no such thing as empty space to begin with'. Is empty space, like phlogiston, simply an outdated idea with no need of existence?

In a later passage in *The Rings of Saturn*, Sebald reflects on a different view of space, seen from the window of a small aeroplane leaving Amsterdam on a short flight to Norwich in the east of England.

> Spread out beneath us lay one of the most densely-populated regions in Europe, with endless terraces, sprawling satellite towns, business parks and shining glasshouses which looked like large quadrangular ice flows drifting across this corner of the continent where not a patch is left to its own devices. Over the centuries the land had been regulated, cultivated and built on until the whole region was transformed into a geometrical pattern. The roads, water channels and railway tracks run in straight lines and gentle curves past fields and plantations, basins and reservoirs.... Along a line that seemed to have been drawn with a ruler a tractor crawled through a field of stubble dividing it into one lighter and one darker half. (Sebald, 2002: 90–91)

What Sebald sees is an aerial view of post-industrial space produced on geometrical lines; a space 'filled in' over multiple timescales until 'not a patch is left to its own devices'; a space that would in some sense be empty if it had not been filled in. It is a view that reminds us of the degree to which modern space is constructed on the model of Newtonian space;

geometrically laid out, as far as the landscapes inherited from the past allow, in regular blocks of commodified space.

To take an example from the other side of the earth, Australia is said to have been declared *terra nullius* by the British colonial explorer James Cook in 1770. Although *terra nullius* means 'land that belongs to nobody', it is often interpreted as meaning 'empty space'. Indeed, in the absence of any means of demonstrating legal ownership in the European sense, the important question at the time was whether or not there were material signs of Aboriginal occupation, architecture or agricultural cultivation (Kilroy, 2016). Ignoring all evidence to the contrary, the British authorities decided that no trace of Aboriginal ownership was to be found (Pascoe, 2018). Australia was designated as an empty space ripe for colonial exploitation, and when it turned out not to be empty at all, there was often wholesale destruction of Aboriginal material and cultural resources, as colonial agriculture and industry spread across the continent. It was only in the late 20th century that the doctrine of *terra nullius* was abandoned and rights to native ownership were recognised.

In the north of Holland, a space was produced geometrically on the model of empty space. In colonial Australia, the production of space rested on an imagination of empty space. But is Newtonian space only a powerful idea that is made real in the course of the production of the space; a principle of the social production of physical space under capitalism? Casey (1998) and Harvey (1978) approach this question from non-Marxist and Marxist perspectives, respectively. In conclusion to a passionate argument for recognition of the concreteness of 'place', Casey (1998) asks why the idea of infinite space should have proved so attractive to so many Western thinkers. In reply, he argues that it 'suggests the possibility of unlimited control: such space is not only measurable and predictable (hence mathematizable) but altogether "passable"' (Casey, 1998: 338). Armed with this idea, a man can imagine himself, like Kant's dove, 'cleaving the air of infinite space freely and without hindrance' (Casey, 1998). Certainly, it is not difficult to see how, allied to economic and political power, the idea of an infinite empty space proved enormously useful to all kinds of projects in the production of space, from the industrialisation of rural space to the European colonisation of much of the world.

However, Harvey's (1978: 124) observation that 'capital represents itself in the form of a physical landscape created in its own image' takes this observation a step further. Empty space is not simply an ideological principle embedded in the production of space. It is also a social and physical product of the capitalist mode of production. Capitalism sometimes builds into or around previously existing spaces, but this is largely a recent idea fostered by movements to protect 'heritage'. More often, an existing space is emptied and then the production of a new space begins. The first step in the colonisation of Australian lands was always to clear and 'stump' forested land; often land that had been produced by millennia of Aboriginal economic activity, so that it could be produced anew on the model of European agriculture. Most modern construction projects begin by emptying and levelling the space to be built upon, usually a space already inhabited by human or non-human life. The destruction of space is thus a precondition for the production of space in the image of capital. Pockets of empty space such as national parks and open public areas in cities are also an end product of the capitalist production of space; as are disused quarries, landfills and toxic wastelands. Emptiness has a different meaning in each case. Space is never really empty in the absolute sense that Newton intended. But the emptying of physical space, the production of a *tabula rasa*, is a feature of the capitalist mode of production that was unknown to its predecessors.

At issue here, however, is a wider issue of abstraction. Abstraction generates the idea of an entity by stripping concrete objects of their physical forms. As physical form is stripped away, concrete objects lose their specificity; they become variant forms of the abstract homogeneous idea of themselves. Abstraction is not only a mode of thought, but it is also a characteristic process of capitalist production. Capital is wealth stripped of its physical forms, labour is productive human activity stripped of its physical forms and so on. In these cases, abstraction is a social process that allows capital and labour to move freely so that the products of labour can be exchanged as commodities on the market. A commodity is always a concrete object produced by some specific process of production. But within the capitalist mode of production, commodities circulate as quantities of abstract exchange value. Lefebvre (1977, cited in Stanek, 2008: 68) refers to an abstraction of this kind as a 'concrete abstraction'; an abstraction that 'concretizes and realizes itself socially, in the social practice'. Newton's absolute space is also an abstraction, space abstracted from matter, stripped or 'emptied' of its physicality. And it is no coincidence that the history of absolute and relative space coincides with the history of capitalism, because it is as a concrete abstraction that space enters into capitalist production. There is always a physical space to be crossed, built upon or built, but as far as possible capitalist production reduces that space to measurable quantities of distance, area, volume and, ultimately, time. In Lefebvre's (1991: 341–342) terms, capitalist space is 'both abstract and concrete in character: abstract inasmuch as it has no existence save by virtue of the exchangeability of all its component parts, and concrete in as much as it is socially real and as such localized'.

The Fragmentation of Space

In the 1980s, Marxism and post-Marxism, which had been natural poles of attraction for critical academic thought in the 1970s, gave way to postmodernism. At around the same time, the critique of capitalism gave way to the critique of 'neoliberalism', viewed as a particularly iniquitous form of capitalism, and the politics of class gave way to the politics of identity. In retrospect, Marxist geography seems too systematic in its approach to account for the complexities of contemporary social space. While Massey (2005: 55) subscribed to the idea of space as an 'ongoing production', she also insisted that it was an 'open' rather than 'closed' system that 'makes room for a genuine multiplicity of trajectories'. The modern city is the archetypal spatial product of the age of capitalism, but as Amin and Thrift (2002: 8) argue, contemporary cities lack system and internal coherence; they have 'no completeness, no centre, no fixed parts'; they are 'an amalgam of often disjointed processes and social heterogeneity'. Brenner and Schmid (2015: 154) agree that capital accumulation continues to 'reshape places, territories and landscapes at all spatial scales', but they also argue the need to understand how the boundaries of the city 'are being exploded and reconstituted as new forms of urbanization reshape inherited patterns of territorial organization, and increasingly crosscut the urban/non-urban divide itself'.

This view was anticipated by Lefebvre (1991: 88) who wrote of the 'hyper-complexity of social space'. For Lefebvre, the 'pulverisation' of space was the characteristic tendency of 20th-century capitalism. The complexity of contemporary space, however, also touches on the sense in which it is a 'social' space. From a Marxist perspective, social space is social because it is produced under the prevailing social relations of production. These are understood, primarily, as relations among humans. For Massey (2005: 61), interaction defines social space: 'If time unfolds as change then space unfolds as interaction. In that sense space is the social dimension'. Elsewhere, Massey (2005: 184) suggests that if space is relational, it is 'no more than the sum of our relations and interconnections, and the lack of them'; space presents us with the social 'as the challenge of our constitutive interrelatedness' (Massey, 2005: 195). It may be a misreading of Massey to suggest that this is an exclusively human understanding of social space. However, as I am about to turn to humanistic alternatives to the idea of the production of space, I want to leave a marker here for a view of social space that includes the non-human within its conception of the social.

A complex view of the social process seems to imply a level playing field on which entities of all kinds deserve consideration, without prior assumptions as to their nature or roles. For this reason, the complexity of social space cannot be reduced to the complexity of human relations.

From this perspective, the problem with Marxist geography lies not only in an overly reductive account of the production of space. The account is also too humanistic. Social space is complex because it incorporates relations among all manner of entities. This view is often associated with the sociologist Bruno Latour, whose actor network theory emphasises the importance of interactions among non-human actors in the constitution of the social (Latour, 2005). If the social is constituted by networks of non-human and human actors, it is also spatial, and it is mainly for this reason that some see Latour as a spatial theorist (Hubbard *et al.*, 2004). Although it was not central to his work, this view of social space was also anticipated by Lefebvre (1991: 101), who wrote that social space assembled 'everything that there is *in space*... living beings, things, objects, works, signs and symbols'. Taking an environmental view of space, Ingold (2011: 5) also argues that humans come into a world inhabited by 'beings of manifold kinds, both human and non-human' and 'relations among humans, which we are accustomed to calling "social", are but a sub-set of ecological relations'. Without using the term 'social space', Amin and Thrift (2002: 83) take a similar view of the contemporary city, which they describe as 'a swirl of forces and intensities' that 'bring into relation all kinds of actors, human and non-human, in all manner of combinations of agency'.

The Social Construction of Place

The theme of this chapter so far has been the attempt of critical spatial theorists to reclaim the concept of space for what I have called a 'social production of space' perspective, a perspective that favours the idea of objects-*as*-space over that of objects-*in*-space. However, two of the writers who I have cited as critics of Newtonian absolute space propose to abandon the idea of space altogether. For Gibson (1979: 11), 'the environment is not the same as the physical world, if one means by that the world described by physics'. His 'surface geometry' is concerned not with regularity and measurability, but with 'things at the ecological level' as they are experienced by living beings (Gibson, 1979: 5). For Casey (1998), the history of the philosophy of space and place has been a prolonged struggle in which place, having been suppressed for 200 years or more, is now showing signs of revival. In taking the side of place in this struggle, Casey allies with geographers, anthropologists and environmental psychologists whose main concern has been with what Low (2016: 68) calls the 'social construction of space and place', or how individuals and social groups experience, attach meaning to and struggle over the meanings of space and place in the course of their everyday lives.

Geographical work in this tradition begins with Torsten Hägerstrand's (1973) time geography, a behavioural alternative to the quantitative geography of his time that involved the detailed examination of the daily or weekly space-time paths of individuals (Pred, 1977). Other important contributions were made by the behavioural geographer Reginald Golledge (1999), whose work on 'wayfinding' focused on people's unique cognitive mappings of the world around them, and the Chinese-American geographer Yi-Fu Tuan (1977), who focused on the human experience of place. In anthropology and environmental psychology, significant figures include Kuper (1972: 420), who seems to have coined the term 'social construction of space', using the term 'site' to refer to 'a particular piece of social space, a place socially and ideological demarcated and separated from other places'; Richardson (1982), who argued that 'the construction of social reality occurs through the symbolic processes by which human experience and feelings become anchored to elements of the material environment' (Low, 2016: 72); and Rodman (1992), whose work on 'place-making' viewed place as 'a unique reality for each person... made up of all the social constructions of spatial meanings enacted and embedded at the site' (Low, 2016: 73). Ingold's (2011) ecological understanding of the environment, which sets Gibson's work on visual perception in an anthropological context, is also allied to the idea of the social construction of place. Work that focuses on place also tends to have its own antecedents in philosophical work by Heidegger (1977) on building and dwelling, Merleau-Ponty (2012) on phenomenology and embodiment and Bachelard (2014) on the poetics of space. Much of this work has been made available in overviews by Cresswell (2015) and Low (2016), both of whom tend to adopt a humanist preference for place over space.

In writing on space and place, the choice of one word or the other often signals a broad theoretical orientation. It can also signal a focus on either the 'globality' of space or the 'locality' of place (Massey, 2005). In everyday language, just as 'space' tends to mean empty space, 'place' tends to refer to fixed, secure positions or sites in space. Moreover, for humanistic geographers, a place is more than just a point or region in space; place is constructed by human activity as meaningful space. Tuan (1977) is, perhaps, the best-known interpreter of the distinction between space and place. For Tuan (1977: 6), space and place 'require each other for definition'. 'From the security and stability of place', he argues, 'we are aware of the openness, freedom, and threat of space, and vice versa' (Tuan, 1977). However, the idea that 'space is transformed into place as it acquires definition and meaning' (Tuan, 1977: 136) is problematic, in so far as it assumes that there is an empty, undifferentiated space that serves as the starting point of this transformation. Humanistic approaches may also be guilty of romanticising the locality of 'place'. In Tuan's work, especially, space threatens, while place offers security, stability and emotional comfort.

De Certeau (1984: 117) is often seen as having reversed the terms of this distinction in his understanding of space as 'a practiced place'. He argues, for example, that 'the street geometrically defined by urban planning is transformed into a space by walkers' (De Certeau, 1984). But this is not a simple exchange of terms because, for De Certeau, establishing a 'proper place' (*un lieu propre*), a territory from which to operate, is a strategy of power. Resistance to power lies in the tactics of everyday practice that play out within the places of the powerful. Massey (2005: 184) also questions the humanistic emphasis on place, arguing that 'romanticising the local can be the other side of understanding space as an abstraction'. Without an understanding of the substantiality of space itself, socially constructed places tend to become the concrete objects that populate an otherwise empty abstract space. Massey thus points to the problem of understanding the concreteness of global space from a humanistic perspective. The difficulty with Heidegger's (1977: 183) 'reformulation of space as place', she argues, is that the 'notion of place remains too rooted, too little open to the externally relational'.

For researchers who work with the idea of locally constructed place, the idea of global space is too abstract. They argue that space is only accessible through individual experiences of place, which are necessarily local. Place emerges from the physical engagement of living bodies with the world around them. It emanates from the body and, in a social sense, from bodies acting in concert with each other. The human activity of place-making also invests space with individual and social meaning, and involves cultural as well as physical resources. Environmental views of space tend to be grounded in this view of place, because they see space as a perceptual construct (Gibson, 1979; Low, 2016). The environment is, essentially, the place that an individual or group carves out from a space that it perceives, and perception varies from species to species, and among humans from culture to culture, person to person. From a production of space perspective, each individual participates in the production of space in a unique manner, but the spaces they produce are alienated from their participation in the process of production. Individuals and social groups do not produce *their own spaces*. In contrast, Ingold (2011: 4) takes as his starting point, the person as a 'developing organism-in-its-environment, as opposed to the self-contained individual confronting a world "out there"'.

I believe that work on the experience of place has a contribution to make in research on individuals' engagements with language learning environments (Chapter 5). But in my view, it is the production of space, rather than the construction of place, that matters most to an environmental approach to SLA research. Important as the human experience of space may be, space does not exist *for* humans. As human beings, we perceive ourselves as objects-*in*-space, as if we were not ourselves spatial entities. From an objects-*as*-space perspective, human beings *are* space, a view that has important consequences for our understanding of language and its relations to space.

Conclusion

The aim of this chapter has been to introduce SLA researchers to the field of critical spatial theory. The survey is not intended to be comprehensive, but rather to introduce certain ideas that will be important to the argument that follows. Focusing on what Low (2016) calls the 'social production of space' perspective, I have given the social construction of place perspective less attention than it deserves. Partly as a consequence of this bias, I have also left out important work from feminist, postcolonial, indigenous and queer theoretical perspectives that is critical of the 'totalising' tendency of work that calls attention to the global character of the production of space (see e.g. Peake *et al.*, 2018). I have also given more weight to the agency of the impersonal forces of globalisation and late capitalism than I have to the local agency of communities and individuals in the production of space. I would agree that there is a tendency in early Marxist work to reduce the production of space perspective to a single economic cause. However, causality becomes more complex in later postmodern work that emphasises the multiplicity of human and non-human agencies involved in the production of space and the complexity and heterogeneity of its outcomes on the ground.

Nevertheless, I believe that the spatiality of second language learning is shaped *first* by the forces of 21st-century globalisation, which create and distribute both demand and resources for second language learning, laying down templates for who gets to learn which languages in which parts of the world, how they learn them and for what purposes. Importantly, these matters are not resolved primarily in the domains of language policy and ideology; they are shaped by the global mobilities of physical objects (people, goods and information) that produce space on global and local scales. This idea is central to the environmental view of second language learning that I want to develop. At the local and individual levels of second language learning, however, there is room for manoeuvre and the resistant tactics of everyday life (De Certeau, 1984). At the individual level, I see language learning environments as emergent and heterogeneous outcomes of negotiations between individual learners and the global production of space; they are what individuals make of the spaces in which they find themselves. I will have more to say on this in the context of an environmental understanding of second language learning in Chapter 5.

Moving forward, I ask readers to keep two main ideas in mind. First, the social production of space is a global process that produces a differentiated physical space, a space of local environments as Gibson (1979) conceived them. Second, there is a distinction to be made between a modernist Newtonian objects-*in*-space view of the world and a postmodern objects-*as*-space view. In the next chapter, I want to apply these two ideas to the production of the disciplinary space of linguistics and its view of language as an object-*in*-space.

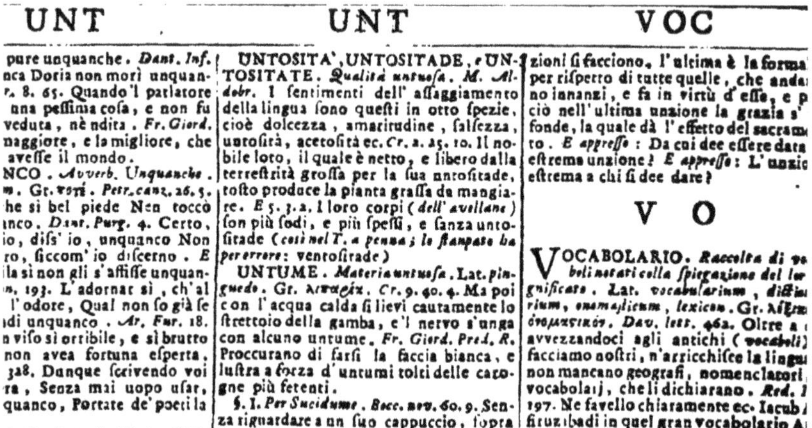

UNT UNT VOC

pure unquanche. *Dant. Inf.* ... nca Doria non morì unquan- ... r. 8. 65. Quando 'l parlatore ... una pessima cosa, e non fu veduta, nè udita. *Fr. Giord.* maggiore, e la migliore, che avesse il mondo. ... NCO. *Avverb. Unquanche.* ... Gr. ποτέ. *Petr. canz. 26. 5.* ... he sì bel piede Non toccò ... nco. *Dant. Purg. 4.* Certo, ... io, diss' io, unquanco Non ... ro, siccom' io discerno. *E* ... la sì non gli s'affisse unquan- ... 193. L'adornar sì, ch'al ... l'odore, Qual non so già se ... di unquanco. *Ar. Fur. 18.* ... n viso sì orribile, e sì brutto non avea fortuna esperta. ... 328. Dunque scrivendo voi ... ra, Senza mai uopo usar, ... quanco, Portate de' poeti la

... MAI, *che anche si scrive* UN- ... *Avverb. Giammai, Mai* ... *nquam.* Gr. ποτέ. *Dant. rim.* ... e ogni augel, che 'l caldo ... rese d'Europa, che non per- ... telle gelide unque mai. *Nov.* ... questo si scrisse per lo mi- ... ch'egli facesse unque mai. ... *red. S.* Chi è in peccato, e per mala via, unquemai ... bbe, se la misericordia non

... *Lo stesso, che Ugnere, Un-* ... *gere.* Gr. χρίειν. *Red. an.* ... 34. Prosciugandole con un ... ntano o di zibetto, o di ...

... *Add. da Untare.* Lat. ...

O. *Add. Dim. d'Unto; Al-* ... *Benv. Cell. Oref. 33.* Per tal ... tt' opera diviene alquanto ... orda. ... IO. *Superl. d'Unto. Tratt.* ... Vogliono averne lo stoma- ... l ventre untissimo. ... *st. Cosa unta, e che ugne.* ... Gr. τὸ κεχρισμένον. *Bocc.* ... a' nell' orto appiè del pesco

UNTOSITA', UNTOSITADE, *e* UNTOSITATE. *Qualità untuosa. M. Aldobr.* I sentimenti dell' assaggiamento della lingua sono questi in otto spezie, cioè dolcezza, amaritudine, salsezza, untosità, acetosità ec. *Cr. 2. 25. 10.* Il nobile loro, il quale è netto, e libero dalla terrestrità grossa per la sua untositade, tosto produce la pianta grassa da mangiare. *E 5. 3. 2.* I loro corpi (*dell' avellane*) son più sodi, e più spessi, e sanza untositade (*così nel T. a penna; le stampate ha per errore:* ventositade)

UNTUME. *Materia untuosa.* Lat. *pinguedo.* Gr. λιπαρία. *Cr. 9. 40. 4.* Ma poi con l'acqua calda si lievi cautamente lo strettoio della gamba, e 'l nervo s'unga con alcuno untume. *Fr. Giord. Pred. R.* Proccurano di farsi la faccia bianca, e lustra a forza d'untumi tolti delle carogne più fetenti.

§. I. *Per Sucidume. Bocc. nov. 60. 9.* Senza riguardare a un suo cappuccio, sopra il quale era tanto untume, che avrebbe condito il calderon d'Altopascio. *Bern. rim. 1. 96.* Se non gli desse noia già l'untume. *Malm. 5. 62.* Ovunque egli è, d'untumi fa un bagordo.

§. II. *Per Untuosità. But.* Le cose ante ardono superficialmente tanto, quanto dura l'untume, cioè l'untuosità.

UNTUOSITA', UNTUOSITADE, *e* UNTUOSITATE. *Astratto d'Untuoso; Untosità. But.* La fiamma è untuosità, che esce della materia, e convertesi in fummo. *Zibald. Andr. 113.* Dolcezza, amaritudine, salsezza, ed untuosità. *Tratt. segr. cos. donn.* In cotali loro untuositadi pensano di rinvigorire.

UNTUOSO. *Add. Che ha in se d.ll' unto, del grassume.* Lat. *unguinosus, pinguis.* Gr. λιπαρός. *Cr. 1. 4. 14.* Le sue triache sono le cose untuose, e dolci. *Ricett. Fior. 14.* Ha in se (*l'allume rotondo*) un certo che di giallo, e d'untuoso, ed in oltre non è pietroso, ed è facile a tritarsi. *E 85.* Certi semi, che hanno del viscoso, e dell' untuoso. *Buon. Fier. 3. 5. 6.* Untuoso, e grasso vivere Regni eterni suol prescrivere (*qui figuratam.*)

UNZIONCELLA. *Dim. d'Unzione.*

zioni si facciono, l'ultima è la forma per rispetto di tutte quelle, che anda... no innanzi, e fa in virtù d'esse, e p... ciò nell'ultima unzione la grazia s'... fonde, la quale dà l'effetto del sacram... to. *E appresso:* Da cui dee essere data estrema unzione? *E appresso:* L'unzio... estrema a chi si dee dare?

V O

VOCABOLARIO. *Raccolta di vo... boli notati colla spiegazione del lor significato.* Lat. *vocabularium, dictio... rium, onomasticum, lexicon.* Gr. λέξικ... ὀνομαστικόν. *Dav. lett. 462.* Oltre a ... avvezzandoci agli antichi (*vocaboli*) facciamo nostri, n'arricchisce la lingu... non mancano geografi, nomenclatori, vocabolarj, che li dichiarano. *Red. I... 197.* Ne favello chiaramente ec. Iacub ... situzibadi in quel gran vocabolario A... bico, che da esso con voce Egizia fu in... tolato Alcamus, cioè a dire Oceano.

VOCABOLISTA. *Vocabolario.* Lat. *vocabularium, dictionarium, onomasticum, lexicon.* Gr. λέξικον, ὀνομαστικόν. *Var. Ercol. 211.* Egli non si potrebbe credi... quanto alcuni (dico ancora di coloro, c... fanno regole, e vocabolisti) s'ingann... in esse. *Lasc. rim. 3. 319.* Un tuo vocabo... sta, ser Ruscello, M'ha chiarito alla f... che se' pedante. *Infar. sec. 303.* Rivolga... pure i vocabolisti.

VOCABOLISTARIO. *Compositore Vocabolarj.* Lat. *nomenclator.* Gr. ὀνομ... τολόγος. *Carl. Fior. 71.* Ne fosse info... mato per vostra lettera, come da sopr... stante segreto de' vocabolistarj. *Dep. D... cam. 139.* Che direm noi d'alcuni nuo... chiosatori, e vocabolistarj, che tanta, sì larga libertà si hanno presa sopra tant... delle nostre voci?

VOCABOLO. *Voce, o Nome, con cui denota ciascuna cosa particolare.* Lat. *vocabulum.* Gr. λέξις. *Bocc. nov. 2. 9.* Qual... Iddio, lasciamo stare il significato de' vo... caboli, ma la 'ntenzione de' pessimi su... mi non conoscesse. *E nov. 79. 36.* Il medi... co, che a Bologna nato, e cresciuto era non intendeva i vocaboli di costoro

Figure 3.1 Standardisation and spatialisation. The *Vocabolario degli Accademici della Crusca*. The definition of 'vocabolario' reads: 'Raccolta di vocabili notati colla spiegazione del lor significato'. A collection of words notated with the explanation of their meanings' (Source: Internet archive https://archive.org/details/vocabolariodegl00crusgoog/page/n218/mode/1up)

3 Linguistics and the Spatiality of Language

> It would be absurd to try to draw a panorama of the Alps as seen from a number of peaks in the Jura simultaneously. A panorama must be taken from just one point. The same is true of a language. One cannot describe it or establish its norms of usage except by taking up a position in relation to a given state. When the linguist follows the evolution of the language, he is like the observer moving from one end of the Jura to the other in order to record changes in perspective.
>
> Saussure, 1983: 81–82

This chapter shifts the focus from critical theories of space to the spatiality of language and the discipline of linguistics. It builds on an insight from the literature on the social production of space: although there is no empty space, space is often produced in the image of empty space. Physical space is emptied of its contents and replaced by a grid of self-contained spaces, each with its own systemically organised content. Modern linguistics, from which second language acquisition (SLA) derives its basic conception of the nature of language, has no explicit theory of the spatiality of language, of how language fits into space. But, I argue, it does work with an implicit conception of language as a self-contained, systemic object-*in*-space. I explore this view through two histories of emergence: first, the emergence of linguistics as an object in the disciplinary space of the social sciences and, second, the parallel emergence of the idea of language and its internal systems, structures and networks. Lastly, I look at how the idea of the language system connects to a history of the physical production of languages as self-contained systems through the semiotic geometries of standardisation, grammars and dictionaries.

The Spatiality of Language and Linguistics

Massey (2005: 65) writes that a particular way of imagining space as 'already divided up' has 'underpinned the material enforcement of certain ways of organising space'. But the end result is not a neatly ordered space of separated and bounded places, but a heterogeneous amalgam of layered spaces, reflecting the dynamics of the complex sets of social relations under which space has been produced over historical time. In order to make sense of the spatiality of language, we need to look at a particular layer of socially produced space: the disciplinary spaces that partition and organise knowledge, and especially the disciplinary space of linguistics.

By the spatiality of language, I mean two things: first, the distribution and circulation of languages and language varieties across geographical space (which will be discussed in Chapter 4) and, second, how language, more generally, 'fits into' space, which is the focus of this chapter. Fowler and Hodge (2011) observe that

> It is deeply entrenched in the thinking of most language researchers and language theorists that there is an object, 'language', that consists of forms and phonotactic and syntactic constraints on how the forms can compose utterances. (Fowler & Hodge, 2011: 150)

Here, Fowler and Hodge allude to two important aspects of the way in which modern linguistics represents the spatiality of language. First, language is seen as an object in the space of the world. Second, it is seen as a self-contained object that holds a certain content of its own. This view is held by almost all linguists. In the specific form that it is stated by Fowler and Hodge, it is a Chomskyan view, but almost all language researchers agree that language has some kind of content and some kind of internal patterning, expressed in terms of system, structure or network. From the viewpoint of modern linguistics, language has a definite 'outside' and 'inside'. Externally, it is one of many objects in the space of the social sciences; internally, it is an object with its own systemic spatiality.

However, linguistics has no explicit theory of the spatiality of language. Instead, we have to infer an implicit theory from metaphors that are present both in models of the language system and in the practices of the language professions. This implicit theory also has its correlates in everyday experience. We confront our own languages as objects that are so internally complex as to be beyond everyday understanding. We look to experts to tell us how to use language grammatically, while the task of second language learning is often construed as one of penetrating and absorbing the inner mysteries of some alien object in the space of the world.

A minority of linguists see language differently, as something that is integrated with and follows the contours of the world (e.g. Harris, 1990; Larsen-Freeman & Cameron, 2008; Pennycook, 2018; Thibault, 2011). In the following chapters, I will develop a version of this integrated view around the notion of language learning environments. In this chapter, however, I want to explore the mainstream view of the spatiality of language. This is a view with deep historical roots, and for this reason I take a historical approach, beginning with a brief consideration of how the production of language as an object-*in*-space is tied in with the production of the disciplinary spaces of the social sciences from which linguistics has emerged.

The Production of Disciplinary Space

Linguistics is the study of language or, more accurately, the study of languages in order to develop theories of language. But if we travel back in time, we reach a point around the beginning of the 17th century where there was little or no theorisation of language, only the study of languages for the practical purposes of foreign language teaching and translation. A history of the spatiality of language needs to explain, then, how the practical study of languages became the study of an abstract theoretical object, language. And because the object language was not already there, waiting to be studied, it also needs to explain both the production of language as an abstract object and the production of a disciplinary space in which this object became a focus of study. Moreover, the history of linguistics shares this problem with the history of the wider field of social sciences, which is not so much a history of the division of an existing field into discrete sub-fields, but more a history of the production of objects of inquiry within emerging realms of disciplinary space.

Disciplinary space is a classificatory space of objects and fields of inquiry. In the 17th century, it also became a space of abstraction in which the idea of thing began to stand in for the thing itself. In 1687, Isaac Newton (1962) came up with a theory of mechanics in which the abstract idea of space became space itself. It was also around this time that the idea of language began its journey into objecthood. By the 21st century, the social sciences had emerged as a comprehensive space of 'concrete abstractions' (Lefebvre, 1976), a space in which we might talk about, for example, the relationship between language and society as if we could hold language in one hand and society in the other. Organised around concrete abstractions of these kinds, disciplinary spaces are spaces in which ideational objects are produced and circulated. In De Certeau's (1984: 38) terms, a disciplinary space is a *lieu propre*, a place of power, in which there is 'an elaboration of theoretical places (systems and totalising discourses)… capable of articulating an ensemble of physical places in which forces are distributed'.

In Chapter 2, I took the view that space is physical. Here, I want to emphasise that disciplinary spaces are also physical spaces that are typically distributed across academic institutions and a host of allied professional and industrial facilities. As such, disciplinary spaces are not ivory towers, but globally distributed sites of concrete academic, professional and industrial labour. At these sites, ideational objects and spaces of inquiry are mutually constitutive. Disciplinary spaces form around ideational objects, as linguistics has formed around the idea of language, but they also produce their objects of inquiry, both as abstract ideas and as concrete objects in the world.

For Lefebvre (1991: 129), the social relations of production of an era 'project themselves into space', and in the process they produce space itself. The capitalist mode of production separated out three fields of space: the space of social practice ('social space'), the space of sensory phenomena ('physical space') and logico-epistemological space ('mental space') (Lefebvre, 1991: 11–12). Historically, the separation of mental space from social and physical space begins with the division of mental and material labour, which Marx and Engels (1970) connected to the separation of town and country. This was a prolonged process that began, perhaps, with the 12th-century figure of 'the professional, town-dwelling scholar who, though usually a cleric, yet devoted the substance of his life to writing and teaching' (Panofsky, 1957: 25). By the 17th century, the urban universities of Europe, and in some cases its monasteries, had become sequestered spaces – 'heterotopias' (Foucault, 1986) – in which abstract thinking could run free. It was at the University of Cambridge, for example, that Newton came up with the secular idea of an abstract empty space in the late 17th century. Earlier in the century, the monastery at Port-Royal-des-Champs, near Paris, provided a similar space for the emergence of an abstract conception of language, although it was not until the early 20th century that language reached the level of abstraction of Newton's empty space.

The Renaissance university was a point of departure both for the multilayered educational systems of the present day and an ever-increasing array of disciplines, sub-disciplines and areas of study. It was also a point of departure for the gathering of professional and industrial practices around academic spaces and their objects of inquiry. Around the object language, for example, we now have an immense physical apparatus of university departments, laboratories, lecture halls, academic associations, international conferences and academic publishing. We also have the various language professions, including dictionary-making, writing of grammars and style guides, editing, translation and language teaching, and the industrial production of the texts that these professions generate. Of equal importance to the disciplinary space of modern linguistics are the networks that connect the parts of this apparatus to each other on a global scale. In other words, we need to understand the emergence of the idea of language as a process that is fully integrated with the production of space under capitalism and globalisation.

The disciplinary spaces of the social sciences emerged in the 19th century in conjunction with the overthrow or decline of western European monarchies, the rise of democracy and social consensus, and the expansion of the colonised world. At the same time, Darwin's evolutionary theory aligned inquiry into human affairs with the natural sciences as individual and collective life became an object of empirical, as well as philosophical, interest. Key to the scientific treatment of the human world was the rooting out of objects of social inquiry from their embedding in the space of the world. As De Certeau (1984) puts it, the constitution of a scientific space requires the transfer of objects of study into the space and the leaving behind of others. 'Only what can be transported can be treated', he argues, and 'what cannot be uprooted remains by definition outside the field of research' (De Certeau, 1984: 20). By the turn of the 20th century, language, society, culture and the mind had each been successfully abstracted from the realities of social life, and each would become firmly established as a self-contained systemic object at the centre of its own disciplinary space: linguistics, sociology, ethnography/anthropology and psychology. From the mid-20th century onwards, two new trends emerged in the social sciences: interdisciplinarity and the proliferation of sub-disciplines.

Although linguistics abstracted language from the world, many linguists insist that it can only be understood in the context of society, culture or the mind. This has led to the emergence of what might be called the 'interdisciplines' of sociolinguistics, anthropological linguistics and psycholinguistics. More recently, computational linguistics and neurolinguistics have built bridges to the applied and natural sciences. Yet, this interdisciplinarity often misses the point that the objects that are combined have *already* been separated out from the world. Sociolinguistics, for example, brings together two well-established objects of inquiry, language and society. Yet, it has failed to produce its own third object of inquiry, say 'language-in-society', and as a result it always falls back into either linguistics or sociology. In this context, Lefebvre (1991: 335) refers to 'laboured interdisciplinary or multidisciplinary montages which never manage to fit any of the pieces back together'. Although this is a rather jaundiced view of interdisciplinary endeavour, it highlights how difficult it is to integrate the ideational objects of the social sciences to the point where they collapse into one another. Above all, it is their self-containment – their internal systems, structures and networks – that holds the external boundaries of these objects firm. The object of inquiry of sociolinguistics can only be the *relationship between* the object language and the object society, because the language *system* is of a quite different order to the social *system*.

The proliferation of sub-disciplinary spaces is related to what Lefebvre (1991: 86) called the 'pulverisation' of space, or its reduction to smaller and smaller volumes. Lefebvre was thinking of the pulverisation of urban space, but he also noticed the same tendency in social life, which is broken down into sectors – the transportation system, the school system, the money market, the banking system and so on – each subject to its own regime of expertise. Step by step, Lefebvre (1991: 311) suggests, 'society in its entirety is reduced to an endless parade of systems and subsystems, and any social object whatsoever can pass for a coherent entity'. In the disciplinary space of linguistics, language has fragmented into a set of interconnected subsystems, each a relatively self-contained object of inquiry for sub-disciplines such as phonetics, morphology, semantics, grammar and pragmatics. A phonetician might be an expert in articulatory, acoustic or auditory phonetics, which would be quite different to being an expert in phonology or speech perception. Linguistics is also fragmented into schools of thought, which no longer succeed each other in historical time, but continue to coexist side by side in disciplinary space. Language now has as many grammars as there are schools of thought on the matter of grammar. Structuralism, generativism and functionalism are, perhaps, the three major 20th-century schools of linguistics, but there are hundreds of variations on these three themes, each occupying its own micro-space within the disciplinary space of linguistics.

Ultimately, fragmentation lends heterogeneity and a lack of coherence to disciplinary spaces. There is a political logic to the unity of a discipline such as linguistics. Members of university linguistics departments typically self-identify as people who study 'language', an object large enough to sustain the physical apparatus of a university department. But linguists also affiliate to sub-disciplines beyond their departments, so that there are often as many sub-disciplines within a linguistics department as there are faculty members. Sub-disciplines organise themselves through scholarly associations, conferences and academic journals, leading to the production of cross-institutional spaces. In this sense, disciplinary spaces are never systematically organised. There is often the principle of a system, but in place of an actual system, we typically find a patchwork with more than a few loose threads. There is both a centripetal tendency for disciplinary spaces to establish their *lieux propres*, and a centrifugal tendency to subdivide and form webs of interdisciplinary connections that ensure that no disciplinary space is ever entirely isolated from its neighbours. Like the contemporary city, disciplinary space could aptly be described as 'an amalgam of often disjointed processes' with 'no completeness, no centre, no fixed parts' (Amin & Thrift, 2002: 8).

A Brief History of the Spatiality of Language

From languages to language

I have suggested that a history of the spatiality of language will need to explain how practical inquiry into languages became, from the 17th century onwards, theoretical inquiry into the abstract object language, and how this transition interacted with the emergence of the disciplinary space of modern linguistics. My version of this history will involve three distinct phases: 17th- and 18th-century grammar, 19th-century comparative philology and 20th-century linguistics. As a full history is beyond the scope of this book, I will examine these phases through a selective reading of three representative texts: the *Port-Royal Grammar* of 1660 (Arnauld & Lancelot, 1780), Müller's (1864) 1863 *Lectures on the Science of Language* and Saussure's (1983) *Course in General Linguistics*, first published in 1916.

Writing in the mid-17th century, the English poet John Milton (1644: np) declared, in a treatise on education, that language was an 'instrument convaying to us things usefull to be known'. In the context of its times this was a radical idea. Indeed, Milton's is the earliest citation for the word 'language' in the *Oxford English Dictionary* to view language as a means of communicating ideas. In earlier centuries, language seems to have meant either the use of words in speech or writing, or a specific language such as English or French. From the 17th century onwards, it becomes commonplace to refer to language, in the manner of Milton, as an object to be contemplated independently of its embedding in speech, writing or a specific language. Language becomes, in effect, something more than what it is – words, speech or the collection of words that makes a particular language. In addition, it becomes a means to the end of expressing and communicating thought. Milton's words thus prefigure an important theme of the European Enlightenment: the relationship between language and thought, which each became more abstract and more object-like as time went by.

Four centuries later, Lightfoot (2006: 3), a linguist in the Chomskyan tradition, suggested that if one were to ask how many languages there are, a plausible answer would be one, 'the human language'. From this perspective, 'language' is not just a word that we apply to the collectivity of languages; it is a distinct, ultimately definable, object in the world. However, this is to take several more steps along the road of spatialising language than Milton and his contemporaries were yet ready to take. The main problem for a history of the spatiality of language then, is to trace a path from Milton to Lightfoot. Milton abstracts the idea of language from the concrete specificity of languages and their use, but not to the degree of asserting the identity of language as a distinct object in the world. We begin, then, in the 17th century in an era in which the shape of the object language could be vaguely discerned, but was yet to fully emerge in its present-day form.

The *Port-Royal Grammar*

By Milton's time, inquiry into languages had already produced two important tools for the spatialisation of language: the dictionary and the grammar. I will return to the significance of these tools later in this chapter. For the present, I want to note that languages already possessed a certain spatiality, which 17th-century grammarians took as their starting point for a more general inquiry into what languages had in common.

At this point in history, a language such as English or French was, essentially, a collection of words, which could be grouped into word classes. Words could be decomposed into the sounds of a language, and there were known rules governing how the sounds and words of a language could be put together. Lastly, it was known that the major languages of Europe, including Latin and ancient Greek, were similar in these respects. The significance of the *Port-Royal Grammar* lay in the way it connected the spatiality of language to the spatiality of thought.

The *Port-Royal Grammar* was the product of a unique collaboration between a grammarian, Claude Lancelot, and a philosopher, Antoine Arnauld, who also co-authored a companion work, the *Port-Royal Logic* (Arnauld & Nicole, 1662). Lancelot had already published pedagogical grammars on Latin, Greek, Italian and Spanish, and Arnauld helped him to connect his observations on the similarities and differences among these languages to the work of the philosopher René Descartes. In a tract published in 1637, Descartes (1850: 97) observed that the use of 'words or other signs' to express thoughts was a characteristic of all men, no matter how 'dull and stupid' (Descartes, 1850: 98). This use of words to make thought understood (note that Descartes says 'words', not 'language') was, thus, evidence of a uniquely human 'reason'. It was also evidence of the hand of God, who had endowed humanity alone with reason. Descartes (1850: 100) was a materialist, but not in his belief in God or in the matter of 'the Reasonable Soul', which, he asserted, 'must be expressly created'.

The *Port-Royal Grammar* elaborated on this relation between language and reason with numerous examples of the rational basis of language forms. Grammar, the authors explained, was the art of speaking, and to speak was to explain one's thoughts using signs invented by men. A language was thus a 'marvellous invention' designed to make an infinite number of words using a small number of sounds (Arnauld & Lancelot, 1780: 64). But because words had only been invented to make thought known, one could not understand grammar without first understanding thought. The *Port-Royal Grammar* was a 'general grammar', because it was based on commonalities among several languages. That the *Port-Royal Grammar* turned out to be a grammar of French (with a sprinkling of examples from Latin) reflects, perhaps, a failure of this attempt to build generality upon comparison. However, it is the thought that counts, and in the case of the *Port-Royal Grammar* quite literally so. For Lancelot and Arnauld, commonalities among languages could only be explained by an underlying universality of thought, or reason, itself. The *Port-Royal Grammar* was thus '*raisonnée*' in a double sense; it explained grammar rationally, and the explanation lay in the reasoning mind.

Chomsky (1966) looked back to Descartes and the *Port-Royal Grammar* as sources for his own conception of language as an object of mind. But it should not be thought that this was an isolated current in

17th-century intellectual thought. We have to consider, instead, the emergence of new ways of thinking about languages that could make possible a statement by a writer such as Milton (who is unlikely to have read Descartes in 1644), where it had not been possible before. Why should Milton be able to see what his predecessors had, apparently, not seen: that language was a means of conveying ideas? Arguably, this has much to do with the growing division between mental and material labour at the time, as well as a certain secularisation of intellectual life that would soon transform the infinite space of God into the absolute empty space of Newtonian physics.

For early 17th-century Europeans, language was a gift of God that had been spurned by the builders of the Tower of Babel. For many scholars, it would remain so into the 19th century. In this sense, language was not a 'means' of doing anything at all. Milton and Descartes were, thus, making a radical claim, and to make such a claim was to set up a productive tension between theological and secular thought. The *Port-Royal Grammar*'s almost secular view of language as a 'marvellous invention' was reconciled with its theology in the belief that language was the product of a God-given reason. If reason were a gift of God, then language might be an invention of humans. That the relationship between language and thought should become a theme of the Enlightenment also had much to do with the rise of vernacular languages and the decline of Latin and Greek. Descartes chose to write in French, rather than Latin, because he believed that natural reason was best expressed in the native tongue. 'Those who make use of their unprejudiced natural Reason', he wrote, 'will be better judges of my opinions than those who give heed to the writings of the ancients only' (Descartes, 1850: 117–118). But for later philosophers, including John Locke and Gottfried Wilhelm Leibniz, vernacular languages were poor vehicles for the expression of rational thought and stood in need of improvement.

So important did the relationship between language and thought become, that Locke (1690) devoted one of the four books of his *Essay Concerning Human Understanding* to it. Although Locke and Leibniz agreed that language was bound up with rational thought, Locke took the view, against Descartes, that the mind was a *tabula rasa* (a philosophical counterpart to Newton's empty space) and that all knowledge was derived from experience. In a work completed in 1704, but not published until 50 years later, Leibniz (1896) refuted Locke's *Essay* chapter by chapter. He reasserted the innateness of reason, and in doing so provided Chomsky with the metaphor of language as 'mirror of mind'. Leibniz and Locke agreed, however, on the all-important problem of the imperfection of language as a vehicle for complex, abstract ideas, a pressing problem for the emerging scientific and political discourses of the time.

For Locke (1690), the imperfection of language was demonstrated by the comparison of equivalent words in different languages, which, he pointed out, rarely stood for the same precise idea. Leibniz also thought that language often made reasoning obscure. This view was widespread and led to a new prescriptive style in the writing of dictionaries and grammars. Concern about the imperfection of vernacular languages also led to proposals for artificial languages (Eco, 1995; Lewis, 2012). Wilkins' (1668) universal language, based on a division of the universe into 40 categories, subdivided according to type, was an early example of an artificial language based on rational thought and designed for cross-lingual use. Leibniz also proposed an artificial symbolic language in which all human concepts would be perfectly represented, based on the principle that complex ideas were derived from and reducible to combinations of simpler concepts (Kulstad & Carlin, 2013).

In the context of fears for the adequacy of language as a vehicle for rational discourse, linguistic inquiry reached an unprecedented level of intensity in the 18th century. As a result, language began to emerge as a concrete abstraction with a distinct exterior and interior. European languages, at least, had enough in common to be examples of a single general object, which was increasingly called 'language'. On the outside, language interfaced with thought. Closely related as language and thought were, the fact that there were many languages but only one reason demonstrated the boundary between them. By the end of the 18th century, the basic internal patterns of language, with its inventories of sounds, words, word classes and patterns of sentence formation, were also reasonably clear. Yet, the tight relationship of these patterns to the patterns of rational thought, not to mention the lack of an explanation for the *irrational* aspect of natural languages, meant that language could not yet emerge as a fully formed object in its own right.

Bouzée's (1767) *Grammaire Générale* came close to resolving the problem of the irrationality of natural language by making an explicit distinction between language (*'langage'*) and languages (*'langues'*). For Bouzée, language was subject to an immutable and universal 'general grammar' that belonged to the nature of reason itself. Languages, on the other hand, were subject to 'particular grammars'; they depended on arbitrary and mutable conventions that gave birth to the different languages of the world. From this point of view, natural language was not so much an imperfect mirror of mind, as a two-sided entity with an interior, pointed towards an inner regulatory reason, and an exterior, pointed towards an outer world of arbitrary and ever-changing conventions. A language such as French was, thus, a product of the interaction between its general and particular grammars, or its inner rationality and its exterior environment. This view of the spatiality of language prefigures the secular notion of the self-contained language system and its environment by more than a century. It was also separated from it by the radical changes in the nature of linguistic inquiry that took place in the 19th century.

Comparative philology and the science of language

It is in Saussure's (1983) *Course in General Linguistics*, published in 1916, that language first emerges, under the name *la langue*, as a fully fledged, self-contained object in the disciplinary space of linguistics. Before this, came a quite different kind of inquiry into languages called comparative philology. The question to be asked of 19th-century comparative philology, then, is what part it played in the transition from the object of Bouzée's general and particular grammars to Saussure's *la langue*. One interesting feature of the *Course in General Linguistics* is the presentation of Saussure's ideas as if they articulated an entirely new view of language. A brief historical survey at the beginning of the book clears the ground by identifying, and dismissing, three phases that the study of language had passed through 'before coming to terms with its one and only true object of study' (Saussure, 1983: 1).

The first phase, called 'grammar', is summarily dismissed as a 'prescriptive discipline, far removed from any concern with impartial observation' that 'offers no scientific or objective approach to a language as such' (Saussure, 1983: 1). The second phase, 'philology', is dismissed as being concerned with texts, rather than living language, although it is acknowledged as having paved the way for the third. The third phase, 'comparative philology', is credited with having discovered that languages were comparable and that 'connexions between related languages could furnish the data for an autonomous science' (Saussure, 1983: 2). Ultimately, however, the comparative philologists failed 'to define exactly what it was they were studying' (Saussure, 1983). In fact, comparative philology did not discover the comparability of languages; comparison was fundamental to the work of the grammarians and Bouzée (1767) consulted work on 17 different languages. We need to tease out, therefore, exactly what the break between comparative philology and general grammar entailed, which was, I suggest, Saussure's production of a space that could accommodate the whole of language, in both its generality and its particularities.

As we saw in Chapter 2, the 19th century was the era in which historical explanation came to the fore (Foucault, 1986; Soja, 1989). Language study took on a historical character in its concern with relations between the languages of the present and the languages of the past. It also took on a wider geographical scope as European colonial expansion led to an expanded awareness of the diversity of the languages 'spoken in every part of our globe' (Müller, 1864: 1). A noted oriental scholar, Max Müller was to become Oxford University's first professor of comparative philology in 1868. Five years earlier, he had delivered a series of popular lectures to the Royal Institution of Great Britain in which he made a bold bid for the recognition of 'the science of language'. Decidedly imperialist in its gathering together of a host of languages from every corner of the earth – from Tahiti to the Caribbean, Greenland to southern Africa, and China to the rainforests of Brazil – Müller's opening lecture was a cornucopia of linguistic detail in which no language was left unturned. If they did not discover the comparison of languages, the comparative philologists certainly compared more languages than anyone before them. And in its attention to the minutest detail of the most remote languages of the world, comparative philology articulated an entirely new outlook on language in which rational thought could play no part.

The risk in comparative philology, however, was that the unity of language, which had formerly been guaranteed by reason, would be lost in this return to the particularities of languages. From a spatial perspective, therefore, the significance of the historical turn was the renewal of this guarantee in the form of a single historical process of divergence. The hypothesis that all languages shared a single ancestor led to intense comparison of the sounds and morphological composition of words across languages, in which particularities of grammar were no longer seen as accidental imperfections, but as evidence of an historical space in which languages had diverged from a single individual. This was a hypothetical space that not only unified the 'rational' languages of Europe, but also accommodated all of the languages of the world and all of their forms. Significantly, it was also a space that belonged to the science of language alone, a *lieu propre* in which language was governed by historical laws that were internal to language itself. After Newton, the objective of a science was to formulate general laws governing its object of inquiry. The formulation of linguistic laws was, thus, crucial to the bid for a 'science of language', which was in turn crucial to the formation of an autonomous disciplinary space around language as an object of inquiry.

At the beginning of his first lecture, Müller painted a remarkable picture of the new science of language.

> [T]he language which we speak, and the languages that are and that have been spoken in every part of our globe since the first dawn of human life and human thought, supply materials capable of scientific treatment. We can collect them, we can classify them, we can reduce them to their constituent elements, and deduce from them some of the laws that determine the origin, govern their growth, necessitate their decay; we can treat them, in fact, in exactly the same spirit in which the geologist treats his stones and petrifactions – nay, in some respects, the same spirit in which the astronomer treats the stars of heaven, or the botanist the flowers of the field. (Müller, 1864: 1)

This statement is remarkable both for the way that it places language on the same ontological plane as rocks, stars and plants, and for its sense of the interiority of language as an object of science. The grammarians had lapsed into prescriptivism, because they had sifted the materials of language through the sieve of rational thought, discarding the particularities that did not pass through. They failed, in other words, to view the materials of language with the objectivity with which a geologist, say, views the materials of the earth. Yet, Müller also suggested that the science of language needed *only* the materials that languages provide. The laws governing language change have never been formulated systematically – there are just too many languages to accommodate – nor have they led back to a single original language. What was important, however, was the emergence of a self-contained space of inquiry, in which language was explained by the materials of language itself. Language was conceptualised, for the first time, as an object of the same order as the self-contained objects of the natural sciences, as an object with its own 'materials' and its own 'laws'.

Saussure and structuralism

In the *Course in General Linguistics*, Saussure (1983) offered up a new object of inquiry, *la langue*, for a new discipline, *la linguistique*. Although the *Course in General Linguistics* may no longer be widely read, it is a marker for the birth of modern linguistics. It is also often cited as the source of key ideas such as the language 'system', the arbitrariness of the linguistic sign and the distinction between synchrony and diachrony. Most importantly, the *Course in General Linguistics* offers one of the clearest accounts that we have of language as a self-contained object-*in*-space, an object that has been freed from its dependence on both reason and history. This object was *la langue*, and although this term is rarely used nowadays, it corresponds very closely to conceptions of language in modern linguistics. I will rely on Roy Harris' excellent English translation (Saussure, 1983), but before proceeding further, I want to note an issue in the translation of the term *la langue* that will prove important to what follows.

Translators of Saussure must struggle with the problem of finding English equivalents for two French words that could both be translated as 'language': *le langage* and *la langue*. In modern usage, *le langage* corresponds to 'language' used without a determiner ('the', 'a', 'this', etc.) to refer to language in general (a usage that seems to have emerged in English in the 17th century). *La langue* corresponds to 'language' used with a determiner to refer to a specific language (e.g. *la langue française*, the French language). This distinction corresponds, more or less, to Bouzée's (1767) use of *le langage* to refer to the object of general grammar and *langues* as the object of particular grammars. In modern French, also, linguistics is the study of *le langage*, not *la langue* (Maingueneau, 2009) and to say that linguistics is the study of *la langue* ('the language') would be to prompt the question, '*Quelle langue?*' ('Which language?'). The point is that *la langue* is used in a non-conventional manner in the *Course in*

General Linguistics to open up a new disciplinary space around an object that could not be grasped by any existing term.

Harris translates the well-known distinction between *la langue* and *la parole* as a distinction between 'language' and 'speech'. But Saussure's distinction between *la langue* and *le langage* is more difficult to pin down in English. Harris solved this problem by translating *le langage* as 'language' and *la langue* as 'linguistic structure'. This is problematic for two reasons. First, there is no explicit reference in the original French text to the 'structure' of language. Second, and more important from a spatial perspective, 'linguistic structure' does not quite capture the sense in which Saussure saw *la langue* as a concrete object in the world.

For Saussure, *le langage* was not so much language in general as language in its entirety, a concept that he inherited from comparative philology. *Le langage* was 'at the same time physiological, physical and psychological' (Saussure, 1983: 10). An illustrative figure of the 'speech circuit' (Saussure, 1983: 11) represents the elements of *le langage*. The figure shows two human heads facing each other, with lines leading from the brain and mouth of each into the ear and brain of the other. The association of 'concepts' with 'sound patterns' (*images acoustiques*) in the brain of the speaker (and the triggering of similar associations in the brain of the hearer) is 'entirely psychological' (Saussure, 1983: 12). The transmission of an impulse from brain to speech organs in the speaker, and from ear to brain in the hearer, is physiological, while the transmission of sound waves between the two heads is purely physical. In the communities of 'individuals linguistically linked in this manner' (*reliées par le langage*) (Saussure, 1983: 13), we have the space of *le langage*, a physical space of the world. But this space was far too crowded with objects of diverse kinds to constitute an autonomous space of linguistics. Saussure was concerned, therefore, to tease out the purely psychological aspect of the speech circuit as an object that linguistics could call its own. The space of *la langue* was purely psychological, or more properly social-psychological because it entailed conventional or collective agreement among a group of speakers and hearers on the association of concepts with sound images.

Viewed in this way, *la parole* is not speech or language-in-use, but whatever is left of the speech circuit when *la langue* has been extracted from *le langage*. As Saussure (1983: 77) put it: 'Linguistic structure [*la langue*] we take to be language [*le langage*] minus speech [*la parole*]'. *La langue* is language conceived as a system of signs; specifically, 'a grammatical system existing potentially in every brain, or more exactly in the brains of a group of individuals' (Saussure, 1983: 13). This grammatical system has three important spatial features. First, it is 'a system in which all the elements fit together, and in which the value of any one element depends on the simultaneous coexistence of all the others' (Saussure, 1983: 113). To think of a sign as no more than an arbitrary combination of concept and sound image, he wrote, 'would be to isolate it from the system to which it belongs' (Saussure, 1983: 112). Second, Saussure (1983: 15) emphasises that *la langue* is 'no less real than speech'. Linguistic signs are 'not abstractions', they are 'realities localised in the brain' (Saussure, 1983). Third, *la langue* is a system of differences and oppositions that divides up and makes sense of the 'vague shapeless mass' of thought (Saussure, 1983: 110). Crucially for an autonomous science of language, *la langue* had gained the upper hand over thought. Language no longer expressed thought; on the contrary, because *la langue* organised thought, it was thought that expressed language.

Saussure's unprecedented use of spatial metaphors and analogies is one of the most striking features of the *Course in General Linguistics*. To cite only a few examples (Saussure, 1983: 10, 13, 15), *la langue* is described as an 'institution', composed of 'acoustic images' that are 'stored' (*enmagazinée*) in a 'repository' (*dépôt*), or as a 'fund' (*trésor*) accumulated by the members of a community who are 'linked' by 'the social bond' of *la langue*. In contrast to *le langage*, which is 'heterogeneous', *la langue* is 'homogeneous' (1983: 14). At the same time, it is a 'complex mechanism' with 'workings' that cannot be intuitively grasped (1983: 73). And in a metaphor that Harris' translation misses, *la langue* is described as a totality of imprints (*empreintes*) deposited in each brain (*déposée dans chaque cerveau*), which remains beyond the conscious control of the depositaries (*en dehors de la volonté des dépositaires*) (1983: 19). The language system is also compared to a game of chess (1983: 87), the quincunx design of an orchard (1983: 91) and the structure of a building (1983: 122), while the inseparability of thought and sound in the sign is illustrated by comparing *la langue* to a sheet of paper with thought on one side and sound on the other. Several of Saussure's metaphors are supported by visual images, including diagrams representing the 'two-sidedness' of the linguistic sign (1983: 67) and the relationship between language (*la langue*) and the speech community (*la masse parlante*) (1983: 77–78). The difference between synchrony and diachrony is illustrated by a cross-section of a plant stem (1983: 87), and the division of thought and sound into signs is illustrated by a sketch showing how air pressure produces waves on the surface of the sea (1983: 156). Saussure also observes a curious feature of *la langue*:

> It has no immediately perceptible entities. And yet one cannot doubt that they exist, or that the interplay of these units is what constitutes linguistic structure [*c'est leur jeu qui la constitue*]. (Saussure, 1983: 105)

I would argue that Saussure's representation of *la langue* as a spatial entity has much to do with the sense he is able to convey that the units of *la langue* really do exist despite all evidence to the contrary.

Saussure's use of spatial metaphors, analogies and images is worth noting as a move that was to become characteristic of 20th-century linguistics. As we will see, Chomsky and Halliday both made prodigious use of spatial metaphors in their writing. In the quotation at the beginning of this chapter, Saussure compares a view of a mountain range from the summit of a single peak to the shifting perspective of an observer travelling from one end of the range to the other. Let us note, first of all, that the mountain-top view was a popular Romantic conceit of the 19th century (Macfarlane, 2003). Note also that, although Saussure uses this conceit to illustrate the difference between synchronic and diachronic views of language, it serves well as a contrast between the viewpoint of the scientific linguist, who views language from above, and that of the language user, who views it from within. As De Certeau (1984: 36) argues, a place of power implies 'a mastery of place through sight', a panoptic view in which objects can be observed, measured and brought within the scope of vision. Visualisation is, in this sense, of the utmost importance to the establishment of a disciplinary space; the object of inquiry must be visible from 'above', as it were, as an object-*in*-space and its internal spatiality must also be open to view.

Saussure's distinction between synchrony and diachrony is also important in this context. *La langue* was, he argued, both 'an institution in the present and a product of the past' (Saussure, 1983: 9). However, *la langue* only changes over time as a result of changes in *la parole* and, for this reason, the history of language was a matter for the study of *la parole*. For Saussure (1983: 99), then, linguistics proper was synchronic linguistics, or the study of language in the present, by which he meant 'a period of time of varying length, during which the sum total of changes occurring is minimal'. By separating *la langue* from *la parole*, Saussure separated language from time and history and turned it into a space. Synchrony is also the key to the relationship between Saussure and his predecessors. Saussure (1983: 82) dismissed the grammarians for their prescriptivism and reliance on logic, but he praised their 'strictly synchronic' programme. He praised the comparative philologists for having drawn attention to a new order of historical linguistic phenomena, but dismissed their abandonment of synchrony for diachrony. However, Saussure did not dismiss the historical approach entirely (having himself carried out important work on the history of German). He simply excluded it from the autonomous disciplinary space of linguistics, which required a purely spatial conception of language to guarantee its autonomy. Viewed synchronically, language was now, as Saussure (1983: 11) put it, 'a self-contained whole'.

As the main argument of this book is that SLA research should pay more attention to space, it might be asked whether Saussure's spatialisation of language was not, in fact, a good thing. Saussure's linguistics had a considerable influence on the 20th-century social sciences, where it was seen as a source for the various forms of structuralism (see, especially, Lévi-Strauss, 1963). And Soja (1989: 18) saw in structuralism 'one of the twentieth-century's most important avenues for the reassertion of space in critical social theory'. Massey (2005), however, disagrees. In a chapter entitled 'The Prison House of Synchrony', she observes that spatial framing was a way of 'containing the temporal', of holding 'the world still in order to look at it in cross-section' (Massey, 2005: 36). Though the structuralist intention of avoiding translating geography into history was a good one, she argues, structuralists 'rob the objects to which they refer of their inherent dynamism' (Massey, 2005: 38). In this sense, *la langue* flattened out the historical space of comparative philology. The space of language became, as it were, a snapshot of a space visualised from above, rather than a space that is experienced with all the senses from within. More than this, however, the assumption of a synchronic, immobile space entailed the idea that language could *only* be as it is at any given moment in time: a closed and completely interlocked system.

Ballard (2016: 13) observes that Saussure is 'generally regarded as the founder of modern linguistics'. This is largely due to his identification of *la langue*, the language system, as the proper object of linguistics. However, one could also argue that Saussure did little more than identify the *principle* of a language system, leaving the details of its description to his successors. With the rise of structuralist linguistics, the idea of a describable internal structure took hold. The *Oxford English Dictionary*, for example, now defines 'linguistics' as the 'scientific study of language and its structure'. A language, the dictionary tells us, is a 'system of communication… typically consisting of words used within a regular grammatical and syntactic structure'. The basic idea of *la langue* has thus become a fact about language itself: structure is an intrinsic property of language. To view language as a structure, however, is to view it as a particular kind of space. Structured physical objects are not interwoven with each other, they do not blend into each other, their parts do not move independently of the whole. But in contrast to the physical structure of, say, a building or the human body, the structure of a language is a purely metaphorical construct. It is an ideational tool that holds an ideational object together at the centre of a disciplinary space.

The assumption that language has structure, then, turns language into a self-contained object-*in*-space with its own internal spatiality. In this sense, Saussure's spatialisation of the language system is his most abiding contribution to modern linguistics, which now conceptualises language in much the same way as he conceptualised *la langue*. Freed from its attachments to rationality and history, language, in the 20th century, finally reached the level of concrete abstraction that Newtonian empty space had achieved two centuries earlier. It was also, for the first time, an autonomous object in a disciplinary space modelled in the image of Newtonian space.

Twentieth-century linguistics

One way to trace the history of the spatiality of language in modern linguistics would be to examine the increasing depth and complexity of spatial representations of the language system since Saussure. The name 'structuralist' was applied to linguists who took on the task of mapping out phonological, morphological and syntactic structures and their hierarchical relations (Bloomfield, 1933; Hjelmslev, 1961; Jakobson & Halle, 1956), although they were not all followers of Saussure. Bloomfield (1924, 1936), for example, viewed language as a highly complex behavioural response to stimuli and was critical of Saussure's idea of *la langue*. Nevertheless, he was designated a 'structuralist' for his models of 'constituent analysis', which broke sentences down into their grammatical components and represented them in the form of inverted tree diagrams. Bloomfield's approach was structural in that it began not from pregiven word classes, but from the relations of the components of a sentence to the grammar of the sentence as a whole.

Two major schools of linguistics dominated the latter half of the 20th century: Chomskyan generativist linguistics and, in a minority capacity, a range of functionalist approaches, among which Halliday's systemic-functional linguistics (SFL) is probably the best known. Although Chomsky (1957) was critical of structuralism, he named his pioneering work *Syntactic Structures* and the distinction between surface and deep 'structures' was central to his early work. Chomsky (1975: 3–4) later wrote that 'by studying language we may discover abstract principles that govern its structure and use'. It was on the point of the spatiality of language that Lefebvre (1991) took Chomsky to task. By insisting that a sentence was not simply a sequence of elements generated from left to right, but, instead, a set of levels ordered from high to low, Lefebvre argued, Chomsky (1975: 5) postulated 'a mental space endowed with specific properties – with orientations and symmetries' that 'completely ignores the yawning gap that separates this linguistic mental space from that social space wherein language becomes practice'. Halliday (2003: 2), on the other hand, tended to avoid the term 'structure', but he echoed Saussure in describing language as a 'semiotic system', or a 'system by which meaning is created and meanings are exchanged'.

One of the main innovations in late 20th-century linguistics, however, was a shift away from the essentially closed system of Saussure's *la langue* to more open, generative structures and networks. Chomsky has posited a grammar that is capable of generating an infinite number of well-formed sentences of infinite lengths, while Halliday (2003: 6) views language as a network of systems 'that makes it possible for a language to expand its meaning potential more or less indefinitely'. For Chomsky (2006: 62), language is an 'abstract system underlying behaviour'. While Chomsky has persistently sought out the most economical grammar,

Halliday's grammar is far from economical, mainly because it incorporates choices at the level of words. Halliday (2003: 2) describes language as a 'fuzzy' system, 'the most complicated semiotic system that we have': 'its own limits are unclear' and 'its internal organization is full of indeterminacy'. For both Chomsky and Halliday, then, language is much less self-contained and internally cohesive than Saussure's *la langue*. The closed systems of structuralism are increasingly giving way to the open systems of the natural and computational sciences.

Yet, Chomsky and Halliday also make liberal use of spatial metaphors and analogies to describe language structures, systems and networks. Chomskyan linguists have spatialised grammar to an extraordinary degree, beginning with Chomsky's 'transformations', which are essentially spatial rearrangements of the grammatical components of written sentences, although they are assumed to take place deep within the mind. Lantolf (1996: 727) noted a list of terms used by Chomskyan linguists, including 'dominance', 'command', 'government', 'binding', 'subjacency', 'barriers', 'constraints', 'dependency' and 'chains'. For Lantolf, these were 'conceptual metaphors of power and control'. They are also metaphors of space that illustrate the dependency of modern linguistics on spatial representations of language.

Halliday (2003) is a retrospective overview of his key ideas on language titled 'On the "Architecture" of Human Language'. The inverted commas around 'architecture' suggest that Halliday did not think that language was *actually* designed in the fashion of a building. Yet, there is ample evidence in the article of a highly spatialised lexicogrammar. Simple sign systems, Halliday (2003: 5) suggests, can be 'expanded' on four 'dimensions': they can be 'combined', 'uncoupled', 'layered' or 'networked'. The systems that make up networks of choice are described as 'organizational spaces', and lexical items are described as occupying 'the more delicate regions of one continuous lexicogrammatical space'. The evolutionary development from protolanguage to language, in which language lost its dependence on the ecosocial environment, is described in explicitly spatial terms: 'a space was created in which meanings could be organised in their own terms, as a purely abstract network of interrelations' (Halliday, 2003: 14). In this observation, we have a remarkable analogue of the Newtonian conception of space, in which the lexicogrammar takes the place of absolute empty space and 'meanings' take the place of physical objects in relative space.

For their followers, Chomsky's generative linguistics and Halliday's SFL are very different in kind. Yet, both Chomsky and Halliday posit a self-contained object, language, with an internally systematic grammar (Chomsky) or lexicogrammar (Halliday). For Chomsky, language is an object of mind that generates grammatically well-formed sentences. For Halliday, who has done more than most linguists to bridge Lefebvre's 'yawning gap' between mental and social space, grammar emerges from the use of language resources to express functions essential to social life. There is a clear spatial difference here. In Chomsky's account, language leans towards mind, whereas in Halliday's account it leans towards the environment. For Chomsky, grammar is interior to mind (although not equivalent to 'reason'), whereas Hallidayan grammar follows the contours of social communication and practice within contexts of culture and situation. In this sense, Chomsky and Halliday point language in different directions, with profound consequences for linguistic theory at multiple levels. However, they also share a certain common ground.

Halliday (1970: 142) writes that '[t]he particular form taken by the grammatical system of language is closely related to the social and personal needs that language is required to serve'. Referring directly to Chomsky's ideas on language acquisition, he suggests that 'the very specific properties of language are not innate, and therefore the child is more dependent on his environment… for the successful learning of his mother tongue' (Halliday, 1978: 17). It is worth noting, however, that Halliday is concerned here with the 'particular form' of the grammatical system and the 'specific properties' of language. He acknowledges that children possess the mental 'ability to process certain highly abstract types of cognitive relation which underlie (among other things) the linguistic system' (Halliday, 1978). Chomsky (1980: 44), on the other hand, writes that although it is 'reasonable to assume that the language faculty… develops in the individual along an intrinsically determined course', it also develops 'under the triggering effect of appropriate social interaction and partially shaped by the environment'. The difference between Halliday and Chomsky, in other words, becomes a difference of emphasis. Both acknowledge the importance of mind and both acknowledge the importance of the social and cultural environment. Importantly, neither wishes to dissolve the object, language, into mind or the environment. For Chomsky, there is still language *and* mind. And although Halliday (1978: 192) writes that 'language has had to be taken out of its glass case, dusted, and put back in the living environment', there is still language *and* the environment.

Producing Language as Space

Saussure's *Course in General Linguistics* marks both the birth of language as a self-contained, internally patterned object and the birth of a disciplinary space that would take language, so conceived, as its object of inquiry. Saussure was, thus, both the founder of modern linguistics and the founder of the modern concept of language. After Saussure, linguists went to work on the internal structure of language, consolidating and amplifying the space of linguistics as they went about the task. Chomsky and Halliday opened up both the internal structure and, to some degree, the external borders of language, abandoning structuralism, if not the broad idea of structure, in search of more open and more complex systems or networks. At the same time, linguistics opened up to interdisciplinary endeavours in fields such as psycholinguistics and sociolinguistics and to a wide variety of perspectives on the internal patterns of language and its links to the world beyond. The basic idea of language as a self-contained object in space was now so firmly established at the centre of the disciplinary space of linguistics that such risks could be taken. Chomskyan linguistics could even locate a language module inside the mind without fear that it would dissolve into the domains of psychology that surrounded it. The point is, perhaps, that the social sciences no longer needed a Saussure to tell them that language exists independently of their own objects of inquiry. Language was now clearly visible in the space of the social sciences *as* the object that linguistics studied. Where a certain conception of the spatiality of language once stood as guarantor for linguistics, linguistics now stands as guarantor for the spatiality of language.

If we find ourselves thinking of language as a kind of planet, inhabited by words and grammatical structures and floating in a solar system in which the other planets have names such as mind, society and culture, we might blame linguistics. Linguistics certainly bears a significant portion of the responsibility for how we conceptualise language in everyday discourse. But linguistics has not acted alone, and in conclusion to this chapter, I want to sketch out another history in which linguistics develops in tandem with a range of professional and industrial practices that also have language as their object. The significance of these practices is that they do not simply conceptualise language as a self-contained object-*in*-space, they *physically* produce language as such an object. A fuller history of the relationship between these practices and the emergence of the disciplinary space of linguistics would need to explore practices such as language standardisation and translation, the invention and use of artificial languages, second language teaching and learning, editing and publishing, the production of pedagogical grammars and style manuals and the compilation of encyclopaedias, atlases and other reference works, especially, dictionaries. This brief sketch focuses on grammars and dictionaries, which have historically been the strongest influence on theoretical conceptions of language.

Grammars and dictionaries

Coulmas (2013: xi) writes that 'the very concept of a language, in the sense of one language being distinct from another, is indissolubly bound up with writing'. To make sense of this statement historically, we need to keep in mind that the 'general grammars' of the 17th and 18th century inherited a rudimentary analytical apparatus from several centuries of second language pedagogy (Howatt, 1984; Kelly, 1969). This apparatus was based on a small number of written languages. Arnauld, the co-author of the *Port-Royal Grammar*, had written pedagogical work on Latin and Greek, which were mainly known as written languages, and the three European languages that had developed significant literatures by the mid-1600s: French, Spanish and Italian. The written forms of European languages were already undergoing standardisation, especially in regard to word choice and spelling, but more important from a spatial perspective were the bodies of literary texts that the major languages now possessed. Semiotically speaking, French literature stood for the French language; it told the world, and French speakers themselves, that French existed separately from Spanish and Italian, which were represented by their own literatures. More than this, however, the body of French literary texts, dispersed across the territory of France and beyond its borders, represented the objectivity of the French language in physical form. The existence of French could hardly be doubted when a book written in French could be held in the hand. And before long, the physical body of the French language would also incorporate a body of metalinguistic texts in which the language described, defined and delimited itself.

In order to understand why the idea of 'general grammar' emerged in the mid-1600s, we need to look at the state of publishing at the time. Although printing presses had been at work across Europe for more than 100 years, the 17th century witnessed a flowering of the book trade and newspaper production, mainly as a consequence of the rise of vernacular languages, the secularisation of publishing and a relaxation of state controls on licensing and freedom of expression. European languages were now embodied in vast quantities of published text, raising concerns, discussed earlier in this chapter, about the adequacy of natural language to discourse in the public sphere. Sixteenth-century dictionaries and grammars were mostly bilingual and designed as aids to second language learning or translation. Nobody would consult a dictionary or grammar in order to learn about their native tongue. But in the 17th century, attention turned to documentation of the native tongue itself in monolingual dictionaries and grammars.

The Italian Accademia della Crusca was established in 1583 and published its dictionary of Italian in 1612. The Académie Française (established in 1635) published its dictionary in 1687. However, these authoritative national dictionaries were only the tip of an iceberg. In England, where there was no academy, a series of monolingual dictionaries were published in the 1600s, beginning as quasi-bilingual texts designed to explicate, and sometimes introduce, Latin, Greek and French loanwords – so-called 'inkhorn' words (Benson, 2001). A number of English dictionaries were already in circulation when Samuel Johnson's (1755) authoritative *Dictionary of the English Language* appeared. By this time, dictionaries had taken on a more regulatory role and Johnson's dictionary, which also incorporated a grammar, was part of a wider project to 'fix' the English language. Like the dictionaries of the European academies, it aimed to distil a purified version of the language from the work of the 'best' writers of the past, who were liberally cited throughout Johnson's dictionary. In the social project that lay behind these authoritative dictionaries, we see the seeds of Saussure's synchronic view of language. For the prescriptivists of the time, European languages were falling into decline as a consequence of their more widespread use in printed text. The project of standardisation used the spatial forms of the dictionary and grammar to hold language still at a point where it was deemed to best reflect rational thought. Before long, every national language in Europe had an authoritative dictionary – the pinnacle of its body of literature and an object that could stand for the language as a whole. Like dictionaries, grammars were increasingly produced for native speakers and they also became increasingly prescriptive, imposing a degree of homogeneity on the language itself. Importantly, this was achieved as much by representation as by prescription.

Space is key to understanding the sense in which dictionaries and grammars represent language. If literature, or the collectivity of published texts, constitutes the tangible physical form of a language, grammars and dictionaries are, in a sense, the essence of this form – metalinguistic works in which the language is represented comprehensively but economically and in an orderly spatialised fashion. In modern terminology, grammars lay out the structure of a language in categorical and classificatory lists and tabulations. The dictionary, on the other hand, aspires to represent the whole of the language, segmenting it into words and tabulating their forms, pronunciations, senses, usages and so on. Although the dictionary never succeeds in capturing the whole of a language, it is important that it appears to do so. This entails a complex semiotic geometry of inclusions, exclusions and markings, as well as networks of word–word relations that emerge as words are defined by other words, that are themselves defined elsewhere in the dictionary (Béjoint, 1994; Benson, 2001). In both the grammar and the dictionary, the language is represented geometrically; arranged within, and at times forced into, the cells of a reticulated empty space. The spatial forms of the grammar and dictionary thus become the spatial forms of the language. Long before Saussure, the dictionary and grammar were producing language as a self-contained systemic object in space.

Discussing the 'invention of monolingualism' in Europe, Gramling (2016) points to the way in which language standardisation rendered European languages mutually translatable. Languages were standardised on the assumption that any word or sentence in any language could be readily translated into a word or sentence in any other language without loss of meaning. If this assumption did not hold, then language needed to be changed. For Gramling, monolingualism is not so much the condition of knowing only one language as the principle, which emerged over several centuries of standardisation and translation, that anything can be said in any language and, therefore, one really does not *need to know* more than one language. This is, perhaps, the principle that underpins Lightfoot's (2006) view that there is only one language, the human language. We all speak this one language, we just use different words. Grammars and dictionaries played a crucial role in language standardisation and we can readily see what they contributed to Gramling's principle of translatability. They did not only stand for the languages they described, but they also furnished spatial templates into which any language could fit or, perhaps, be forced. The grammar and the dictionary thus became spatial representations of the idea of a standard language, and all the more so as their production was industrialised with all the implications of standardisation that industrial production entails.

Standardisation and modern linguistics

Saussure levelled the playing field of language variety. From the perspective of *la langue* there were no hierarchies of language or language variety; every variety was a language system. But this modern egalitarian view obscures the history of language standardisation and its formative influence on modern linguistics. For the British linguist Wyld (1907: 357), standard English was 'the channel of all that is worthiest in the national literature and the national civilisation'. It had an 'absolute superiority over any of the dialects' (Wyld, 1907), because it had been refined over two centuries of standardisation. Wyld's view can now be dismissed as an elitist view, but we can nevertheless acknowledge that standard languages are not simply fished out of the sea of dialects and language varieties. A dialect is selected, but it is then *produced* as a standard language. Moreover, the work that goes into the production of the standard is spatial work. In Chapter 2, I argued that the Newtonian conception of space is not just an idea. Under the capitalist mode of production, space is produced in the image of the Newtonian conception. This is equally true of the production of language. The word 'standard' implies measurement; standard languages are, thus, measurable entities that fit within the geometries of the grammar and the dictionary. They also have a homogeneity that conforms to the mathematical logic of general grammar and stands opposed to the heterogeneity of non-standard languages. By a 'non-standard' language, here, I mean a language that has not been subjected to standardisation, not a language that is somehow inferior to standard language. Crucially, however, grammars and dictionaries represent standard language as if it were language itself. In doing so, they furnish evidence that language 'possesses' a system or structure that allows it to be accommodated within the spatial framework of the grammar or dictionary. As a result, 'non-standard' languages seem to be inferior, because they lack the system or structure that is assumed to be inherent to language itself.

Ballard (2016: 29) observes that, '[o]ur feeling that language "exists" is perhaps reinforced by the evidence of specific languages having been embodied, so to speak, in dictionaries and grammar books'. Everyday conceptions of language are shaped as much by our experience of authoritative representations of our languages as they are by direct experience of language use. We also learn to mistrust our own use of language and to measure it against the language of the grammar and dictionary. Is it possible that this is also true of modern linguistics? There is certainly some evidence that Saussure put the cart of *la langue* before the horse of *la parole*. One of Saussure's great influences was the American comparative philologist William Dwight Whitney (1875). Whitney was also a dictionary editor and he made the following observation:

> No one can define in the proper sense of that term, a language; for it is a great concrete institution, a body of usages prevailing in a particular community, and it can only be shown and described. You have it in its dictionary, you have it in its grammar… (Whitney, 1875: 157)

For Whitney, the grammar and the dictionary were the closest that one could come to a definition of a language, which begs the question of how one could define a language that has no grammar or dictionary. Among his many spatial analogies, Saussure also compared *la langue* to a dictionary:

> A language (*la langue*) as a collective phenomenon, takes the form of a totality of imprints in everyone's brain, rather like a dictionary of which each individual has an identical copy. (Saussure, 1983: 19)

This observation provides an answer of a kind to my question. One could define a language that had no grammar or dictionary, perhaps, by writing a grammar and dictionary for it. In fact, this is what many 20th-century linguists did, giving all kinds of languages spatial form by providing them with a writing system and a certain representation of the standard. To get back to the point, however, there is more than a hint in Saussure's comment that the synchrony of *la langue* is, in effect, the synchrony of language as it is 'fixed' in the dictionary. At the very least, the orderly spatial representations of languages that appear in dictionaries suggest the idea of a synchronous language system. And, of course, by the end of the 19th century most educated Europeans actually did possess a dictionary of their native language, if not in their brains, at least in their homes.

The establishment of the disciplinary space of linguistics in the 20th century led to a reordering of the hierarchies of theory and practice. Although we now assume that theoretical linguistics informs the language professions, this was by no means always the case. In this context,

Saussure made a second interesting comparison between *la langue* and the dictionary or grammar.

> Our ability to identify elements of linguistic structure (*la langue*) in this way is what makes it possible for dictionaries and grammars to give us a faithful representation of a language. A language is a repository of sound patterns and writing is their tangible form. (Saussure, 1983: 15)

This comment raises the old chicken or egg question. Which comes first, the language system or systematic representations of language in metalinguistic texts? Here, Saussure seems to suggest that the dictionary and grammar express the inner spatiality of *la langue*. Yet, this is surely an error to the extent that it ignores the prolonged history of language standardisation, in which European languages were forced, often uncomfortably, into the spatial frameworks of dictionaries and grammars. There is, in other words, a certain sleight of hand involved in the claim of modern linguistics that all language varieties are equal. Without the spatialisation of language involved in standardisation, modern linguistics might not exist at all.

Modern linguistics has moved on from straightforward analogies between the spatiality of language and the spatiality of the grammar and dictionary. Nevertheless, in a current widely used introductory textbook on Linguistics, Fromkin *et al.* (2018: 11) can still write: 'The grammar, together with a mental dictionary that lists the words of the language, represents our linguistic competence'. Linguists such as Chomsky and Halliday, on the other hand, now see language less as a reflection of its representation in grammars and dictionaries, and more as an open system that is capable of generating an infinite expanse of sentences or meanings. In this, they make an analogy with computer systems and their capacity to generate vast quantities of information from a limited set of instructions. Chomsky and Halliday both worked with computational linguistics and their spatial metaphors are often drawn from that field. To paraphrase Saussure, language is no longer like a dictionary, but more like a computer program installed in everyone's brain. The problem for linguistics is to work out how the program works. In our everyday lives, we also see computer programs processing, generating and translating almost inconceivable quantities of text on the internet. Digital representation is producing language as a new kind of object in the world, and this object will undoubtedly have its impact on conceptions of language within the disciplinary space of linguistics.

Conclusion

The main argument of this book is that SLA should pay attention to the *where* of language learning; it should take space more seriously than it does at present. What I hope to have shown in this chapter is that this means challenging and finding alternatives to the implicit theory of the spatiality of language that already underpins SLA research and practice. The problem that I have identified in modern linguistics is not that it neglects space – linguistics is awash with spatial metaphors and analogies. Rather, linguistics spatialises language without explicitly acknowledging that it does so and without reference to spatial theory. I have suggested that linguistics is underpinned by a Newtonian objects-*in*-space view of the world. But it is more important, perhaps, to identify the particular form in which this conception is applied to language.

Language is not a physical object in motion in empty space, but linguistics conceptualises language as if it were such an object. What exactly does this mean from an object-*as*-space perspective? First, linguistics defines language as what it is not – language is not society, culture, mind and so on. But what this really means is that language is *ideationally* produced as the self-contained object of a vast *physical* disciplinary and professional apparatus – what I have called the disciplinary space of linguistics. Second, language is conceptualised as an internally structured space – a space *sui generis* that contains and organises a content of its own. And once again, there is the production of a *physical* space – the professional and industrial production of representations of standard languages as spatially structured objects.

Although I have not dealt directly with SLA in this chapter, it will be clear that SLA draws its basic conception of language from modern linguistics. Moreover, linguistics spatialises *language* by spatialising *languages*, and as it does so it makes them available to be learned as *second languages*. Historically, these are three aspects of a single process, although it is worth noting that second language learning seems to have driven the process up to the 17th century. One of the consequences of this is that second language learners tend to confront the languages they learn as self-contained objects in space, and often as neatly organised standardised objects, packaged in textbooks, learners' dictionaries and grammars, and other language learning materials. From the next chapter onwards, my task is to elaborate an alternative to the objects-*in*-space perspective on the spatiality of language: an 'objects-*as*-space' or 'environmental' perspective that might serve as a basis for a different view of what second language learning entails. In the next chapter, I begin the task by exploring the sense in which language becomes physical and is set on the move.

Figure 4.1 A multilingual language-bearing assemblage in motion, Kennedy Town, Hong Kong (Source: Author's photograph)

4 Language-Bearing Assemblages

> [T]here is no language in itself, nor are there any linguistic universals, only a throng of dialects, patois, slangs, and specialized languages. There is no ideal speaker-listener, any more than there is a homogeneous linguistic community. Language is, in Weinreich's words, 'an essentially heterogeneous reality'. There is no mother tongue, only a power takeover by a dominant language within a political multiplicity. Language stabilizes around a parish, bishopric, the capital. It forms a bulb. It evolves by subterranean stems and flows, along river valleys or train tracks; it spreads like a patch of oil.
>
> Deleuze and Guattari, 2013: 6

In Chapter 3, I critiqued what I called the objects-*in*-space conception of the spatiality of language that has developed within the disciplinary space of modern linguistics. One of my main concerns with this conception in regard to second language acquisition (SLA) research is that it encourages us to think of second language learning as a matter of any learner learning any language anywhere. In effect, the objects-*in*-space view frees language from its spatial constraints, such that the *where* of second language learning becomes unimportant. This is a conception of space that says that space does not matter. What matters are the universal processes that hold true under any spatial circumstance at all. This book, on the other hand, argues for an environmental approach to SLA research in which the spatial circumstances of second language learning matter a great deal.

The critique of the objects-*in*-space conception of language has, in a sense, cleared the ground for an environmental or objects-*as*-space view of language. In order to outline the main features of this view, I need to introduce three new concepts: flat ontology, assemblage and mobilities. The idea of flat ontology helps us explain what language is and how it becomes present in the world. From assemblage theory, I develop the idea that language becomes spatially present in the particular forms of language-bearing assemblages: people, goods and information. Mobilities theory helps explain how language-bearing assemblages are put into motion on a global scale and how languages get into language learning environments.

A Spatial Ontology of Language

I have suggested that the spatiality of language is a matter of how language fits into space. I now want to reframe this as a question of spatial ontology. Ontology is broadly concerned with how things exist, or the nature of their being. By spatial ontology, I mean how things exist spatially or the nature of their relations to space. The objects-*in*-space and objects-*as*-space views are, essentially, contrasting spatial ontologies. The objects-*in*-space view of language posits a spatial relation between two entities: one entity, language, exists *inside* another entity, space. This implies a dualistic opposition between objects and space; objects are always something other than space itself. In the objects-*as*-space view, objects *are* space, or rather space is a property of objects and their interrelations. In the objects-*as*-space view, space is also a *physical* reality. It makes little sense from this point of view to say that a non-physical object occupies space. Non-physical objects can only occupy the space of other, physical, objects. The problem for a spatial ontology of language that adopts an objects-*as*-space view is, then, to explain the relation of language to the physical world.

I want to begin from three propositions that I believe to be almost self-evident, based on our everyday experience of language: (i) language exists; (ii) language is ubiquitous; (iii) language exists physically, but it is not a physical object. The first two points should not be controversial. First, language exists if only in the sense that it is something, rather than nothing. When Deleuze and Guattari (2013: 6) write that there is 'no language in itself', they do not really mean that language does not exist at all. In fact, they recognise the heterogeneous 'reality' of language only a few lines further on. What they mean is that the abstract object that linguistics proposes as language does not exist. Second, language is ubiquitous in the sense that we find it everywhere that we find humans. It is the stuff of thought, speech and writing, and social action and interaction. Language is inextricably bound up with social processes of all kinds, from the day-to-day management of family relations and friendships, to the lives of institutions, cities and nations. And of particular importance in the context of second language learning, language is crucial to global mobility and relations. Language is also a ubiquitous presence beyond the purely human world in the names of things, processes, emotions, identities and experiences. As Ochs (2012: 144) puts it, we live in a world of 'saturated entanglement of experience and language'. We experience Gibson's (1979) physical environments as already 'languaged', as environments in which things already have names and differ from each other because they have different names.

The third proposition, that language exists physically but not as a physical object in its own right, may be less self-evident. Michael Dear (1997: 49), a postmodern geographer, suggests that space is 'nature's way of preventing everything from happening in the same place'. Language, however, seems to defy this principle by always occupying the space of something else and never a space of its own. We always encounter language physically, but always in the physical form of something other than language: as electrical impulses in the brain, as vibrations in the air or as light reflected from a surface or projected onto a screen. It might be argued, on this view, that language *only* exists physically; that it does not exist at all outside of the physical forms in which it is made manifest. This is, however, a non-intuitive view. We could read Adrian Mitchell's poem 'Tell Me Lies about Vietnam' silently and then watch a video of the poet reading 'Tell Me Lies about Vietnam' aloud in live performance. The printed poem and the spoken poem are clearly different objects, with very different spatialities, but it would make no sense to say that they are two different poems. In other words, 'Tell Me Lies about Vietnam' exists as a *non-physical* entity independently of the different *physical* forms in which it is spatially manifested. This also has much to do with the ubiquity of language. Language is made up of a finite number of non-physical entities (for the sake of brevity, I will call them 'words') which can be put out into the physical world in multiple forms simultaneously, and time and time again. The ontological problem that needs to be addressed, then, concerns the non-physicality of linguistic entities and their ubiquity in physical space.

Object-Oriented Ontology and Assemblage Theory

As a source of ideas for a spatial ontology of language, I draw on the work of a loose alliance of contemporary philosophers who are sometimes described as 'speculative realists' (Bryant *et al.*, 2011). Western philosophy is dominated, they argue, by dualist oppositions between mind and external reality, subject and object, or more generally, the human and the non-human. Speculative realism challenges this dualism through the idea of flat ontology, or an assumption that all entities, human and non-human, are ontologically equal. In this, speculative realism connects to a number of recent calls for attention to the agency of non-human entities (Barad, 2007; Bennett, 2010; Bogost, 2012; Bryant, 2011; Garcia, 2014; Latour, 2005; Morton, 2013).

Object-oriented ontology (also known as OOO or 'triple O') is the brain-child of the philosopher Graham Harman (2016, 2018). It grew out of his interest in the 20th-century German humanist philosopher Martin Heidegger and the French sociologist Bruno Latour's (2005) actor-network theory (ANT) and it is now closely allied with Miguel DeLanda's (2006, 2016; DeLanda & Harman, 2017) assemblage theory. DeLanda's assemblage theory elaborates on ideas originally proposed by Deleuze and Guattari (2013), but it is in many ways independent of their work. Although Harman and DeLanda deploy very different conceptual vocabularies, they hold similar views on the ontology of objects and assemblages. The following brief outline is selective and focuses on three key ideas: (i) flat ontology, (ii) the rejection of the ontological distinction between humans and non-humans and (iii) the complexity of objects and assemblages. I will also highlight three characteristics of assemblages: (i) their emergence from the interaction of their component parts; (ii) the detachability of parts; and (iii) downward causality, or the retroactive effects of assemblages on their parts. These ideas contribute to my understanding of the spatiality of language by providing an ontological framework for the proposition, which I will develop later in this chapter, that language becomes spatial only in the physical forms of 'language-bearing assemblages'.

OOO borrows the idea of flat ontology from Latour's (2005) ANT, which holds that 'anything is real insofar as it *acts*' (Harman, 2016: 2). Traditional ontologies use the spatial metaphor of ontological 'planes', or hierarchically arranged levels on which different kinds of entities exist. Religious ontologies, for example, often posit one or more transcendental planes that are situated above the plane of human experience on which only spiritual entities exist. Modern secular philosophies, on the other hand, tend to posit ontological divides between, for example, mental and material, subjective and objective, or human and non-human planes. Flat ontology recognises no *a priori* hierarchies or divisions of these kinds. There is only one ontological plane on which all objects exist equally. In spatial terms, we might posit distinct physical, social and mental 'fields' of space (Lefebvre, 1991), but from the point of view of flat ontology, there is only one space that is physical, social and mental at the same time.

For Harman (2016: 54), the point of a flat ontology is that it 'initially treats all objects in the same way, rather than assuming in advance that different types of objects require completely different ontologies'. In this respect, OOO is highly inclusive in regard to what counts as an object. One of Harman's (2016: 2) lists includes 'supersonic jets, palm trees, asphalt, Batman, square circles, the Tooth Fairy, Napoleon III, al-Farabi, Hillary Clinton, the city of Odessa, Tolkien's imaginary Rivendell, an atom of copper, a severed limb, a mixed herd of zebras and wildebeest, the non-existent 2016 Chicago Summer Olympics, and the constellation of Scorpio'. Harman (2016, 2018) also treats larger-scale entities and events as objects, including the Portuguese East India Company, the American Civil War and a mid-air aeroplane collision. Although Harman does not address language from an ontological viewpoint, there seems to be no reason why language and other linguistic entities (languages, poems, words, etc.) should not be considered as objects. OOO imposes only two conditions on objects: that they should not be reducible either to their component parts or to their effects. Harman's main point is that there is a 'surplus' beyond the parts of an object and its effects, which is the existence of the object itself. Beyond these conditions, no object is more of an object than any other, and all objects 'must be given equal attention, whether they be human, non-human, natural, cultural, real or fictional' (Harman, 2018: 9).

One of the main features of flat ontology is its avoidance of the dichotomy between the human subject and the external world. Harman makes a distinction between the 'sensual' object, or the object as it is perceived sensually by other objects, and the 'real' autonomous object, which is only accessible via the sensual object. He also insists that this distinction applies not only to the relationship between humans and the external world, but also to non-human–non-human interactions, which take place on the same ontological plane as human–human and human–non-human interactions. Reality does not exist 'outside the mind', he argues, 'as if humans were the only entities with an outside' (Harman, 2016: 17). Objects interact with each other even in the absence of humans, and OOO thus 'needs to be aware of relations between objects that have no direct involvement with people' (Harman, 2016: 6).

For OOO, most objects are composed of other objects. But complex objects are also more than the sum of the parts that comprise them, because new properties emerge from the interaction of the parts. If no new properties emerge, there is simply an aggregate of existing objects. An apple, a pear and an orange sitting side by side on a table, for example, form an aggregate. They are three objects, not one. A bowl of fruit, on the other hand, is an object in its own right, an emergent whole that is greater than the sum of its parts. DeLanda (2016) views assemblages in a similar fashion as emergent wholes that are irreducible to the sum of their component parts. For Harman (2016: 41), 'object' and 'assemblage' are, thus, parallel terms that share the ideas of emergence and irreducibility. DeLanda treats virtually all objects as assemblages. And because each component of an assemblage is also an assemblage on a smaller scale, assemblages are typically 'assemblages of assemblages' (DeLanda, 2016: 3). Drawing on the idea of the French historian Fernand Braudel (1982: 458–459) of 'society as a set of sets', DeLanda uses the idea of assemblages of assemblages to develop what he calls a 'materialist social ontology'. Over historical time, 'social assemblages' – communities, organisations, towns and cities, regions and nation states – emerge on new levels of scale, as assemblages with emergent properties that distinguish them from their predecessors. The historical dimension of the emergence of social assemblages involves what Harman (2018: 167) calls a kind of 'compositional causality', in which change is understood as the emergence of new objects from relations among existing objects.

Detachability is the principle that the components of an assemblage retain their own identities and are not absorbed into the new whole. Although assemblages emerge from the relations of their parts, the parts retain their autonomy; they can be 'detached from one whole and plugged into another one, entering into new interactions' (DeLanda, 2016: 10). If this were not the case, the object would be a seamless whole, rather than an assemblage. Component parts can also be replaced without necessarily forming a new assemblage. A human body is an assemblage. Its cells are replaced at varying intervals over the course of a lifetime and some parts of the body can be removed and inserted into other bodies. But none of this implies the emergence of new bodies. Detachability also gives assemblages a dynamic, fluid character. Closer to the issues that I am concerned with in this book, people and things are constantly flowing into and out of cities, buildings are torn down and replaced, older economic activities are replaced by newer ones, cities grow in population and area, patterns in the use of languages change over time and so on. This simply means that cities are dynamic and fluid assemblages, not that there is a succession of different cities on the same site. For reasons I will come to shortly, I am reluctant to think of languages as assemblages in their own right, but languages too are dynamic entities with detachable parts, such as words and phrases that fall in and out of use, or words that are borrowed from and loaned to other languages.

Downward causality refers to the influence that assemblages exert over their parts. DeLanda (2016: 17) observes that, although detachable parts retain their identities, in many assemblages 'the component parts come into being when a whole has already constituted itself and has begun to use its own emergent capacities to constrain and enable its parts'. For example, people are typically born into, or become components of, social assemblages that have existed for some time before their birth. Their abilities, values, attitudes and so on are formed within the social assemblages into which they are born. These assemblages are maintained by the continuous interaction of their component parts, but the character of these parts is also formed within the assemblage itself. This downward causality means that 'once an assemblage is in place it immediately starts acting as a source of limitations and opportunities for its components' (DeLanda, 2016: 21). Harman (2016: 41) calls this the 'retroactive effect' of objects on their parts, to which he adds the idea that objects also generate new parts. Again, we might think of the way in which languages exercise downward causality, or have retroactive effects, on words borrowed from other languages, adapting their pronunciations, spellings and meanings to the constraints of the new linguistic assemblage.

In my view, OOO provides strong support for a view of language and linguistic entities as objects that interact with all kinds of other objects, both human and non-human. Assemblage theory provides a framework for understanding how language, a *non-physical* object, interacts with *physical* objects to form what I call language-bearing assemblages. The kinds of assemblages that I have in mind here are, in a general sense, speech, writing and print, and, more specifically, any artefact that has language as one of its component parts: a chat with a neighbour, a scribbled note on the fridge door, a book of nonsense poems by Edward Lear, a singing birthday card, an episode of *Stranger Things*, an entry in a Chinese-English dictionary, a broadcast of the Reverend Al Sharpton's eulogy at the funeral of George Floyd, a YouTube video of Miley Cyrus' performance of *Old Town Road* at Glastonbury 2019, an automated instruction from a supermarket checkout machine, Patricia Highsmith's signature on a first edition of *The Talented Mr Ripley* or the text of Ezekiel 25:17 as quoted by Samuel L. Jackson in the film *Pulp Fiction*. Language-bearing assemblages, I want to argue, are crucial to the spatiality of language. It is in the form of assemblages, and assemblages of assemblages, that language makes its way into physical space and takes on the forms of languages and second languages.

Is language an object?

At the beginning of Chapter 3, I cited Fowler and Hodge's (2011) observation that most language researchers believe that there is an object, language. Elaborating on this observation, I suggested that modern linguistics views language not just as an object, but also as a self-contained, internally patterned object-*in*-space. The alternative view that I want to develop challenges this view of the spatiality of language, while retaining the idea that language is an object. Critics of mainstream linguistics, especially those who adopt integrationist, complex systems, post-human or distributed approaches, question the idea that language is an object (e.g. Harris, 1990; Larsen-Freeman & Cameron, 2008; Pennycook, 2018; Thibault, 2011). They argue either that language is a process or that language does not exist at all. I believe that these approaches have much to offer an environmental view of language learning, but I find these arguments problematic for two reasons. First, to begin from the assumption that language does not exist makes discussion of language unnecessarily difficult. Second, they ignore certain self-evident senses in which language clearly exists. OOO and assemblage theory, I believe, offer a way of treating linguistic entities as objects, without falling prey to the fallacies that these critics point out.

Harman (2016: 40) refers to a common understanding that objects must be 'inanimate, durable, nonhuman, or made of physical matter'. For this reason, most of us would be comfortable with a description of bricks, cups, mobile phones, cars and skeletons as objects, but less comfortable with the application of this word to a plan, an ideology, a city, water, air, wind, a rainstorm, a dog or a child. A particular reluctance to describe people as objects may reflect the difficulty of thinking beyond the human (subject) and non-human (object) ontological divide. A reluctance to describe language as an object may also reflect an underlying feeling that language is a distinctively human phenomenon, as well as its failure to meet Harman's common understanding of an object. It could be argued that OOO views all of the above as 'objects' for want of a better term to capture anything that exists, in whatever form ('entity' might be a better term, 'thing' would probably be worse). Yet, if one were to ask whether any of the items on a OOO list of objects-that-do-not-seem-to-be-objects is 'something' or 'nothing', say wind, an ideology or a child, the answer would clearly be 'something'. There is, in other words, an everyday category – let us call it 'something rather than nothing' – that corresponds to the idea of an 'object' in flat ontology. The idea that language does not exist, on the other hand, begs the question of what language *is*, if it is not something.

Larsen-Freeman and Cameron (2008: 1) suggest that 'in our theories we everywhere find processes converted into objects'. In contrast to the view that language is an object, they suggest that language is 'a process in which we participate' (Larsen-Freeman & Cameron, 2008: 109). Thibault (2011: 211) also sees language as a process – so much so that he is reluctant to use the word 'language' as a noun, preferring terms such as 'languaging behaviour' or simply 'languaging'. But is there a principled difference to be made between objects and processes? European languages signal the difference between objects and processes in the word classes of noun and verb. But there is also a fluidity in these relationships as objects and processes cross the boundaries of word classes. The idea of a sunrise, for example, can be expressed as 'the day dawned' (process) or 'the dawn of the day' (object). Whorf (1956: 215) pointed out that the existence of nouns and verbs implies 'a bipolar division of nature' that does not exist in nature itself. Why, he asked, is 'fist' a noun when it is also a temporary event? It turns out, Whorf argues, that an event is no more than 'what our language classes as a verb' and that to define something as an event, thing, object relationship and so on 'always involves a circuitous return to the grammatical categories of the definer's language' (Whorf, 1956).

The distinction between 'object' and 'process' implies the same bipolar division. A process has duration, it lasts for a period of time, and involves change; an object lacks duration and simply exists unchanging as time passes. As far as OOO is concerned, however, there are no 'static' objects of this kind, fixed in space and immutable over time. Discussing the relationship between events and objects, Harman suggests that a hurricane has a short duration in comparison to a grain of sand, but many things happen both in a hurricane and in a grain of sand. For this reason, 'durability is not a good criterion for sorting things into one pile called "objects" and another called "events"' (Harman, 2018: 53). Nor would adding a pile called 'processes' to account for language help very much.

Harris (1990: 45), on the other hand, doubts that the concept of language 'corresponds to any determinate or determinable object at all'. If there is 'no such object' as language, he suggests, modern linguistics is based on a 'myth'. Deleuze and Guattari's (2013: 6) comment that there is 'no language in itself' is echoed by DeLanda (2016: 52), who qualifies it by saying that there is no such thing as 'language in general', by which he means language as the abstract object-*in*-space posited by modern linguistics. But if there is no such thing as language in general, what are we to make of this object? There are two answers to this question. For the integrationists, it is the multimodality of action, interaction and communication, in which language is inextricably entangled that matters. Block (2014a), for example, writes of a 'lingual bias' in linguistic analysis of verbal communication. Linguists who extract language from verbal communication fail to take account of its embodiment and multimodality. On this view, if there is an object that we can call 'language', it is so deeply entangled in situated social interaction that there is little to be said of it independently of communication as a whole.

The second answer lies in Deleuze and Guattari's (2013: 6) 'throng of dialects, patois, slangs, and specialised languages'. DeLanda (2016: 52) suggests, similarly, that 'we must replace the reified generality "language" with a population of individual dialects coexisting and interacting with individual standard languages'. In making this point, DeLanda highlights an important distinction between the general concept of an object and its individual cases. In DeLanda's version of a flat ontology, generalities have no place. Particular marketplaces and bazaars are acceptable entities in historical explanation, but 'the market' is not. Similarly, 'there is no such thing as atoms in general, only populations of individual atomic assemblages' (DeLanda, 2016: 147–148). DeLanda's ontology, thus, only accepts historically unique entities that exist independently of how they are conceived, and of the categories to which they are supposed to belong. Crucial to this argument is a materialist insistence that populations of individual markets, atoms, languages and so on are not to be thought of as multiple instantiations of concepts or categories, but as similar products of parallel but unique histories.

The view of the spatiality of language that I am proposing holds that language is never an object apart from the world; it is always embedded in some specific physical and social environment, where it is bound up with a multiplicity of objects other than itself. However, from the point of view of assemblage theory, being bound up with other objects does not make an object less of an object. Language is an integral component of verbal communication, but it is not inseparable from it. I also agree with DeLanda that language is neither the abstract concept of language nor the category to which all languages, dialects and so on belong. Yet, I also find his reasoning on this point somewhat unclear. If 'language in general' is a *reified* generality, then it is surely an object or assemblage of some kind. The more important point, however, is that to insist that language is not an object seems unproductive. It leads either to futile discussion of the distinction between objects and processes, or to self-contradictory discussions of non-existent entities. Against this, I argue that language is an object, which implies little more than its existence as an entity that cannot be reduced to its component parts or its effects in the world.

Is language an assemblage?

DeLanda (2015, 2016) has written a good deal about language, which plays a crucial role in his social ontology. He acknowledges that it is difficult to incorporate language into assemblage theory, because 'linguistic entities operate at several levels of scale at once' (DeLanda, 2016: 15). He then suggests three ways of looking at language that I will reduce to two. First, language is a 'variable': words and sentences are component parts of social assemblages, interacting with material and non-linguistic expressive components. It is also a 'parameter': linguistic entities such as religious discourses and written constitutions code the components of an assemblage. Because the distinction between variable and parameter relates to the kind of contribution that language makes to a social assemblage, I will consider this as *one* way of looking at language – language as a component of social assemblages. The second way is to view language as an assemblage in its own right. I will mainly be concerned with the first view, here, and will comment on the idea of language as an assemblage only briefly.

DeLanda (2016) includes an interesting, if problematic, account of the evolution of language as an assemblage, which draws on the work of Zelig Harris (1981). In brief, this account shows how the complexities of modern languages may have emerged from interactions among simpler linguistic entities: 'sounds or letters interact to form words, with irreducible semantic properties of their own, and words interact to form larger wholes, sentences with their own semantic and syntactic properties' (Harris, 1981: 52–53), and so on. This account of the emergence of the complexity of modern languages avoids the necessity for a Chomskyan generative linguistic competence. The problem I see with this account, however, is that language seems to emerge from interactions among components that already belong to language itself. Words, for example, surely emerge not from interactions among sounds alone, but from interactions between sounds and non-linguistic objects in the environment. A word must be thought, spoken or written, and it must name or refer to some object in the world. And as the name of an object is put into thought, speech or writing, an assemblage emerges that includes language, but is not language itself. In brief, in treating language as an assemblage in its own right, there is a risk of falling back into the objects-*in*-space view of language as a self-contained system made up of objects that are specific to language itself. A more productive line of inquiry follows words into the language-bearing assemblages that make up social assemblages.

Language-bearing assemblages

By a language-bearing assemblage I mean any physical object that has language as one of its component parts (examples were listed above). Typically, a language-bearing assemblage can be broken down into three components: language itself (words, phrases, etc.); whatever it is that the language refers to (meaning); and the vehicle that carries it into the world (speech, writing, etc.). By carrying language into the world, language-bearing assemblages give language spatiality. A friendly 'Beautiful day!' spoken to a neighbour while leaving home is a language-bearing assemblage. A Facebook post saying, 'Beautiful day!', perhaps accompanied by a photograph of the garden in the morning sunshine, is a different kind of language-bearing assemblage. The point about language-bearing assemblages, in contrast to language, is that they always occupy a certain physical space. Although they carry the same language – the words 'Beautiful day!' – these two assemblages occupy different spaces. Two aspects of language-bearing assemblages are particularly important in this respect: first, reference, or the *non-physical* relationship between language and objects in the world, and, second, attachment, or the relationship between language and the *physical* objects that carry it into the world.

By reference, I mean the ways in which pieces of language connect to particular objects in the world; in broad terms, the names of objects and the meanings of words. For the sake of brevity, I use 'word' here as shorthand for any piece of language – a conventional word, phrase, lexical chunk (Lewis, 1993), formulaic sequence (Wray, 2008), sentence or longer stretch of discourse – that names, describes or invokes another object. Referential relationships are typically probabilistic, contested and dynamic. Objects also exist independently of their names, while many objects do not have names at all. Reference is concerned, then, with the ways in which language picks out objects from the world; a process that divides up the world and, at the same time, divides up language correspondingly. Reference produces non-physical assemblages, which I will call 'word-object relations'.

Word-object relations have some similarity to Saussure's (1983) two-sided signs, which he conceives as relationships between concepts and acoustic images. But I do not see them as objects of mind (thought is only one of the physical forms that they can take on), nor are they necessarily systematically related to each other. As a matter of convenience, different objects have different names, but this is by no means always the case, and reference does not in any sense imply a system of differences. Objects may have more than one name, and the same word may refer to more than one object, but this is only a matter of irregularity if one assumes the existence of a regular system in advance. The primary relationship is not the relationship among signs, but the relationship of reference, a complementary relationship between a word that is picked out of language by its meaning and an object that is picked out of the world by its name. Thus, language enters language-bearing assemblages indirectly in the form of word-object relations. A word-object relation is, essentially, a word-and-its-meaning. When people speak, they do not say a word and then decide on its meaning. They say a word-object relation, or a word that already has meaning, and for this reason I will again use 'word' as shorthand for 'word-object relation'.

There are two important points to be made about the relationship between words and language-bearing assemblages that relate to the principles of downward causality and detachability in assemblage theory (see above). First, words exist before they are spoken, but on an evolutionary scale it is inconceivable that words preceded speech. On the contrary, words, and language itself, could only have emerged from the act of speaking. To the extent that written language differs from spoken language, it is likely that written language also emerged from the act of inscription. Within the physical spaces of thought, speech and writing, new words constantly emerge, their meanings are contested and changed, and old words disappear. This is a matter of downward causality, or the retroactive effects of language-bearing assemblages on their linguistic components.

According to the principle of detachability, the components of an assemblage must be detachable and available for use in other assemblages. Words are, thus, detachable from language-bearing assemblages, such that any word is, in principle, available for use in any assemblage. The detachability of words is limited only by the retroactive effects of speech and writing, which cause certain words or expressions to 'belong' either to speech or to writing. This view of the relationship between speech and writing marks an important difference with the modern linguistic view of speech as the primary mode of language. In consequence of this view, linguists often treat speech as if it were language, and writing as if it were more or less a transcription of speech. From the perspective of assemblage theory, writing and speech share language as a detachable component, and the differences between them lie in their other component parts.

A second important difference with modern linguistics concerns the relationship of language to thought. Thought, speech and writing are the three basic physical forms in which language appears in the world. Of the three, thought seems to be the most difficult to conceptualise as a language-bearing assemblage, partly because we tend to view language as a means of expressing thought. By thought, I have in mind, not the general operation of the brain or mind, but the specific action of 'thinking'. I want to suggest that thought is, in this aspect, analogous to speech or writing, or using language to speak or write; it is a matter of 'thinking words', or using words to think, a physical action that has language as one of its components. The physicality of thought is now widely accepted, in the sense that all cognitive activity emerges from physical processes involving the brain, the body and its immediate environment (Lakoff, 2013). However, the argument that I want to make also depends on a conceptual distinction between the conscious thinking of words and the knowledge that such thinking calls upon. I can, for example, leave home and think 'Beautiful day!' without saying it out loud. This implies, first, that I know the words 'Beautiful day!' and, second, that I call on this knowledge to actively bring them to mind. The knowledge of language that I call on is the same knowledge that I call on to say or write 'Beautiful day!'.

The idea that thought is a language-bearing assemblage on the same level as speech and writing implies two important points of difference with an object-*in*-space view of language. First, language does not express thought. On the contrary, thought expresses language. Second, nor do speech and writing express thought. Speech and writing draw on knowledge of language, but there is no reason to believe that words must be actively thought before they are spoken or written. This calls for a reconsideration of the route taken by language into the language-bearing assemblages of thought, speech and writing. I have suggested that language enters these assemblages in the form of *non-physical* word-object relations. However, this needs to be modified to take account of the storage of knowledge of language in the brain. As we learn language, we find words in the world, in language-bearing assemblages based on speech and writing. But when we think, speak or write language, we use words that are already in mind or close to hand. This knowledge is also the basis for understanding what we hear or read. We need, therefore, to posit an intermediate kind of assemblage corresponding to knowledge of words. Whereas words themselves are non-physical entities, knowledge of words is a physical property of the brain. Thus, to say that thought, speech and writing have language as one of their components is to refer, more precisely, to an interior knowledge of word-object relations that already has the character of a language-bearing assemblage.

To return to the spatiality of thought, two points are relevant to the manifestation of language in the environment. First, thought is a private activity to the extent that it is not communicated to others. In this respect, its capacity to enter larger-scale language-bearing assemblages is strictly limited. Although thought is not expressed in speech and writing, it can be translated into speech or writing in much the same way that speech can be translated into writing, or vice versa. Second, thought is evanescent and leaves no trace of itself. However, thought can generate new thoughts, which can be stored in memory. To the extent that these thoughts involve words, they may add to, or modify, the individual's knowledge of language and become available, in this form, to speech, writing or further thought. All of this is possible, not because of any direct relationship between thought and its expression in speech and writing, but because the linguistic components of thought are detachable and available for use by other language-bearing assemblages.

Speech and writing, then, share knowledge of language with thought. In the act of speaking or writing, language is assembled with the relevant parts of the body and its surroundings. As a product of speaking, speech combines language with the physical substance of sound, while writing combines language with a surface and a medium of inscription. Viewed as acts of communication, speech and writing enter into larger-scale assemblages such as conversations and meetings or the publication of printed texts, in which the components involved in the production of a text are assembled with the parts of the body used by hearers and readers, as well as other elements in the setting. As assemblages, speech and writing are perhaps best understood in this more holistic manner as acts of communication.

As acts of communication, speech and writing have well-defined spatial characteristics. Speech is a physical entity that co-occupies the space of its physical components, whereas written texts occupy discontinuous spaces of production and consumption, in addition to the space of the text itself. Like thought, speech is evanescent, leaving no trace of itself beyond memory, whereas a written text is a durable record of the action that produced it. As Coulmas (2013: 34) puts it, once a written message leaves its originator, it 'begins a life of its own'. The spatial range of speech is limited to the space between speakers and hearers, whereas a written text is a portable space that can, in principle, be transported anywhere at all. In practice, the spatial range of a handwritten text is limited by its production as a unique object. Assemblages in which speech and writing are reproduced by modern technologies, on the other hand, have much wider ranges. Telephones project speech across vast distances; microphones, amplifiers and speakers distribute speech to audiences of hundreds or thousands; speech can also be audio- or video-recorded and broadcast, not only across vast distances, but also to mass national and global audiences. Using print technologies, a handwritten text can be reproduced and circulated on a much wider scale; technologies for digital display expand the range of written texts further still.

Perhaps the most important characteristic of speech and writing, then, is their capacity to enter into assemblages on ever-increasing scales to the point where any given social assemblage – a community, institution, city, nation state, etc. – is both saturated with and spatially defined by language-bearing assemblages. A conversation is an assemblage that emerges from the speech of a small number of individuals. A meeting is an assemblage that emerges from conversations on a larger scale. A city corporation is an assemblage of local meetings. A national parliament is an assemblage of city corporations and so on. This is, of course, an oversimplification, in that there is no straightforward progression from one level of scale to the next. Also, social assemblages draw in a multiplicity of new assemblages – both language bearing and non-language bearing – at each level of scale. A meeting, for example, is much more than an assemblage of conversations. Although it is principally in the form of conversation that language plays its part in a meeting, there are also agendas, minutes, documents to be discussed, regulations governing the conduct of the meeting and so on.

There seems to be a principle, however, that the scale of a social assemblage is constrained by the language-bearing assemblages on which it is based. Gamble *et al.* (2014) suggest that in the early stages of human development, increases in the size of social groups depended, first, on the storage of social relationships in objects, ceremonies, places and architecture, and, later, on speech. In their estimate, the maximum size of a social group held together by spoken language is around 1500, which is typically the upper limit of the number of people we can name. Writing is not simply a more efficient means of storing social relationships than speech, but it also allows for the emergence of more expansive language-bearing assemblages (religious discourses, laws, constitutions, etc.) and larger social assemblages on the scale of a religious order or a city-state (Coulmas, 2013). Without writing, social assemblages on the scale of a pre-modern city could not exist. Without print technologies, modern cities and nation states could not exist. And the sense that our lives are governed not only by nation states, but also by global entities of various kinds (Beck, 2000), depends largely on the ways in which present-day broadcast and digital communications systems – producing the most complex language-bearing assemblages that we have witnessed to date – enable the circulation of language-bearing assemblages on a global scale.

Mobilities and Mobility Systems

The French philosopher Tristan Garcia (2014: 1) writes that we are currently experiencing an 'epidemic of things'. We are increasingly aware of objects at multiple levels of scale; that an incomprehensibly large universe is ultimately made up of infinitesimally small sub-atomic particles. At the human scale, this epidemic of things is also an epidemic of language-bearing assemblages. To say that we live in a language-saturated world, therefore, is to say that we live in a world saturated with language-bearing assemblages. This is the world in which second languages are learned and the mobility of these language-bearing assemblages lies at the root of second language learning. Space matters in SLA research for one reason above all others. Second language learning depends on the coming together of learners and languages in space. In Chapter 5, I describe these spaces as language learning environments. In SLA research, the language-to-be-learned is often called the 'target language'. This term conveys a sense of distance between learners and the languages they learn. But if learning is to take place, the learners and the target language must come together. Either the target language must come to the learners, or the learners must come to the target language; or, perhaps, there will be movement in both directions. SLA research tends to assume that the learners and the target language are already in the same place. From an object-*as*-space perspective, however, the spatial relationship between the learner and the target language is a circumstance that needs to be explained. From the perspective of assemblage theory, this is a relationship between language-bearing assemblages of different kinds. The idea of 'mobilities' is key to understanding the spatial circumstances that govern this relationship.

Introducing his seminal work on mobilities, Urry (2007: 9) explained how, in earlier work, he had developed 'a sociology which focuses upon movement, mobility and contingent ordering, rather than upon stasis, structure and social order'. His more recent work aimed not only to deepen this analysis of mobilities, but also to focus on 'mobility systems', or the infrastructures that 'enable the movements of people, ideas and information from place to place, person to person, event to event' (Urry, 2007: 12). Urry also linked the idea of mobilities and mobility systems to Massey's (1994) view of space as being 'comprised of various materials, of objects and environments that are intermittently in motion' and 'assembled and reassembled in changing configurations and re-articulated meanings' (Urry, 2007: 34). From this perspective, 'places' are also dynamic assemblages, 'economically, politically and culturally produced through the multiple mobilities of people, but also of capital, objects, signs and information moving at rapid yet uneven speed across many borders, only contingently forming stable places of spectacle' (Urry, 2007: 269). Urry does not propose an unmoving space in which objects are in constant motion. He proposes, instead, a space that is constantly in motion, in a state of turbulence. Linking this view to the notion of language-bearing assemblages, I want to suggest that the places in which we live and learn languages are, like Amin and Thrift's (2002: 7) urban spaces of 'mobility, flow and everyday practices', contingently stable environments in which there is a constant coming and going of language-bearing assemblages.

A second key idea in Urry (2007: 52) is that mobilities are only made possible at the expense of the construction of large-scale immobile infrastructures. In any society there is a dominant process of circulation, or a system of 'routeways' through which people, goods and information are moved from place to place, including 'networks of bridleways, of footpaths, of cycle tracks, of railways, of telephone lines, of public roads, of networked computers, of hub airports'. As mobilities become more global in scale and significance, Urry argues, there is a corresponding increase in the scale, organisation and complexity of immobilities. Mobilities depend on the production of large-scale immobile assemblages such as the increasingly vast airports on which modern cities depend.

Mobility systems are, in this sense, central to globalisation. Globalisation, understood as 'the widening, deepening and speeding up of worldwide interconnectedness in all aspects of contemporary social life' (Held *et al.*, 1999: 2), involves processes that go beyond the 'international', or interconnections among nations. For Beck (2002: 4), this involves a tension between the nation state, which is always attached to a particular place, and a putative 'world society' that is coming into being 'because a multiplicity of social circles, communication networks, market relations and lifestyles, none of them specific to any particular locality, now can cross the boundaries of the national state'. Urry's (2007) point is that such transnational spaces are produced by mobility systems that extend beyond reciprocal interconnections among nation states. He argues, for example, that without extended systems of mass air travel, 'what is now termed "globalization" would be utterly different, possibly non-existent' (Urry, 2007: 149). Global space is 'something that is made' (Urry, 2007: 149) by the global mobilities of people, goods and information and the massive immobile infrastructures that put them into motion.

As is often the case with spatial theory, Urry's work on mobilities tends to take language for granted. Although Urry mentions the importance of English to the development of air travel, the wider question of how language is implicated in mobilities on national and transnational scales is not addressed. This question has been tackled in several ways in recent work on the sociolinguistics of globalisation, which foregrounds language mobility and at times addresses issues of second language learning (Blommaert, 2010; Pennycook, 2012). A point that I want to emphasise, however, is that language mobility is not additional to the mobilities that Urry (2007) discusses. Rather, the mobilities of people, goods and information are largely mobilities of language-bearing assemblages. Moreover, it is the mobility of language-bearing people, goods and information that explains the emergence of the global map of languages and of second language learning as we know it today.

The mobility of language-bearing assemblages

Arguing for a sociolinguistics of globalisation, Jan Blommaert makes the following observation:

> We now see that the mobility of people also involves the mobility of linguistic and sociolinguistic resources, that 'sedentary' or 'territorialized' patterns of language use are complemented by 'translocal' or 'deterritorialized' forms of language use and that the combination of both of them accounts for unexpected sociolinguistic effects. (Blommaert, 2010: 4)

The mobility of people, in other words, puts language into motion. The deterritorialisation of languages problematises the modernist idea of geographically based national languages and regional dialects, calling for a shift of attention to the global mobility of language resources. In a similar vein, Pennycook (2012: 20) highlights the ways in which, in spite of 'sets of expectations about language and place, about things being in their right place', language turns up in 'unexpected places'. However, interesting as accounts of the unexpected consequences of global language mobility are – and Pennycook's point is really that the unexpected is now the sociolinguistic norm – they create a misleading impression that language mobility is something radically new. It is as if the modernist map of the world, on which each language sat comfortably in its own territory, was somehow a product of the immobility of language. To be sure, this map is now being torn apart by an unprecedented acceleration of language mobilities. New, more complex, more dynamic maps are being created. What is missing from the sociolinguistics of globalisation, however, is a sense of how the map that is being torn apart was itself a product of language mobility. Here, I want to suggest that there is a need for a better spatial understanding of the mechanics of language mobility – of *how* language moves from place to place – and of the consequences of mobility for the emergence of languages, their mapping on to geographical space and their availability as second languages.

If Urry's (2007) work on mobilities is to incorporate the mobilities of language, two points must be emphasised. First, the objects that are put into motion by mobility systems are, by and large, language-bearing assemblages. These include not only people, but also goods and information. From the perspective of assemblage theory, people are language-bearing assemblages, who carry knowledge of languages and capacities to use and learn them wherever they go. Goods are labelled and documented, and they also include commodities that have value because they contain language (books, magazines, audio and video recordings, etc.). Information is largely linguistically encoded, often in multimodal forms in which language is combined with sounds and visual images, and transmitted through broadcast and digital media. In addition, mobility systems, themselves, are composed of language-bearing assemblages and are highly dependent on language for their operation.

Second, language-bearing assemblages are *inherently* mobile. A spoken utterance is projected into space at the very moment of its production; a handwritten letter is placed in an envelope and sent off in the mail; a newspaper is printed and immediately circulated around the city; digital texts are added to social media platforms and mailing systems and are automatically distributed to global networks of computer screens and mobile devices. The differences lie not in the mobility or immobility of language-bearing assemblages, but only in the degrees to which they are mobile: the speed at which they move, the distances they travel, their capacity to travel in multiple directions simultaneously, their durability and capacity to self-reproduce and so on. Language mobility is not a matter of languages moving by themselves. In order to move, language must be attached to some mobile physical object and the factors of its mobility (speed, range, distribution, durability and reproduction) are a function of the physical objects to which it is attached. The history of language mobility is one of regular increases in all of these factors: language travels faster, further and to more and more people over historical time. It is also a history in which developments in the mobilities of language are entangled with the social production of space itself. What is most interesting from this point of view is how patterns in the circulation of language-bearing assemblages are related to the emergence of languages and their availability as second languages.

It is worth noting that all language-bearing assemblages carry information, or word-object relations. In contrasting information with people and goods, therefore, I mainly have in mind digital and broadcast information, or the products of media and information technologies. Digital and broadcast information are, like people and goods, physical entities and there are costs involved in their transmission from place. However, these forms of information differ from the information carried by people and goods in that they are to all intents and purposes 'weightless'. From this point of view, a movie streamed on the internet or broadcast on a global television network is a very different object to the same movie stored on a disc, packaged and loaded onto a container ship. In this sense, the rise of global communications networks has heralded an entirely new order of mobilities for language-bearing assemblages of many kinds.

Earlier in this chapter, I observed that there is a relationship between the scale of a social assemblage and the means of linguistic communication available to it. A family can get by with spoken words and the occasional written note pinned to the fridge door. However, many families have added mobile phone calls and messages to their multimodal repertoires, and this goes hand in hand with new uses of space inside and outside the home (children spend less time in shared rooms, stay out later at night). This will not do for a nation state, however, which needs more sophisticated and expansive means of storing language and moving it from place to place. Cast in terms of mobilities and mobility systems, this means that social assemblages emerge and develop in conjunction with technologies for the circulation of language-bearing assemblages. Historically, the scale of social assemblages increases in tandem with their capacities to produce and circulate the language-bearing assemblages that hold them together. But this also implies the emergence of conventionalised sets of word-object relations as language travels along regularised routeways within a social assemblage. In this way, the emergence of the language of a social assemblage is inseparable from the emergence of the social assemblage itself. Each social assemblage develops its own language or language variety depending on its scale and relationship to other social assemblages on the same and higher/lower levels of scale.

It is in this sense that I believe that languages are not assemblages in their own right. They are, instead, products of the downward causality, or retroactive effects, of social assemblages. The circulation of language-bearing assemblages within a social assemblage engenders degrees of conformity in the forms of words and their uses at a corresponding level of scale. This conformity is also produced within specific relations of power and centralisation. The larger the social assemblage, the more it seeks to establish its *lieu propre* (De Certeau, 1984) – a place of its own – so that language becomes embroiled in triangular 'power geometries' (Massey, 2005) involving language, social institutions and space. These power geometries fix the language in place, so that it becomes *the* language of the social assemblage: a language that differs from the languages of other social assemblages. As language-bearing assemblages circulate within a social assemblage, their circulation marks out the boundaries of a space, which becomes the territory of the language itself. The important point to note here is that that territorialisation is just as much an outcome of language mobility as deterritorialisation is.

The nation state is currently the largest and most complex territorial assemblage that we know. Despite globalisation and the power of transnational organisations (Beck, 2000), the nation state continues to provide the primary framework for the regulation of our lives. As territorial units, nation states also regulate the mobilities of language-bearing assemblages (people and goods, more so than information). Language-bearing assemblages tend to circulate more freely within nation states than between them. We have thus become accustomed to thinking of languages and geographical space in terms of a one-language-one-state model: French in France, Russian in Russia, Japanese in Japan and so on. This is the typical European model in which nation states and national languages co-emerged as regional languages or dialects were worked up as standard written languages and languages of print. Key to the emergence of national languages were more or less planned manipulations of language involving the production of metalinguistic texts – the grammars and dictionaries discussed in Chapter 3. Equally important was the imposition of standard languages and varieties through social institutions that are contiguous with the territorial boundaries of the state, especially government and public administration, the law, education and the media. Over several centuries, a typical hierarchical structure emerged, in which a single standardised national language reigns supreme over minority languages, regional dialects and 'intermediate' language varieties (Cerruti & Tsiplakou, 2020), all of which have diminished in status over time.

In the 19th century, vast numbers of languages were identified and documented by missionaries, colonial officials and explorers. These became the treasure trove of comparative philology. Many were written down and standardised on the European model and gained some degree of territorial status. In the postcolonial world, new national territories were carved out of highly multilingual spaces. In these new nation states, the diversity of languages and dialects was put into order either by the adoption of colonial languages or the elevation of one or more local languages to the status of national language. This process has varied considerably from nation to nation, but in all cases there has been an intensified circulation of national languages and a diminished circulation of local and indigenous languages.

Each nation state has its own particular history in regard to the emergence of its national language, and in some cases two or more national languages share territorial space, often unequally (e.g. Switzerland, Canada, South Africa). But there is no language whose history and present-day status has not been shaped by the formation of nation states. For some sociolinguists, this calls into question whether national languages are really just ideological constructions that support the idea of the nation state, but bear little relation to the language use on the ground (Blommaert, 2010; Cameron, 2006; Piller, 2016). Cameron (2006: 145), for example, argues that 'the notion of a national language is an ideological fiction', or in the Marxist historian Eric Hobsbawm's (1990: 57) words, 'a sort of platonic idea of the language existing behind and above all its variants and imperfect versions'. This argument comes in a variety of guises, and to tackle it in detail would be a diversion from the line of argument I want to develop. However, I would argue that national languages are by no means imagined or ideal. They are, on the contrary, very real retroactive effects of intensive circulations of the language-bearing assemblages in which they are embedded.

Globalisation and second languages

Language-bearing assemblages escape the boundaries of nation states in two main ways. In a typical situation of language contact (Matras, 2009), languages from adjacent or nearby territories circulate within a shared space, either as a consequence of histories of conquest and settlement, or in the context of trade and labour mobility. From the co-emergence of nation states and national languages in Europe, a number of powerful standardised languages arose that also began to circulate as *second* languages in adjacent and nearby territories: notably, Portuguese, Dutch, Spanish, French, German, English and Russian. Glück (2014) and Sánchez (2014), for example, show how materials for teaching German and Spanish as second languages first developed outside Germany and Spain. More characteristic of the current era, however, is a process that might be called dispersal, in which languages travel far and wide, rather like seeds floating on the wind. This is often referred to as language 'spread', of which the global spread of English is the prime example (Trudgill, 2017).

Metaphors such as spread and dispersal, however, tend to obscure the actual mechanisms by which languages are moved around the world. Languages do not float on the wind. Instead, they are carried by multidirectional flows of language-bearing assemblages along the global routeways of Urry's (2007) mobilities. The dispersal of European languages began in earnest with the long sea voyages of the Age of Discovery in the 16th century and the subsequent era of imperialism and colonisation. As such, the global mobility of languages has a residual colonial character, witnessed by the retention of colonial languages as national or official languages by many postcolonial states. But in its present-day form, global language mobility is associated more with the flows of social, economic and cultural globalisation (Appadurai, 1996; Held *et al.*, 1999) that have so disrupted the modernist language map of the world.

The effects of globalisation on language mobility in the early years of the 21st century are easily underestimated. However, statistics point to an extraordinary acceleration in the mobilities of language-bearing assemblages of all kinds over the past 10–20 years. Aggregated statistics published by the World Bank (2020) show, for example, that the number of air passengers doubled between 2006 and 2018, reaching a figure of 4.3 billion annually. The quantity of air freight increased by 87% between 2000 and 2018, while the quantity of container port traffic increased by 250% over the same period. The number of individuals using the internet doubled between 2009 and 2017, reaching 49.7% of the world's population. Whereas global growth in internet use was at one point constrained by lack of access to basic infrastructures and electricity in Africa, South and Central America and much of Asia, there is now much wider access through mobile networks. Between 2009 and 2017, the number of mobile phone subscriptions increased by 80%, reaching 1.06 subscriptions per head of population globally.

Globally, mobile people include migrants and refugees (Canagarajah, 2017), business travellers and transnational workers (Garrido & Sabaté-Dalmau, 2020), students studying abroad (Benson *et al.*, 2013; Kinginger, 2009) and tourists (Goethals, 2015; Phipps, 2007). Many of these people cross language borders, carrying multilingual competences with them, and developing them as they travel. While we can be sure that individuals who cross language borders are a significant proportion of globally mobile populations overall, it is difficult to tease out their numbers. Individuals can also cross language boundaries within national territories, or be linguistically mobile at a distance, using print, broadcast and digital materials. We are also aware of increased use of multilingual packaging and documentation, growth in exports of texts across language borders and the increasingly multilingual character of broadcasting and online communication, although these are also difficult to quantify. There is, therefore, a need for more statistical research on the global mobilities of languages to back up the largely anecdotal evidence that we have to date of the normality of languages turning up in 'unexpected places' (Pennycook, 2012). The best evidence that we have to date is, perhaps, the growth of the language industries themselves.

The global mobility of languages depends on the mobility systems that set people, goods and information in motion (Urry, 2007). This is not so surprising, because the mobilities of people, goods and information are, by and large, mobilities of language-bearing assemblages. It should also be borne in mind that the operations of, for example, international air travel depend on the mobilities of multilingual workers and multilingual documentation. However, there are also mobility systems that are specific to language: notably, the translation, interpreting and localisation industries that facilitate the movement of goods and information around the world (Bielsa, 2005; Cronin, 2003); language-testing regimes that control migration, education and employment across language borders (Hogan-Brun et al., 2009); and second language teaching and learning industries at both points of departure and points of arrival. One of the most powerful indicators available for this area is the size of the global language services market (mainly translation and localisation), which is estimated to have doubled between 2009 and 2018 (Mazereanu, 2019), a growth that broadly corresponds to the growth in overall global mobility indicators reported above.

Statistics on language testing and teaching are easier to find for English than for other languages. The International English Language Testing System (IELTS) is the most widely taken 'high-stakes' English language test. According to IELTS own statistics, it is used by more than 10,000 universities, schools, employers and immigration departments. The number of IELTS test takers increased from 1.7 million to more than 3 million between 2011 and 2017, while the number of test centres around the world increased from 50 to 140 (IELTS, 2012, 2017). An important point to bear in mind is that global mobility creates demand for language teaching and learning both at points of arrival (the places that mobile individuals travel to) and points of departure (the places that they are leaving, or potentially leaving). Thus, the rapid growth of English language education and testing in schools around the world (which has crept down from secondary school to kindergarten in many countries over the past 30 years or so) (Chik & Besser, 2011; Nunan, 2003) does not necessarily involve mobilities of learners, but it is largely a consequence of the increased mobility of English language-bearing goods and information in the countries in which English language education is on the rise. The growth of English teaching also creates its own demands for mobility, not only for language teaching and learning materials, but also for language teaching professionals. East Asian countries have imported English-speaking teachers for several decades, and as Japan, Korea and China, in particular, have opened up channels for migration from other parts of Asia, the sources of teachers have diversified. In 2018, for example, China and the Philippines signed an agreement allowing 300,000 Filipino workers to work in China, including 100,000 English language teachers (International Organisation for Migration, 2019: 80).

The available statistics may give the impression that the global mobility of language is mainly a matter of West to East, or global North to global South, flows of language resources and, especially, English language resources. However, there is also evidence that global language mobility involves multiple languages and multidirectional flows on a global scale. Migrant workers, for example, overwhelmingly move from lower-income to higher-income destinations, but not necessarily to Western countries (International Organisation for Migration, 2019). In some parts of the world, internal, rural to urban migration also involves language mobility. The sociolinguistic effects of diverse streams of migration on 'multilingual cities' (King & Carson, 2016) around the world also point to the importance of multidirectional flows of people, goods and information. It is also important to bear in mind that the multilingual city phenomenon is produced not only by the presence of linguistically diverse migrant populations, but also by a much wider availability and circulation of linguistically diverse goods and information.

Europe accounts for around half of the global language services market (Mazereanu, 2019). This is partly explained by the need for translation across European languages, including recently recognised minority languages in the European Union. One of the consequences of this is the growing number of 'new speakers' of languages such as Catalan, Galician and Irish beyond their traditional territories (O'Rourke & Pujolar, 2015). The rapid growth of globally accessible online language learning resources on websites such as Duolingo may also prove to be an important factor in fostering multidirectional flows of language resources. Duolingo, for example, offers courses in 34 natural languages (not to mention High Valyrian and Klingon), including Irish, Welsh and Scottish Gaelic. Almost half of Duolingo's claimed 30 million users use the site to learn languages other than English (Chik, 2020).

Conclusion

The most important idea that I want to carry forward from this chapter is the idea that it is the extraterritorial circulation of language-bearing assemblages that lies at the root of second language learning from a spatial perspective. In Chapter 5, I will set this idea within the notion of language learning environments, or environments in which global and local circulations of language-bearing assemblages bring learners into contact with the languages they learn. As Matras (2009: 3) argues of the sociolinguistic concept of language contact, 'the relevant locus of contact is the language processing apparatus of the individual multilingual speaker and the employment of this apparatus in communicative interaction'.

However, I believe we are too ready to slip into a terminology whereby languages are seen as being mobile independently of their attachments to the physical substance of the world. I have argued, therefore, that it is important to base our understanding of language mobility on an understanding of the ways in which language is attached to physical objects – human and non-human – of various kinds.

Bearing in mind that learners are also language-bearing assemblages who come to second language learning situations with language knowledge and capacities for language learning, language contact becomes a matter of two or more mobile language assemblages (one of which is the learner) meeting and interacting with each other. Such meetings and interactions constitute spaces for second language learning (I will call them 'settings'), or spaces that are constituted by the coming together of mobile language-bearing assemblages in the learner's environment. However, it is also important to bear in mind that, in order to be a second language, a language must in some sense be present in the environment of a person who intends to learn it. From a spatial perspective, this means that the language must be *produced* as a second language within the global circulation of language-bearing assemblages.

Figure 5.1 In the year 2000: At School, by Jean-Marc Côté (1901) (Source: WikiMedia Commons: https://commons.wikimedia.org/wiki/File:France_in_XXI_Century._School.jpg)

5 Language Learning Environments

> He walked with equipoise, possibly in either city
>
> Miéville, 2009: 295

The foregoing chapters have been concerned with the spatiality of language. This chapter shifts the focus to the spatiality of second language learning environments. The idea of language learning environments connects the objects-*as*-space view of language outlined in Chapter 4 to the *how* of language learning by addressing the question of *where* second languages are learned. Second languages are learned in language learning environments, or spaces in which mobile language-based assemblages meet and become available as resources for second language learning. More importantly, it brings the question of where second languages are learned to front of stage, because the *how* and the *where* of language learning are inseparable from an environmental point of view.

Ecological approaches to learning (Bronfenbrenner, 1979) and language learning (van Lier, 2004) provide a strong basis for understanding the *how* of language learning. In this chapter, however, I want to argue that these approaches are insufficiently explicit on the spatial character of the environment. In particular, the fact that second language learning resources are more or less *scarce* resources calls for more attention to the ways in which they get into language learning environments and how learners' access to them is shaped by experiences and uses of space. Ecological approaches tend to use the terms context and environment interchangeably. The framework that I propose uses the term environment to ground context in space. I will discuss two perspectives on language learning environments – an 'areal' perspective in which the environment is viewed as a geographical area (e.g. a campus, a city or a region) and an 'individual' perspective in which the environment is viewed as a configuration of settings assembled by an individual learner. This chapter also discusses the multilingual city as a relevant areal unit and the place of online resources in language learning environments. Lastly, I touch on some issues related to inequities in second language learning that I believe can often be explained in terms of uneven patterns in the global distribution of second language learning resources.

The Ecology of Learning

In the objects-*in*-space view of language (Chapter 3), a language is a systematically organised whole that can be acquired piecemeal through mastery of its systems – phonology, morphology and syntax, vocabulary, etc. This view implies a transmissive view of language learning in which language knowledge is fed into the minds of the learners, in the manner of Jean-Marc Côté's imagined school in the year 2000. On this view, learning depends on instruction and the classroom is the best place for instruction and learning to take place, as classrooms are, after all, designed for that purpose. Outside the classroom, learners practice the language they have learned and develop skills in its use. The transmission metaphor is closely associated with the idea of second language learning as 'developing monolingual competence a second time around' (Ortega, 2014: 33) and the idealised model of a bilingual speaker as one who has a perfect and equal command of two languages. In conjunction with the social turn in second language acquisition (SLA), however, a more participatory view of second language learning has taken hold (Block, 2003; Douglas Fir Group, 2016). From this point of view, learning depends on the learners' interaction with the language both inside and outside the classroom. Second language knowledge develops experientially and the goal is to develop 'multicompetences' (Cook, 1992) or 'truncated' multilingual repertoires (Blommaert, 2010) that match learners' needs and are situated in language use.

The objects-*as*-space view of language (Chapter 4) supports a participatory approach to teaching and learning and is closely aligned with ecological views of learning (Barron, 2004, 2006, 2010; Bronfenbrenner, 1979, 1999; Kramsch, 2008; van Lier, 2002, 2004). The idea of ecology can be traced back to late 19th-century thinking on interdependencies among living organisms and inorganic matter (Stauffer, 1957). The view that space is composed of physical objects and their relations has much in common with ecological views of the perception of the environment by living organisms (Gibson, 1979). In the 20th century, social ecologies explained human behaviour ecologically, often in terms of an environmentally deterministic opposition between human and non-human worlds. The idea of flat ontology that I introduced in Chapter 4 helps us think of the environment as a space of ontologically equal, human and non-human objects or assemblages. From an ecological perspective, learning is adaptation to such an environment and development is not an exclusively human characteristic. All kinds of objects 'learn' in the sense of environmental adaptation and development.

In SLA research, we are, of course, concerned with human learning and development. As Bronfenbrenner (1979: 3) puts it, human development is 'a lasting change in the way in which a person perceives and deals with his environment'. Because we live in a language-saturated world – a world of language-bearing assemblages – learning a second language is a matter of seeing and dealing with the world in new ways. Second language learning is also a physical process with physical effects, including changes to the neuroplasticity of the brain and to bodily dispositions (Block, 2014a; Lakoff, 2013). In childhood and adolescence, learning is intimately bound up with physical growth. Learning a second language also implies change not only in the learner, but also in the learner's environment.

Published in 1979, Uri Bronfenbrenner's (1979) *The Ecology of Human Development* remains an important source on the psychology of learning. It is also an explicitly *spatial* account of the ecology of learning focusing on settings for development and their inter-relations. Bronfenbrenner criticised laboratory research for its failure to recognise the influence of the laboratory setting on observations. He was also critical of research that focused on the developing person, 'with only the most rudimentary conception and characterization of the environment in which the person is found' (Bronfenbrenner, 1979: 16). He commented that, 'to the extent that we have theories about *how* environmental influences affect behavior and development, they are theories about interpersonal processes' (Bronfenbrenner, 1979: 18). This comment has a wider resonance for present-day critical approaches to SLA, which tend to view context as *social* context, and learning as an emergent property of interactions among people. Bronfenbrenner (1979: 169) argued that the first step in an ecological approach to human development 'entails a systematic description and analysis of the settings in which development takes place'. In my view, this implies a *spatial* view of context that does not exclude people, but treats them as one kind of object in spaces that are made up of many kinds of objects.

Bronfenbrenner (1979: 4) modelled the environment for human development as 'a set of nested structures, each inside the next, like a set of Russian dolls'. He also conceptualised it as a set of systems, or patterns of activities, roles and interpersonal relations experienced within settings. This set of systems consisted of (i) the immediate setting (the microsystem), defined as 'a place where people can readily engage in face-to-interaction – home, day-care center, playground, and so on' (Bronfenbrenner, 1979: 22); (ii) interconnections among these settings (the mesosystem); (iii) events occurring in settings in which the developing person is not present that are brought into the immediate setting by others (the exosystem); and (iv) the culture or sub-culture, which provides a kind of 'blueprint for the organization of every kind of setting' (Bronfenbrenner, 1979: 4) (the macrosystem). The idea of a 'chronosystem' was later added to the model to account for temporal relations among settings over the course of development. This nested model was developed mainly with early childhood development in mind and, although Bronfenbrenner used it to generate hypotheses on adolescent and adult development, it does not map directly onto second language learning beyond early childhood. The main idea that I draw from it, however, is the value of detailed investigation of the settings in which languages are learned and of mapping out their inter-relationships within wider language learning environments.

Bronfenbrenner makes two important points about the environment and human development: first, what matters is 'the environment as it is *perceived*, rather than as it may exist in "objective" reality' (Bronfenbrenner, 1979: 4) and, second, the environment extends 'far beyond the immediate situation directly affecting the developing person—the objects to which he responds or the people with whom he interacts on a face-to-face basis' (1979: 7). Development is, in effect, spatial development. The perceived environment expands spatially with the child's 'dawning realization of the relations between events in different settings' and, with the development of spoken and written language, 'events in settings that he has not yet entered himself', such as foreign lands and fantasy worlds (1979: 10). Throughout the lifespan, Bronfenbrenner (1979: 212) hypothesises, development is enhanced 'as a direct function of the number of structurally different settings in which the developing person participates', especially 'when the settings occur in culturally diverse environments'. The idea that learning is an expansion of the learner's phenomenological environment lends substance to the often-made claim that second language learning widens horizons and opens up new worlds.

An ecological view of development implies that learning is environmentally constrained, but not environmentally determined. The developing person is 'a growing, dynamic entity that progressively moves into and restructures the milieu in which it resides' (Bronfenbrenner, 1979: 21). In her work on adolescents' self-directed learning projects, Barron (2010: 114) emphasises the roles of agency and engagement in an ecological view of 'learning as becoming that takes place across longer scales of time and within and across the multiple life spaces that a learner inhabits'. She emphasises the learner's influence on the learning environment, arguing that the ecological perspective 'foregrounds the fact that adolescents are simultaneously involved in many settings and that they are active in creating activity contexts for themselves within and across settings' (Barron, 2006: 199). As children grow older, opportunities to develop unique developmental trajectories expand, and growing independence 'affords greater opportunity to adapt one's environment and to more directly influence how others respond' (Barron, 2006: 196).

The Ecology of Language Learning

There is a good deal of published work on the ecology of language learning (Kramsch, 2002, 2008; Lai, 2015; Palfreyman, 2014; Singleton &

Aronin, 2007; Tudor, 2003; van Lier, 2002, 2004). However, the specifics of the ecological approach are difficult to pin down, largely because it is yet to be developed as an independent approach. Kramsch's (2002) collection of papers might have led to the development of an ecological research agenda for SLA, but among the contributors, only van Lier (2002) was fully committed to an ecological view. The most cogent account that we have to date, van Lier (2004), relies a great deal on Vygotskyan learning theory. Kramsch (2008) subsequently linked the ecological approach to complex systems theory, and it is in the context of complexity that ecology is most frequently referenced in recent work. The key idea in the ecology of learning is that of learning through interaction with the environment. My concern here is to pick out insights from the literature that contribute to a spatially oriented view of this interaction.

Kramsch (2002: 8) saw the ecological perspective as a post-structural alternative to the traditional dichotomy between language acquisition and language socialisation; an alternative that encompassed 'the totality of the relationships that a learner, as a living organism, entertains with all aspects of his/her environment'. For Tudor (2003: 4), this approach meant exploring language teaching and learning 'within the totality of the lives of the various participants involved, and not as one sub-part of their lives, which can be examined in isolation'. He described the language classroom as an 'ecosystem', but also called for attention to the meaning of learning and teaching for the participants within and beyond the classroom. More recently, Lai (2015) has emphasised how learners traverse out-of-class and in-class learning and the ecological balance they seek among activities carried out in different settings. For van Lier (2004: 11), an ecological approach 'looks at the entire situation and asks, what is it in this environment that makes things happen the way they do?'

The key ecological idea in van Lier's (2004) account of language learning is Gibson's (1979) concept of affordance. For Gibson, organisms co-perceive the world as it relates to themselves and an affordance is a relationship between an organism and its environment. In the context of second language learning, affordances are objects in the environment that are perceived as resources for learning. Affordances are the resources the environment offers and what learners do with them. Language learning depends on an active, attentive learner who is in tune with the semiotic resources – including language, other modes of expression and things to talk about – that the environment makes available. Language learning is the emergence of language out of interactions between learners and these semiotic resources. Contrasting the ecological view with an 'input-based' view in which the learner internalises 'pieces of language that are selected, sequenced and transmitted in language curricula', van Lier (2004: 52–53) suggests that, from an ecological perspective, language learning 'occurs as a result of meaningful participation in human events'. For van Lier, the ecological view is also an 'activity-based' view. Language learning occurs in the course of activity, in which 'language is part of action, of physical artifacts, of the actions of others' (van Lier, 2004: 53).

An additional point, which van Lier (2004) touches upon but does not address explicitly, concerns the learner's relation to the environment. This is a spatial question that is often resolved metaphorically by placing the learner *opposite to* the environment, as if the learner and the environment were two different objects. However, there is also good reason to view the language learner as *part of* the language learning environment, especially in the spaces of activity in which learning occurs. Taking an ecological view of 'third' language learning, Singleton and Aronin (2007) argue that multilinguals' language awareness is an affordance for further learning. Multilinguals do not simply possess 'a stock of languages', they also make use of their 'capacity to deal with the languages at their disposal and challenges and opportunities connected with them' (Singleton & Aronin, 2007: 84). This is a question of the resources that learners bring to the learning environment, which vary considerably from learner to learner. Palfreyman (2014: 178) calls attention to the whole range of resources in the environment, including 'enabling' resources such as books and people that give access to 'learning resources' such as knowledge and motivation. He also refers to 'discursive resources', including 'approaches, expectations, and identities related directly and indirectly to learning', which are individual to the learner, but also shaped by social and cultural discourses on teaching and learning. From the point of view of assemblage theory, the relationship between the learner and the environment could be seen as a meeting up of mobile language-bearing assemblages, one of which is the learner. As these assemblages interact with each other, a new assemblage emerges of which the learner is a component part. This new assemblage is likely to comprise multiple components relevant to the learning that emerges, some of which are brought by the learner while others come from elsewhere.

In my view, van Lier (2004) offers a strong account of *how* language learning occurs from an ecological perspective, but he does not explain the key spatial question of how the necessary semiotic resources get into the environment. Partly because he does not make a strong distinction between second and first language learning, van Lier (2004: 55) assumes that the language to be learned 'surrounds the learner in all its complexity and variety', that it is 'embedded in the physical and social world'. Although this assumption makes sense for first language learning and early childhood bilingualism, it is more problematic for second language learning, which often takes place in environments where access to the language is more limited.

Van Lier's (2004) view that first and second language learning are similar from an ecological perspective is shared by more recent critical work on SLA, notably the Douglas Fir Group (2016: 21), who maintain that there is 'good reason to consider the processes involved in the learning of first languages to be largely the processes also at work when new languages are being learned later in life'. However, a spatial perspective suggests that there are clear differences between first and second language learning related to the environments in which they take place. One of the main differences is the presence of the learner's first language as a resource in second language learning. Van Lier (2004: 135) also notes this, but he views the first language as a 'mediator or a support structure' rather than as an environmental resource. In other respects, also, first and second language learning take place under very different spatial conditions. For Vygotsky (1994), first language acquisition is explained by the presence of the language to be learned in the child's immediate environment. The language is present in its mature form from the beginning, and the environment also develops in tandem with the child's language development (Vygotsky, 1994). But in second language learning, the language to be learned is never simply 'there', waiting to be learned. In second language learning, the target language is a *scarce* resource. It must either find its way into the learner's immediate environment, or the learner must go out and construct an environment in which it is present.

Most importantly, whereas the early stages of first language acquisition are undertaken by an infant with limited mobility, second language learners are older and, therefore, more mobile. Infants have no choice but to learn whatever language(s) surround(s) them, but the spatial mobility of second language learners means that they have a degree of choice on which languages they learn and where, when and how they learn them. Second language learning is also a purposeful activity guided by motives and motivations. Choices are constrained, again primarily by spatial factors governing the availability and accessibility of resources, so that, in the longer term, language learning becomes a matter of seeking out settings and resources, mapping out learning environments and developing learning pathways over time. This is why the *where* of second language learning is so important. The presence of the second language in the learner's environment is always a matter to be explained.

There is also a tendency in ecological accounts to describe the environment as a construct of human, non-human and ideational resources, but to focus in practice on human social networks and spoken language interaction. Thus, although van Lier (2004: 5) begins by describing the environment as 'all physical, social and symbolic affordances that provide grounds for activity', he later writes:

> Language learning, if it is to be at all meaningful, and if it is to be tied to the self and the formation of identities, must therefore be embedded in conversation. Worksheets, grammar books, drills and tests can never be more than distancing devices, unless they are integrally connected to acts of speaking, presentations of self, and projections of identity. (van Lier, 2004: 145)

This tendency to separate interaction with people from interaction with things, or to view things only as mediators of interaction between people, makes second language learning seem more akin to first language learning than it actually is. We must be wary of what is, in effect, an ecological tendency for objects of a similar kind to have an affinity for each other. Dogs, for example, are most excited when they meet other dogs. Humans see their interactions with other humans as being somehow more significant than their interactions with other objects in the environment. This tendency is not particularly helpful, however, in understanding second language learning, in which direct interaction with non-human objects plays a much more important part than SLA research allows. This gives us a second reason why the *where* of second language learning is so important. To begin an environmental investigation into language learning with an *a priori* assumption that conversations are more valuable than worksheets, or that worksheets are only valuable if they are embedded in conversation, would be to close off some of the most interesting questions about language learning environments before the investigation even begins. What is needed, instead, are investigations of settings and environments that examine the whole range of human and non-human assemblages that comprise them and then work out how these assemblages are related to each other in the context of learners' engagements with the environment as a whole.

Language Learning Environments

Bronfenbrenner (1979: 12) argued that advances in the study of human development required 'investigation in the actual environments, both immediate and remote, in which human beings live'. However, the spatial compositions and locations of settings and environments tend to be underspecified in ecological studies. For Bronfenbrenner, the environment is made up of spatial units that he calls 'settings', but at higher levels of scale his nested model specifies only relations among settings (mesosystem and exosystem) and a rather vaguely defined cultural context (macrosystem). Human development involves participation in more and more settings over time, but it is not clear that the environment is any more than the aggregate of these settings. A lack of clarity on the nature of language learning environments can also lead to strange conclusions. Van Lier (2000: 253), for example, argued that 'the environment is full of language that provides opportunities for learning to the active, participating learner'. But from the point of view of the second language learner, the environment is clearly *not* full of second languages, which are only contingently present in respect to specific languages and specific locations.

The problem, here, is the sense in which settings are put together as environments. I will come to settings later. Here, I want to focus on environments and suggest, first, that there are two ways in which they are more than simple aggregates of settings. I will call these 'areal' environments and 'individual' environments. From an objects-*as*-space perspective, space and the environment are more or less the same thing. To speak of 'the environment' implies that there is really only one indivisible space, in which everything is in some sense interconnected. Globalisation is, perhaps, producing such a space as I write. But there is also a sense in which spaces and environments are localised. We might ask, for example, whether Barcelona is a good environment for learning Spanish. In this case, Barcelona would be an 'areal' language learning environment, or an environment that corresponds to an identifiable area in space. The area in question could also be of any size or dimension: the area of a city, but also the area of, say, a university campus or a nation state. Often, such environments will correspond to the territorial bases of DeLanda's (2016) social assemblages at various levels of scale.

How one would go about identifying the boundaries of areal language learning environments is a complex issue. The question about Barcelona, for example, implies a person who is considering travelling to Barcelona in order to learn Spanish. But it seems unlikely that anyone would go to Barcelona in order to learn Spanish and not leave the city limits, not use the internet, not watch television broadcasts from Madrid and so on. An areal language learning environment is a problematic concept, in other words, if it does not correspond to the complex ways in which individuals experience or make use of space. Nevertheless, we can imagine that learning Spanish in Barcelona would be a very different matter to learning Spanish in, say, Beijing or Moscow, or, more meaningfully, Buenos Aires or Madrid.

The idea of an environment also conveys a sense of surrounding. An environment is usually the *environment of* a particular organism and to look at the environment from this perspective is to look at what I will call 'individual' environments. However, individual language learning environments are not simply areal environments viewed from 'inside', from the perspective of individuals 'within' them. They are environments that individuals assemble from the spatial resources available to them. To identify an areal environment, we might draw a line around an area on a map, or more likely take a line that has already been drawn such as the boundary of a city. To identify an individual environment, we would need to somehow track an individual and record the places that they go. This distinction is related to the difference between a cartographic approach to space and a wayfinding approach (Golledge, 1999; Ingold, 2011). In both cases, the environment is made up of settings. In an areal environment, they are grouped together as points within a continuous space on a map. In an individual environment, they form a discontinuous space that corresponds to an individual's pathways within, and beyond, the areal environment.

Language learning environments: The areal view

It is now often observed that multilingualism, not monolingualism, is the new sociolinguistic norm (May, 2014; Ortega, 2014). This means two things. First, because there are more multilinguals than monolinguals in the world, there is nothing unusual about being multilingual. For some, monolingualism is the deviation from the norm of multilingualism. Second, monolingualism should not be the model for multilingual competence; a multilingual person is not two monolinguals in one body, but one who uses the resources of two or more languages flexibly according to the context of communication. In my view, these are important correctives to what has been called a 'monolingual mindset', and an expectation that second language learners should aspire to 'native speaker' norms and competence (May, 2014; Piller, 2016). The idea of second language learning as 'becoming multilingual' (Ortega, 2014) fits well with an ecological perspective. However, I also want to consider the contrary view that every human being who is capable of doing so learns at least one language, but only a proportion, albeit a majority, learns two or more languages. Moreover, being multilingual usually means knowing and using a relatively small number of languages that have value for the individual. This is not intended to be a defence of monolingualism. Rather, I want to suggest that we do not really need to look for a cause for each specific case of first language learning; a general environmental cause will do. But we do need to look for causes of specific cases of second language learning, which will most often lie in the particular characteristics of areal language learning environments. While some multilinguals make great efforts to learn remote languages, most learn languages that are present within the environments in which they live, either as the first languages of others or as socially validated second or foreign languages.

Some years ago, in the 1980s, I spent a few days hiking in the rice terraces of Ifugao province in northern Luzon, in the Philippines. At one point, I was guided across a confusing maze of rice terraces by a 10-year-old girl who told me she knew five languages. These were, as she named them: Batad, the language of her village; Ifugao, the language of the nearby town in which she went to school; Illocano, the major language of northern Luzon; Filipino, the national language; and English. Although she did not have 'monolingual' competence in all of these languages, to my ears, she had an extraordinary multilingual competence. The reason I bring up this example is that, remarkable as this young girl's multilingual competence was, it was shaped by the particularities of the language learning environment of her locality. Moreover, this language learning environment was shaped both by local circumstances and by national and global circulations of language-bearing assemblages that were bringing both Filipino and English to a remote mountainous region that was, at that time, just beginning to develop as a tourist destination.

From an areal perspective, then, language learning environments, like social assemblages (DeLanda, 2016) and space itself (Smith, 1991), have a scalar character. Indeed, if there is a relationship between the formation of social assemblages and the circulation of language-bearing assemblages, as I suggested in Chapter 4, the scales of social assemblages might be a good guide to the scales of language learning environments. Geographically, language learning environments may be shaped and divided from each other by patterns in the global flow of language-bearing assemblages at national, regional, urban and local scales, the lower levels of scale being nested with the higher levels, with opportunities for language learning being variably distributed at each level.

Language learning environments differ from each other laterally (e.g. from city to city) mainly as a consequence of variations in the densities of language-bearing traffic and the routes along which this traffic travels. They are also shaped by language policy regimes that regulate the use of languages in domains such as the law, education and the media. Language policy regimes impose an official or dominant language on these regimes and also rule on issues such as which languages are taught in schools, provision of translation services, display of languages in public space and so on, with retroactive effects on the flow of languages in and out of the environment. Global and national circulations of language-bearing assemblages also tend to concentrate in metropolitan hubs, rather than smaller towns, regions and rural areas. This means that language learning environments can be evaluated across levels of scale in respect to both languages and localities. All else being equal, and taking no account of the individual learner, Sydney is almost certainly a more favourable environment for learning English that it is for any other language. It may also be a more favourable environment for learning Italian, Japanese or French than it is for Burmese, Dinka or Welsh. For learning English, it might be difficult to choose between Sydney and London, but both are probably more favourable environments than Shanghai, which is, in turn, probably more favourable than, say, Nanchang, an inland city approximately 700 kilometres to the west of Shanghai. These are conjectures, of course, but they can, at least in principle, be empirically tested. In order to do so, we would need to consider the idea of language learning environments in conjunction with those of resources and settings for language learning.

Resources and settings

When language-bearing assemblages circulate in a multilingual environment, they become resources for language learning. These assemblages include people, goods and information, each of which acts somewhat differently as language learning resources. From an SLA perspective, these are resources in the sense that they are sources of language input: people who speak the target language, who can teach it or act as conversation partners; goods and information that carry multimodal texts that can be read, listened to and enjoyed. In addition to being sources of spoken language, people are also producers of language-bearing assemblages of all kinds. People also include learners of the language and all of the inner resources (knowledge, motivations, capacities for learning, etc.) that they carry with them. Media devices also have the capacity to produce language-bearing assemblages or, more often, to bring remote informational resources into the environment from elsewhere and enable communication across distance. It is the ubiquity of media devices in the modern world, especially, that makes the borders of areal language learning environments difficult to define. Using televisions, radios, computers and mobile phones, language learners can access informational language-bearing assemblages globally so that their geographical location often becomes insignificant. On the other hand, geographical location does seem to matter, when we consider, for example, levels of income, access to devices and facilities such as free Wi-Fi.

In addition to language resources there are other kinds of nonlinguistic resources involved in language learning. Learners do not simply interact with language learning resources as they pass by on the wind. They also require what might be called a certain 'furniture', consisting of places to meet and study, comfortable chairs and tables to sit at, snacks and cups of tea or coffee, things to look at and talk about and so on. These are not necessarily language-bearing resources (although they often are); rather, they represent the infrastructure of the settings in which learners interact with language resources.

In an earlier study, I defined a setting for language learning as 'an arrangement for learning, involving one or more learners in a particular place, who are situated in particular kinds of physical, social or pedagogical relationships with other people (teachers, learners, others) and material or virtual resources' (Benson, 2011b: 13). In plain language, a setting is a place where language learners access and engage with language resources. Settings are assemblages of human and non-human, linguistic and non-linguistic resources, but learning in settings also involves a crucial engagement with space. Language learning does not take place in the undifferentiated space of the environment, but at specific sites at which resources are assembled for the purpose of language learning. Day-to-day, second language learning typically involves comings and goings, movements from setting to setting, within geographically circumscribed areas and the spatial routines of everyday lives.

Settings for language learning include language classrooms and a host of institutional and non-institutional settings beyond the classroom. Some settings are specifically designed for language learning (e.g. language schools, language laboratories, self-access centres) and some are designed for learning more generally (e.g. classrooms, computer laboratories, libraries and learning spaces). Others are everyday spaces in which language learning resources are assembled on the fly. These include cafés, bars and other meeting places; public transport, shopping malls, waiting places, the home, places where the learner can be alone, and so on. They also include online settings where broadcast and digital informational resources are assembled, including television and radio shows, web sites, messaging services and social media platforms. I will discuss these settings in more detail later, but note here that they are, strictly speaking, representations of space that function to all intents and purposes as if they were settings. However, if they are to be viewed as settings, account must also be taken of the devices used and the spaces in the offline world from which they are accessed.

In the sense that I am using the term, settings have something in common with Scollon's (2001) 'sites of engagement' – points in time and space where networks of practices come together; and White and Bown's (2018: 32) 'learner-context interfaces' – points at which learners 'shape space, place and opportunity in language learning'. If a setting is a spatial assemblage of resources, there is a sense in which it only exists for the time that the resources are assembled and language learning is taking place. A classroom is a setting for language learning when language students, language teachers and other language resources are present and interacting with each other. At other times, it may be a setting for other kinds of learning, and when the classroom is locked up and empty at the end of the day it is no longer a setting for anything at all. A bus stop can be a setting for language learning, if a language learner strikes up a conversation in the target language with a fellow passenger. Under other circumstances it is simply a setting for waiting. This suggests that settings have both a spatial aspect and temporal or durational aspects. A classroom is a setting for language learning at a certain time of the day and for the duration of the language lesson. Each lesson, each bus-stop conversation is a unique assemblage of resources and a unique setting. However, if we treat settings spatially, these unique temporal assemblages might be better described as language learning events at sites that become settings because these events occur repeatedly and routinely. What is most relevant to the notion of setting is not the particularity of events (which may of great interest in other ways), but the ways in which their regular occurrence stamps spaces with a particular character over time.

In Bronfenbrenner's (1979) model, settings are the building blocks of environments for human development. However, it may make more sense to think of settings and resources as products of their environments, than vice versa. The number, density, quality and accessibility of settings for language learning provide evidence of the character of an area as a language learning environment. But settings for language learning are so often designed for purposes other than language learning that it is difficult to assess the quality of an areal language learning environment without reference to its use by populations of learners. Settings that are specifically designed for second language learning only arise where the circulation of language-bearing assemblages and the level of language learning activity warrant such specialised uses of space. In this sense, language learning environments are formed by the transformation of spaces into settings for language learning at different timescales and under the pressure of flows of language-bearing assemblages and their use as resources for learning.

The following sections will look more closely at two phenomena arising from accelerated global mobility that are currently shaping language learning environments on a global scale: the multilingual city which has emerged as the principal framework for language learning environments on the ground, and multilingualism online, which both disrupts the relevance of territorially based language learning environments and raises questions about the sense in which the metaphorical spaces of online communication can be thought of as settings and environments in their own right.

Multilingual cities

In 2007, the proportion of the world's population living in urban areas passed 50%. In 2018 it reached 55% and it is projected to reach 68% by 2050 (United Nations, 2018). Trends associated with the growth of urban populations include the transformation of metropolitan cities into global hubs for the mobility of people, goods and information. As much of this mobility involves language-bearing assemblages, second language learning is increasingly concentrated in globally connected cities. However, this is not simply a question of where second language learning takes place. It is also a matter of how flows of language-bearing assemblages transform urban spaces into settings for language learning, and cities into language learning environments. Of particular importance, in this respect, is the phenomenon of the 'multilingual city' (King & Carson, 2016).

In a much-cited passage, Lefebvre (1991: 25) wrote that 'around 1910 a certain space was shattered'. This was 'the space of common sense, of knowledge (savoir), of social practice, political power… the space, too, of classical perspective and geometry… bodied forth in Western arts and philosophy, as in the form of the city and town'. Lefebvre did not explain the significance of the date 1910, but in another much-cited passage from a work published in 1912, the artist Wassily Kandinsky (1946) wrote of a state of spiritual confusion, 'such as would prevail if a mathematically constructed city were suddenly overthrown by uncontrollable forces of nature'. In 1903, the German sociologist Georg Simmel (1997: 175) had already written of the fragmentation, diversity and 'onrushing impressions' of the modern metropolis, which produced an 'intensification of nervous stimulation' and highly individual subjectivities. This view of the fragmentation of the city is persistent. In his novel *The City and the City*, China Miéville (2009) imagined two cities intertwined with each other in one space and, as I was writing this chapter, I glanced at a recently published volume, *Walking Cities: London*, which aims to show 'how the city exists as *many* cities, multi-layered, constructed from a myriad of overlapping cultural, social, historical, political and economic paths' (Joseph-Lester *et al.*, 2020: 1). Fragmentation, diversity and multiplicity have become dominant themes in contemporary work on urbanisation and the city (Amin & Thrift, 2002, 2016; Brenner & Schmid, 2014, 2015; Massey, 2005).

Language is scarcely mentioned in this work. Yet, over the last 20 years or so, there has been a global upheaval in the sociolinguistics of the city, as if the orderly one-language-one-nation linguistic map of the world has been thrown up in the air, depositing fragments of multiple languages in so-called 'global cities' across the world (Sassen, 1991). The multilingual city is, in fact, a consequence of the sharp acceleration in the mobilities of language-bearing assemblages outlined in Chapter 4. A rough-and-ready survey of the percentages of population who are reported to use languages other than English in traditionally English-speaking cities is revealing – Toronto (46%), Los Angeles (41%), London (37%), Sydney (36%) and New York (36%). Although I cannot vouch for the accuracy of these statistics, it seems reasonable to assume that these cities are now no longer 'English speaking'; English is the dominant language, and perhaps the lingua franca, but English shares the space of the city with many other languages. The number of languages used in these cities is typically above 200, and in New York City, possibly the most linguistically diverse location in the world, it has been estimated at more than 800, including many endangered languages (Roberts, 2010).

Manchester, the city in which I grew up in the 1960s, was as I recall it a decidedly monolingual city. My school friends spoke only English and English was the only language to be seen on the streets. Now Manchester is home to more than 150 languages. Almost half of its school students have a home language other than English, and the city's linguistic landscapes are rich in multilingual signage (Matras & Robertson, 2015). In my youth, the local grammar school taught French. The same school now offers qualifications in French, Urdu, Spanish, Arabic, German, Italian, Modern Greek, Polish, Portuguese, Bengali and Persian. There is now a considerable body of published work on the linguistic diversity of London (Block, 2006), New York (García & Fishman, 2002), Sydney (Chik *et al.*, 2019) and many other cities around the world (Boix-Fuster, 2015; Duarte & Gogolin, 2013; King & Carson, 2016; Smakman & Heinrich, 2018). Migration is the main driving force of what has been called the linguistic superdiversity of modern urban settings (Duarte & Gogolin, 2013). However, in so far as we are concerned with multilingual cities as language learning environments, the effects of migration on the circulation of language-bearing assemblages are as important as migration itself. To illustrate what this means, I will take Sydney as an example.

The Australian census publishes statistics on respondents' use of languages other than English (known as 'community' languages) at home (Benson & Hatoss, 2019). These statistics point, first of all, to the concentration of multilingualism in urban areas. Sydney and Melbourne, Australia's two largest cities, have similar populations. In 2016, community language speakers made up 35.8% of the population in Sydney and 32.3% in Melbourne. Sydney and Melbourne accounted for 65% of Australia's community language speakers, but only 38% of the population as a whole. Census statistics also show how Sydney's recent population growth, largely driven by migration, reflects accelerated global mobility. Between 2011 and 2016, the number of community language speakers rose by 21.4%, while the number who speak English only increased by just 3.1%. There were 47 languages with more than 1000 speakers in the city, and 87 with more than 100 speakers. In general, speakers of community languages are dispersed in neighbourhoods across the city, rather than concentrated in language 'ghettoes' (Chik et al., 2019). In addition, Sydney has a large transient international population that is not captured by census statistics. In 2017, there were 194,000 international student enrolments and 3.2 million international short-term visitors in New South Wales, the vast majority in Sydney. Again, there is evidence of a rapid acceleration in mobility over the past decade. International student enrolments increased by 58% between 2013 and 2017, while the number of international visitors increased by almost 50% over the same period.

These developments have had two immediate impacts on Sydney as a language learning environment. On the one hand, recent migrants, international students and short-term visitors use the city as a resource for English language learning. On the other hand, Sydney's multilingual population has become a resource for learning all kinds of languages other than English. It is not just that the city is rich in opportunities for social interaction with speakers of other languages. There is also a more indirect impact of the migration of language professionals and semi-professionals, the establishment of language teaching facilities, including English language programmes for new migrants, private language schools and university language centres, foreign language programmes in schools, officially supported community language schools for young people and a host of community organisations offering language lessons for adults. Though it may be easier to find resources to learn Italian, Japanese and French, language classes in Burmese, Dinka, Welsh and many other languages are available. Sydney has a vast infrastructure for international students taking short English language courses, many within English language testing regimes that act as gatekeepers for migration and admission to higher education. But at the same time, there is also a substantial infrastructure for teaching and learning, formally and informally, the many languages that migrants bring to the city.

In addition to the rise of formal language learning opportunities, there has also been a transformation of everyday resources and settings as the practices and routines of everyday life are woven into the fabric of wider language learning environments. The presence of migrant and transient migrant communities attracts global flows of language-bearing assemblages into the city and creates new transnational flows. Established migrants, in particular, become importers and producers of language-bearing resources, including multilingual products and documentation, books, newspapers and magazines, cultural performances and festivals, and linguistic landscapes. Sydney has, for example, more than 40 community language newspapers, 21 language-based film festivals, television and radio broadcasts in numerous languages and thriving retail sectors with signage and products carrying texts in Chinese, Korean, Arabic, Persian and many other languages. Because the urban economy, especially the service sector, relies on the casual employment of recent migrants and international students, there is a proliferation of multilingual workplaces – construction sites, markets, restaurants, foodstores, etc. (Pennycook & Otsuji, 2015). Less easily documented is the proliferation of informal meeting places, or 'inter-spaces' as Urry (2007: 243) calls them – bars, cafés and restaurants, community centres, campuses and open spaces – that serve as sites for an 'extensive cultural exchange' that is functional in sustaining 'urban sociality' in multilingual cities. In such informal settings, translanguaging, or 'the fluid and dynamic practices that transcend the boundaries between named languages, language varieties, and language and other semiotic systems' (Li, 2018: 9) may also become a context in which languages are informally exchanged and learned. As Pennycook and Otsuji (2015) argue through the idea of 'metrolingualism', informal language use in multilingual cities has as much to do with situated engagement with the spaces of the city as it does with language contact.

Multilingual cities are of interest as language learning environments because they offer rich arrays of resources and settings for learning multiple languages, and also because most language learning takes place in cities. Cities are not self-contained spaces, however, and the language learning affordances they offer may also include connectivity to other spaces, either as hubs for travel to surrounding areas or as locations for inexpensive access to online resources. This does not mean that language learning does not take place in other spaces. Small towns, rural and remote areas, cruise ships, military facilities and prisons can all be investigated as language learning environments. Such investigations would, perhaps, be based on an assumption that a language learning environment is a space in which a certain population or group lead their lives and learn languages. If this is the case, however, account could also be taken of where a language learner might take a trip from a city such as Sydney, and, in addition, their use of digital online resources from beyond the city. These might be thought of as other environments, other spaces or as extensions of the urban environment, which are for many people an important aspect of the urban environment itself.

Online resources and terrestrial space

In 21st-century language learning, online resources are playing increasingly important roles. They complement what we might call 'terrestrial' resources accessed in settings on the ground (Lai, 2017; Meskill & Guan, 2012). There are also reports of people attaining high levels of second language competence using only online resources (Cole & Vanderplank, 2016; Sockett, 2014). Two kinds of online resources seem to be especially important at present. Audio and video hosting and streaming services such as YouTube, Spotify and Netflix have become vast pools of multilingual popular culture resources. Social media platforms such as Facebook, Instagram and TikTok have also become important sites for multilingual communication at a more personal level (Jacquemet, 2012). Other online contexts for informal second language learning include online games, online shopping, interpersonal communication using videoconferencing and text messaging, and web sites and mobile applications designed for language learning. The most important feature of the online world, however, is the multiplicity of language resources that it makes available. For most learners, online resources are more abundant, more easily accessed and less expensive than resources accessed on the ground.

English is the most widely used language online, which means, perhaps, that English language learners benefit most from the availability of language resources online, as well as from the frequent use of English as a lingua franca in online communications among multilingual speakers. But online communication is also highly multilingual (Benson, 2017b; Cunliffe & Herring, 2005; Danet & Herring, 2007; Lee, 2017). Popular online services such as Facebook and YouTube have interfaces in multiple languages. At the time of writing, six of the 10 most viewed videos on YouTube use English. The other four use Korean, Russian and Spanish. The music video for *Despacito* by Spanish singer Luis Fonsi was noteworthy at the time because the number of views (6.9 billion) was approaching the most recent figure for the world's population (7.8 billion). The internet also seems to favour the global dispersion of less-used and minority languages on sites designed for language teaching and in more informal forums for transnational communication among diaspora populations and 'new speakers' (O'Rourke & Pujolar, 2015). Following the adoption of the European Charter for Regional and Minority Languages, the internet has had a particular impact on the dispersal of less-used European languages. Notably, while the number of speakers of Irish is in decline in Ireland, Duolingo reports more than a million 'active learners' of Irish globally. Lee (2017) also highlights the impact of online communication on 'lesser-written' languages such as Cantonese, Luxemburgish and Egyptian Arabic.

The objects-*as*-space perspective that I have adopted views space as a physical entity, and up to this point I have used the terms setting and environment, accordingly, to refer to physical spaces on the ground. For convenience, I will refer to these as 'terrestrial' settings and environments. Terms such as 'cyberspace' and 'virtual space' suggest that online space is metaphorical, not physical. The spatial dimensions of the online world are discussed in depth elsewhere (Ciolfi, 2015; Graham, 1998; Moores, 2012; Wilken & Goggin, 2012). Here, I want to make several points about how online resources fit into the terrestrial world of language learning settings and environments.

Online space is not a domain of space *sui generis*. It *is* physical space in two important senses that arise from the discussion of mobilities in Chapter 4. First, online communications depend on a vast terrestrial network of computer terminals and servers, routers and relay stations, massive data storage units and thousands of miles of fibre-optic and electrical cabling. The online world is, in fact, 'more physical than we think' (Bhardwaj, 2018). Second, the mobility of language-bearing assemblages is inseparable from the mobility of people, goods and broadcast or digital information. In each case, there is a physical transmission of information but, as I argued in Chapter 4, the main feature of broadcast and digital information is their 'weightlessness'. As a result, broadcast and digital information flow more freely and in multiple directions simultaneously.

This has a number of perceptual effects in regard to how we access information online. When we 'navigate' online worlds, we often feel that we are going somewhere to get information, not that the information is being sent to us. This also relates to what Virilio (1994) called 'telepresence', or the experience of feeling as if one were actually present at a remote place when, for example, viewing a live transmission of a sports event or concert, or participating in a video-conference. As Jacquemet (2012: 476) puts it, the almost instantaneous transmission of video images produces a 'new kind of place'. In other contexts, we have the perception that the information is contained within the device we are using, rather than summoned over distance. This perception is particularly enhanced by mobile phones and intelligent assistants, which seem to become sources of knowledge in their own right. In other words, the weightlessness of broadcast and digital information disturbs our sense of space, such that we are not really aware of where information comes from or how it gets to us. We have a sense of information coming to us across frictionless space whenever and wherever we want it. However, in reality, the spatiality of physical mobility infrastructures shapes the circulation of broadcast and digital information, such that its movements are far from frictionless. In particular, online language resources tend to concentrate in global multilingual cities in much the same way as language-bearing people and goods. This means that the terrestrial environment from which online resources are accessed can have a great significance.

Part of the perceptual problem that we have to deal with is that online communications are largely organised through a metaphorical vocabulary of space. Sources of information are divided up into sites, platforms, channels, pages and so on. So effective is this metaphorical representation of information as space (which is visual and auditory, as well as linguistic) that 'going online' seems to be a matter of going somewhere in the world, of being in a space of spaces to be entered, exited, inhabited and explored. This perception is subjectively so real that there may be no harm in thinking of web sites such as Duolingo or social media platforms such as Facebook as settings that offer language resources. On the other hand, although the immersive multimodal experience of being 'in' an online game world may be more visceral, it is essentially the same as the experience of being lost in the fictional world of a good book. Many young English language learners read J.K. Rowling's *Harry Potter* books, treating them as authentic learning resources. Setting would be more a matter of where the learners get the books from (a school library, a local English language bookshop or an online store?) and where they read them (in their bedroom, on the school bus, during dull lessons at school?). Similarly, it seems to make more sense to think of the online world as a resource embedded in the terrestrial environment, and not as a parallel environment. The point is not to be finicky about the use of these words. It is rather to maintain an awareness of how spatial circumstances in which learners go online – what devices they use, where they are located and what other human and non-human resources are assembled in the setting – may impact the learning that takes place (Kuure, 2011).

Lastly, I want to add that these spatial circumstances are extraordinarily varied both in respect to environments and settings. Online resources are accessed at home on a personal computer, on workstations at educational institutions or in the workplace, on mobile devices and phones or on workstations in public spaces while on the move. In multilingual cities there is usually a high level of access to devices and connectivity and individuals are often online throughout the day. I have observed this in work with adult international students learning English in Sydney (Benson *et al.*, 2018), but I have also observed how, in order to save money, students often 'poach' on the resources of others (De Certeau, 1984), by using mobile phones or tablet devices as multifunctional tools to access free Wi-Fi in public spaces. In this way, digital media use is woven into learning environments in which settings for language learning are often settings that afford access to digital resources. Learners also use digital resources to organise their uses of space. Using online maps, text messages and phone calls, they use digital media to navigate urban environments and move from setting to setting. In this way, the environment becomes a configuration of settings and 'inter-spaces' (Urry, 2007), in which meetings and arrangements are made using digital communication on the move (Benson *et al.*, 2018). In a highly 'connected' environment for English language learning like Sydney, the layering of online resources within terrestrial settings is apt to be highly complex. In other environments, however, the situation may be very different. There may be more limited access to devices and internet connections; there may be limited availability of online resources in the language that the learner is learning or, conversely, the internet may be the only source of language learning resources. In these ways, online resources are an important factor in the constitution of settings and variations among language environments that contribute to the spatial inequities I will discuss at the end of this chapter.

Individual Language Learning Environments

The question of who gets to learn which languages where can, ultimately, only be answered at the level of the individual. In some parts of the world, local environments or language policies severely constrain second language learning for young people. Although my young guide in northern Luzon was certainly a gifted language learner, she had little choice in the matter of which five languages she had learned. In Hong Kong, where I taught English for many years, all students learn English and Putonghua (Mandarin Chinese) at school from an early age and opportunities to learn other languages are few before they reach adulthood. In other parts of the world, young people have more choice in the matter of whether they learn second languages or not, and if they do, which languages they learn. Even then, however, choices are constrained by environmental circumstances, related to the accessibility of settings and the availability of resources. From an areal perspective, then, language learning environments both constrain and enable the language learning choices and behaviours of individuals.

From the perspective of the individual, the settings and resources of a language learning environment act as a framework within which choices are made and actions taken. Becoming multilingual is not a matter of acquiring an environmentally determined set of multilingual competences; nor is it a matter of learning any language at all. It is something between these two poles, and it depends largely upon individual learners' uses of environmental resources. Because resources are always accessed in settings, it also depends on the pathways that individuals trace among settings for learning. This means that we have to do with two kinds of language learning environments: the areal environments that frame the learning of populations and the environments that individuals map out in accordance with their circumstances and needs.

This mapping out of individual language learning environments, although it is not exclusive to multilingual cities, has much to do with the individualisation of urban life. Writing in the early years of the 20th century, Simmel (1997: 183–184) pointed to a modern conception of individualism connected to the emergence of the metropolis. The metropolitan citizen, he argued, 'does not end with the limits of his body or the area comprising his immediate activity', but is constituted 'by the sum of effects emanating from him temporally and spatially'. This entailed a conception of individual freedom, based on the particularity that comes from 'the working out of a way of life'. Many years later, White and Siegel (1984: 239) made a similar observation when they criticised the superficiality of the idea that socialisation is a 'universal process through which all children in a society acquire a common stock of knowledge, attitudes, beliefs, and customs'. Because children occupy only a fraction of the space of the towns and cities in which they live, socialisation necessarily involves 'negotiation to find a viable and unique set of social contexts to be used and lived in by the individuals', a process that 'makes children not alike as it makes them alike' (White & Siegel, 1984).

Barron (2010) captures the importance of individual agency in an ecological perspective on learning in the idea of 'learning pathways'. Following Bronfenbrenner (1979), Barron (2010: 117) emphasises how young people adapt their environments as they 'create their own learning opportunities' by choosing to pursue meaningful lines of activity, by developing relationships with mentors and collaborators and by pursuing material resources that sustain interest-driven projects. To this I want to add that the creation of learning opportunities also involves adaptations of space as learners create their own settings for learning. De Certeau's (1984: xii) notion that everyday life 'invents itself by poaching in countless ways on the property of others' captures something of this relationship between language learners the many spaces in which they learn. Agency in language learning begins from uses of space and, as De Certeau (1984) would describe it, the 'tactical' use of the spaces of others. It is, as Bronfenbrenner (1979: 289) puts it, a matter of 'making the world one's own'.

Individual language learning environments have four main characteristics, which I discuss below: (i) they are configurations of settings, (ii) they are both spatial and temporal, (iii) they often extend beyond circumscribed areal environments and (iv) they embrace the learner herself/himself.

First, an individual language learning environment is made up of the settings and resources that an individual uses or creates in the course of their learning. It is an assemblage, rather than an aggregate, in so far as it is put together by an individual in a way that is coherent with their goals, motivations, interests and everyday life. Settings are the spatial building blocks of individual learning environments. The 'whole' of an individual's language learning environment is the configuration of settings in which they engage with language learning resources. Importantly, these settings, and the activities they afford, must fit into the spatial frameworks of everyday lives. Everyday life is a spatial affair, a matter of coming here and going there in order to do this and that. From an environmental perspective, the ways in which language learners fit settings for language learning and use together, and into the spatial frameworks of their everyday lives is of special interest.

Second, language learning environments are both spatial and temporal in two respects. Settings are arranged in space, but because an individual cannot be in two places at the same time, a configuration of settings is also a configuration of times: time spent in one setting on a certain activity, time spent in other settings on other activities. This means that a configuration of settings can never be viewed synchronically; it is always a configuration of spaces and times. To the degree that language learning becomes a routine affair that is blended into the routine mobilities of everyday lives, a language learning environment has something of the character of a timetable that divides up days, weeks and months into time spent in different settings and time needed to get from one setting to the next. There is also a longer-term durational aspect to individual language learning environments, as they evolve over time and in relation to the learner's developing multilingual competence. Configurations of settings develop over time and, in their durational aspect, language learning environments often involve sharp transitions – for example, when a learner relocates from one country to another – in which one configuration of settings is abandoned and replaced by another. These transitions are fundamentally spatial and they are of great interest in contexts of study abroad, international education and migration (Kashiwa & Benson, 2018).

Third, individual language learning environments are not necessarily, or even normally, spatially continuous. If we focus on learners' uses of the space of a city, for example, the configurations of settings that make up their individual learning environments rarely form a continuous space. Drawn on a map, individual language learning environments are more easily represented by lines joining up the sites on which settings are located, than by lines circumscribing an area. Moreover, these lines are likely to extend beyond the city into other, often remote, spaces, either through travel or transnational connections, or through uses of online resources. The long-term durational aspect of language learning environments also means that, over time, environments span spaces that are separated by considerable distances, as well as experiences of learning two or more second languages. In this respect, the individual view of language learning environments is very different to the areal view. Whereas the latter implies a focus on the affordances of settings and resources in a continuous bounded space, the former requires a focus on the assembling of individual environments from discontinuous unbounded spaces. This brings us back to the idea that, from an areal perspective, there is really only one continuous global language learning environment in which everything is somehow connected. As in Bronfenbrenner's (1979) model of human development, language learning implies an expanded experience of this wider environment, or a certain 'globalization of biography' (Beck, 2000: 73). But, as I see it, this can never be an experience of global space in its entirety. It is always a piecing together of a coherent individual environment from fragmentary experiences of global space.

Fourth, language learners are ever-present, integral components of their own learning environments. The learner's self is a language-bearing assemblage and learners carry their selves wherever they go, encountering them as resources in any setting in which they learn a language. The learner's part in mapping out an individual language learning environment is thus shaped by the wealth or poverty of embodied knowledge, experience and skills that they bring to the task. It is also partly a matter of the learner's attentiveness to the affordances of settings. Because language learning so often takes advantage of the circulation of language-bearing assemblages in spaces that are not specifically designed for language learning, it is largely a matter of attentiveness to the potential for spaces to be transformed into settings for language learning.

Many people believe that they cannot learn a second language without being taught the language in a class that is set up for that purpose. From an environmental perspective, we might say they lack confidence in their capacity to transform spaces into language learning settings. Among beginners, this lack of confidence is understandable, because the capacity to create settings for learning is enhanced by knowledge of the target language, skills in the use of second languages and experience of learning. But as the learner's knowledge, skills and experience improve, so does their agency within the learning process. One of the tasks of language instruction, therefore, must be to help learners use their developing abilities to transform the spaces of the wider environment into settings for learning and assemble them into coherent language learning environments that are adaptive to their interests and needs.

Language Learning Environments in an Uneven World

Inequalities in second language learning have been discussed from three main aspects: unequal access to opportunities to learn second languages and unequal outcomes for those who do learn second languages either in respect to competences achieved or in respect to rewards obtained for successful learning. Prior to the social turn in SLA, inequalities were mainly addressed in terms of the influence of individual difference factors on learning outcomes (Larsen-Freeman, 2001). Subsequently, inequalities in second language learning were taken up by socially-oriented SLA researchers who linked them to social inequalities relating to race, ethnicity, nationality, gender, religion, sexuality and social class (Block, 2014b). More recently, these inequalities have been connected to broader inequalities among languages and language varieties under globalisation and neoliberalism (Block *et al.*, 2012; Piller, 2016; Rojo & Del Percio, 2020; Tupas, 2015). In this work, inequalities are linked to discrimination on grounds of multilingual competences (e.g. in migration and employment) (Blommaert, 2010; Duchêne *et al.*, 2013) and the idea of the commodification of language under neoliberal economic regimes (Duchêne & Heller, 2012). A more comprehensive discussion of these different aspects of inequality and second language learning would be worthwhile. My part is limited to making the case for the role of space by suggesting, first, that such inequalities are 'built into' the social production of space under globalisation and capitalism and, second, that they are observable as inequalities among areal and individual language learning environments.

I observed in Chapter 2 that from a production of space perspective, uneven regional development is both a consequence of the social relations of capitalism and a solution to crises as capital is moved rapidly around the globe in search of higher rates of profit (Harvey, 1982; Smith, 1991). Neoliberalism involves financial deregulation and the free movement of capital and goods and, somewhat paradoxically, massive interventions by nation states both to attract capital and to ensure its freedom of movement. One of the consequences of this has been a certain kind of regional specialisation in the uses of space or 'zoning' for particular activities, in which second language learning is often implicated. Examples include the emergence of regional and urban economies that are highly dependent on international tourism, where tourism and the tourist industries become contexts for second language learning and use (Goethals, 2015; Janta *et al.*, 2012; Phipps, 2007); the marketing of cities as international education hubs and destinations for language learning; and the production of low-cost English-speaking labour in Asia for call centres (Friginal, 2009) and international domestic work (Lorente, 2018).

Phenomena of these kinds map second language learning onto regions and channel it into certain purposes and educational structures. It is quite a different matter, for example, to be trained in English for work in tourism, a call centre or domestic service, than it is to study English for university entrance. However, to treat such phenomena simply as examples of the commodification of language would be to miss their essentially spatial character. Indeed, under globalisation, the commodification of language is a much wider phenomenon that occurs whenever people, goods and information cross language boundaries. The global mobilities of people, goods and information are largely mobilities of commodities, whether we are thinking of the buying and selling of goods and information or the labour power of transnational workers. And because most commodities are language-bearing assemblages, there is an added cost attached to their language components as they cross language boundaries. Although the value of the language component is difficult to quantify, goods may require multilingual packaging and localisation, information may need to be translated and, if there is a need for English-speaking labour, it may be advantageous to seek it in a region where both the costs of language training and the overall value of labour power are relatively low. What is important here is the entwining of language with unevennesses in the production of space on a global scale. It is the uneven fragmentation of global space that ultimately shapes who gets to learn which languages where, and the benefits they gain from them.

The linguistic consequences of the uneven production of global space are felt at the level of language-learning environments. Bauman (1998: 2) wrote that mobility is 'perpetually a scarce and unequally distributed commodity' and 'what appears as globalization for some means localization for others'. In many parts of the world, second language learning, and knowledge of national and world languages especially, confers social and geographical mobility. But second language learning does not take place on a level playing field. Language learning environments may be either richer or more impoverished in the resources they offer for second language learning.

From the 1990s, language policies across East Asia sought to position nations advantageously in global flows of English language-bearing assemblages from which they had been largely excluded. These policies sought to create English language learning environments from the inside out – not only extending English language teaching into secondary and primary education, but also running up against a lack of local resources, teachers and texts (Nunan, 2003). In China, for example, English language teachers, texts and expertise in communicative language teaching (CLT) methodologies were imported on a vast scale. However, one of the outcomes was an uneven circulation of English language-bearing assemblages within China, which had pronounced regional effects on how English was learned. Hu (2005), for example, found that while some aspects of CLT methodology had been taken up in more developed areas of China, more traditional teaching approaches prevailed in less-developed areas. Hu attributed this difference to a variety of economic, social and cultural factors. Without diminishing the importance of these factors, it could also be said that the causes of this difference were fundamentally spatial and lay in the production of two very different English language learning environments in China; first, as a consequence of the constricted flow of English resources into the country and, second, due to the uneven circulation within China of the resources that were imported to solve this problem.

It must also be added that, because there are costs to the production of the language components of language-bearing assemblages, however difficult they may be to quantify, a 'rich' language learning environment will be rich in a double sense: full of potential for learning, but also costly to assemble. In highly stratified urban environments, where the gaps between the wealthy and the poor are widening, individuals' access to the resources of a rich language learning environment is not guaranteed. Some years ago, I led a research project in which we elicited English lifelong language learning histories from university students in Hong Kong. Towards the end of the interview, the students were asked to sum up what it was like to learn English in Hong Kong. One student explained that it was extremely difficult because 'nobody in Hong Kong uses English', students simply do not come across English outside English lessons at school. Another said that it was not difficult to learn English at all, that 'English is everywhere', and that learning English was not really something that she did, it was 'more of a feeling'. For a long time, I have wondered how two students who studied at the same university in the same city could have such different impressions of their shared language learning environment. At the time, I thought this was a matter of their perceptions of shared environmental resources; that the first student could not see the affordances for language learning in what the second student saw. Or perhaps the second student had more interest, initiative and determination to transform spaces into settings for language learning. But was it also possible, I wondered, that, like the inhabitants of Miéville's (2009) *The City and the City*, these two students actually lived in two different cities that occupied the same geographical space – one in a city where English was nowhere and the other in a city where English was everywhere? And had the very different spatial circumstances under which they had learned English been shaped by the social and economic circumstances of their lives?

Conclusion

This concludes my own thoughts, for the present, on second language learning and space. What I hope to have provided is a set of ideas, a kind of conceptual toolkit, for thinking about language learning from a spatial perspective: ideas that include the production of space on a global scale and the production of local language learning environments and settings. In the next chapter, I will refer to some data-based studies of my own that have contributed to the development of these ideas, but I mostly want to open up the field to others who are also taking up a spatial view of SLA research.

Figure 6.1 A heritage language learner's experience of learning Macedonian in Sydney. From the interview transcript: So when I think of my experience of learning Macedonian, I think of the alphabet…. One of the things I liked about learning Macedonian was being able to communicate with my grandparents, who didn't speak any English…. I personally did not like going to Saturday school. I found it terrible having to go to school on a Saturday at 9 am, when other kids might have been doing sport or playing with their friends… But coming into my senior years and then finally finishing high school and getting a really good mark going towards my high school certificate, it was like, it was nice, it was a nice thing to know that it actually did pay off, yeah (Source: Author's data)

6 Space and SLA Research

> I am, a stride at a time. A very short space of time through very short times of space.
>
> James Joyce, 1986: 31

This book has argued that second language learning begins with the global mobility of language-bearing assemblages (people, goods and information) and that learning emerges from the encounters among these assemblages (learners and learning resources) in language learning settings and environments. It is because second language learning is inextricably bound up with movements of people, things and information on a global scale that the spatial circumstances of language learning are so important. I have proposed the concept of language learning environments as the key term in a framework to address those spatial circumstances. Chapter 2 introduced work on critical spatial theory, which advances a number of ideas that frame the critique, in Chapter 3, of the view of language as a self-contained systemic object-*in*-space that underpins modern linguistics. Chapter 4 outlined an alternative, objects-*as*-space view, in which language is integrated with physical space in the form of mobile language-bearing assemblages. Chapter 5 combined this understanding of the spatiality of language with an ecological view of learning to develop what I have described as an environmental perspective that grounds contexts of language learning in space.

The main aim of this book, however, is not to insist upon the environmental framework that I have developed, which I see as one of several possible directions for the application of critical spatial theory in SLA. The aim is more to share my understanding of spatial theory and make the argument that 'space matters' (Soja, 2009). Having developed my own view of the spatiality of second language learning, in this chapter I want to bring the work of other SLA researchers into play, in order to consider how SLA might look more deeply into the *where* of second language learning.

This chapter, first, outlines the work of a number of researchers who are making valuable contributions to a spatial perspective on SLA. Some make explicit reference to aspects of spatial theory discussed in this book, while others have explored issues of space without direct reference to it. Then, I will discuss, from an autobiographical point of view, a number of studies that have influenced the development of my thinking on language learning environments, including several projects that I have been involved in. In conclusion, I will make some suggestions pertinent to a research agenda that might lead to a deeper understanding of the *where* of second language learning, including topics and issues that call for further research and innovative research methodologies.

Space in SLA Research

In this section, I want to call attention to a diverse body of studies, mainly published over the last decade, that has addressed issues of space in second language learning. This work is part of a new flowering of ideas in a field in which critical work is moving beyond a somewhat narrow focus on social theory. Although I am critical of some of this work, I believe that researchers who are adopting spatial perspectives will learn more from attending to each other's work than they will from engaging in mutual critique. Moreover, it is difficult to do justice to the work of these researchers in short summaries of this kind. My main aim is to point to work that I hope readers will want to read for themselves.

Sociolinguistics and SLA

Christina Higgins (2015) first called attention to the potential role of spatial theory in SLA in an article published in the journal *Language Teaching*. In this paper, Higgins drew on Appadurai's (1996) work on intersecting 'scapes' in cultural globalisation to examine how global flows of people, media, money, technology and ideologies shape language learners' identity construction in and out of the classroom. A subsequent article on space, place and language in the context of migration covered both sociolinguistic and SLA applications (Higgins, 2017). This paper drew mainly on De Certeau (1984) and called attention to the experience of language and space in migration and its impact on identities. As a sociolinguist whose work embraces the politics of language, multilingual practices, globalisation and identity, Higgins is mainly concerned with sociolinguistic implications of spatial theory, but she also points to the value of spatial analysis in research on policies affecting language learning, the shaping of pedagogical spaces and the performance of institutional identities, and learners' critical responses to the positioning of languages, cultures and people in language learning spaces. Two recent studies show the potential for spatially oriented research to bridge sociolinguistics and SLA. Higgins (2019) explores the complex roles of place in language learning narratives of new indigenous speakers who are contributing to the revitalisation of 'Ōlelo Hawai'i' (Hawaiian). Using actor-network theory (Latour, 2005), Higgins and Ikeda (2019: 123) discuss the emergence of new linguistic practices in tourism sites in Hawai'i and Japan, framing new networks of signs, speech and embodied communication as spatial repertoires and as 'examples of language learning and language change that occurs as an effect of human mobility intersecting with material affordances in new environments'.

Garold Murray and Terry Lamb are established researchers in the field of autonomy in language learning. Murray has made particularly important contributions to research on language learning beyond the classroom, while Lamb is well known for his work on pedagogies for autonomy. Murray and Lamb (2018) are also editors of the first collection of papers on space and SLA, which consists of 14 chapters in which authors address themes of space in their work on autonomy. The book is organised under four headings: urban spaces; teacher education spaces; classroom spaces and beyond; and institutional spaces. Murray's work on social learning spaces is discussed in the next section. Lamb (2015) has also published work on interlinguality in multilingual urban spaces. Lamb and Vodicka (2018) draw on Massey's (2005) conception of place as open and dynamic to highlight the 'throwntogetherness' of languages, cultures and identities in multilingual cities. A monolingual habitus and ambivalent policies on language diversity tend to pathologise the languages of minority communities, leading to their exclusion from formal education and the public spaces of the city. Against this tendency, Lamb and Vodicka (2018: 20) foreground the collective initiatives of communities in Sheffield, England, to create 'autonomous spaces in which their languages can be learnt, used and sustained', including complementary language schools and everyday practices that make community languages visible and encourage a plurilingual habitus through the production of shared interlingual spaces. Lamb's work in this area highlights the potential for research that addresses the interface between the sociolinguistics of language use and informal teaching and learning of community languages in multilingual urban environments.

Michael Baynham (2003, 2015) is a sociolinguist who has written on the role of space in narrative and has also co-authored, with James Simpson, an important paper applying spatial theory to classroom practices in language education for new migrants in the United Kingdom (Baynham & Simpson, 2010). Baynham (2015) makes a number of interesting comments on the role of space as 'backdrop' or 'constitutive' feature in narratives of language in migration. In a conventional account of narrative, stories develop in time, while space is the backdrop to the events that constitute the story. Baynham (2015: 120), on the other hand, is concerned with narratives 'where mobility in space effectively is the story'. Baynham (2015: 123) argues for the 'constitutive, indeed performative, role of space and spatialization practices in narrative' and 'a move in narrative analysis from backdrop to constitutive accounts of space/time orientation'. My interest in this work is twofold. First, Baynham's distinction between backdrop and constitutive accounts of space in narrative fits well with the distinction made in this book between the Newtonian view of objects-*in*-space and an environmental view of objects-*as*-space. Second, Baynham's comments connect to my own work on narrative inquiry, especially language learners' '(auto)biographies' and 'language learning careers' (Barkhuizen *et al.*, 2014; Benson, 2012; Benson & Nunan, 2005), and a sense of frustration with the lack of spatial detail in narrative interviews that sparked my interest in theories of space. Baynham (2015) offers a strong argument for a focus on space in narratives of language learning, given that language learning is essentially a matter of the mobility and displacement of people, goods and information.

Baynham and Simpson's (2010) study of community-based English courses for new migrants in the United Kingdom draws on work in spatial theory by Harvey (1989), Lefebvre (1991) and De Certeau (1984). The authors argue that language classroom research should situate the classroom 'in social and multilingual sociolinguistic space, in the complex and iterative networks of encounters and interactions that make up daily life' (Baynham & Simpson, 2010: 420). The study integrates spatial theory in two main ways. It shows, first, how community-based language teaching for migrants occupies and appropriates the 'liminal material spaces' of community centres for pedagogical purposes – an illustration of De Certeau's (1984: 421) idea of space as a practiced place. Second, it shows how learning is constructed as a spatial process, as movement through the abstract space of a qualifications framework – in Harvey's and Lefebvre's terms, a 'representation of space'. Baynham and Simpson (2010: 425) are also concerned with how the apparently practical issue of student placement in different kinds of classes 'can be understood productively in terms of space and place, positioning and identity' and how the 'material space of the class' relates to abstract understandings of space, placement and progression. In this respect, Baynham and Simpson (2010) raise important issues about relationships between the physical spaces of language learning settings and the spatial metaphors that are invariably overlaid on the learning processes that take place within them.

Suresh Canagarajah and Peter De Costa (2016) borrow the notion of scales from geography (Brenner, 2011; Moore, 2008; Smith, 1991) and sociolinguistics (Baynham, 2009; Blommaert, 2010). They suggest that scale helps answer conceptual questions in SLA research concerning appropriate units of analysis, relationships between context and language and the connections between language and other semiotic resources. They observe that the use of preselected scales (e.g. local, regional, national, transnational, global) is now contentious in geography and they argue that scale is best understood as a 'category of practice': 'it is not scales themselves (as perhaps containers of social and communicative life) that are of interest, but scaling practices' (Canagarajah & De Costa, 2016: 3). They also caution against neglect of temporal context, or the separation of time from space, suggesting that scales are 'spatio-temporal' (Canagarajah & De Costa, 2016: 4). The utility of scale in SLA research seems to lie mainly in making sense of the layered spatio-temporal contexts of local phenomena in language learning and use. Canagarajah and De Costa (2016: 5) suggest, for example, that language classrooms are embedded in larger discourses of neoliberalism, lifelong learning, transnationalism and digital learning, each of which 'rescales' the analysis of learning and teaching processes, with the appropriate unit of analysis changing according to the scale adopted. Their paper introduces a special edition of the journal *Linguistics and Education*, which includes several interesting applications of scalar analysis, including Dong and Blommaert's (2016) study of the ways in which national (formal) and global (informal) language learning scales intersect in the formation of Chinese middle-class identities. Canagarajah (2018) exemplifies the use of scalar analysis in a paper that analyses connections between the 'translingual practices' and 'spatial repertoires' of academics writing a transnationally co-authored paper at a North American university.

Gao and Park (2015) draw on work by Harvey and Blommaert to address the question, 'how are trajectories of language learning under the neoliberal economy shaped in spatial terms?'. The paper brings together two case studies from the authors' earlier work that illustrate how language learning in a global context is not a matter of rational choice or practical need, but spatially grounded in the complex material conditions and inequalities of neoliberalism. Gao's case study focuses on the Chinese village of Yangshuo in southern China, a popular destination for overseas travellers that has branded itself as 'the biggest English corner in China', a destination for Chinese visitors to study English at local English language schools and chat with international visitors. Park's case study focuses on the practice of *jogi yuhak* (early study abroad), which has become increasingly popular among Korean middle-class families over the past two decades. Children are sent overseas, either alone or with a parent, or in some cases as part of a move for the whole family, to complete part of their education in English in order to gain educational advantages on their return to Korea. For Gao and Park (2015: 88), this practice, like that of travelling to Yangshuo to learn English, is an illustration of 'how international mobility becomes appropriated as a strategy for language learning'. In conclusion, the authors make three points about language learning, space and neoliberalism: first, language is an important semiotic resource for branding and repositioning place; second, language learning becomes a spatial project that is mediated by class-based evaluation and comparisons of language varieties and commodified spaces; and, third, as a language learning strategy, geographical mobility serves as 'a neoliberal technology of the self'. Gao and Park's work is especially interesting,

I believe, in beginning from observations of two interesting local cases and linking them to broader currents of globalisation. It also shows how inequities in opportunities for language learning are distributed within the social production of space on a global scale. While certain places are zoned as 'good' places to learn second languages – places in which second language learning becomes part of the commodification of place – others become places where second language learning opportunities are sparse or impoverished – places that must be left if the learner is to sell his or her labour power at a premium in a globalised linguistic marketplace.

Settings for informal and formal learning

In studies focused on a 'social learning space' in a Japanese university, Garold Murray (2018) and his colleagues (Murray *et al.*, 2014) draw on several theoretical sources, including communities of practice, ecological and complexity approaches and mediated discourse analysis. Here, I am particularly interested in his use of work in humanistic geography on the social construction of place (Carter *et al.*, 1993; Cresswell, 2015; Tuan, 1977). For Murray (2018: 94), a social learning space differs from a self-access centre in its 'emphasis on people coming together in order to learn with and from each other'. A key assumption in this work is that 'how people define a space transforms it into a place, determines what they do there and influences their autonomy' (Murray, 2018: 93). The work of Murray and his colleagues points in two directions that deserve more attention. First, research and practice on out-of-class learning in institutional spaces has tended to focus on self-access centres, but a recent special issue of the journal *Studies in Self-Access Learning* (Mynard & Edlin, 2016) reflects a tendency to reconceptualise self-access learning in terms of the wider educational idea of learning spaces (Hobbs & Dofs, 2018). Second, their work points to the potential for the wider application of humanistic theories of the social construction of place in SLA.

Alice Chik (2016) reports on a general education course for English language students at a university in Hong Kong, entitled 'Image of the City'. In groups, the students prepared a presentation on a city of their choice focused on a particular theme, such as London as a literary city, or Beijing as an artefact of political change. The innovative aspect of the presentations was the students' use of Google Maps as a presentation tool, attaching images and a voice-over to produce an online video that was uploaded to YouTube. Chik's paper focuses on how the use of Google Maps fostered creativity by constraining the students to organise and present information within a new environment. I am also interested in the ways in which this course used mapping as a tool to engage students' desires to learn and use languages for travel. Using spatial resources in a rather different way, Antje Wilton and Christian Ludwig (2018) included a task involving linguistic landscapes in a course on English as a global language as part of an English teacher programme in Germany. Students were asked to explore multilingual landscapes in their neighbourhoods and evaluate their potential as language learning resources. The student teachers were largely positive about the potential for linguistic landscapes as authentic resources to foster language awareness and autonomy. Again, I am interested in the way in which this task engaged students in thinking about issues of language and space in their local environments.

Digital games are of interest, here, because they are often based in fictional worlds, which are often described as learning environments. For Reinhardt and Thorne (2020: 410), digital games are *de facto* 'learning environments that are intentionally designed to guide players to higher levels of skill and challenge over time'. The sense of being immersed in an imagined space seems especially strong in single-player world-building games such as The Sims and massively multiplayer online role-playing games (MMORPGs) such as World of Warcraft (Newgarden & Zheng, 2016; Peterson, 2016), in which players become actors in game worlds that involve embodied experiences of place. Importantly, players use languages to interact not only with other players, but also with the space of the game world itself. MMORPGs are often global in their reach and support multiple languages and transnational communication; in addition, many gamers around the world use an second language to participate in MMORPGS which do not support their first languages.

While online gaming provides opportunities for naturalistic learning through chance encounters with speakers of other languages (Thorne, 2008) or use of in-game texts and out-of-game paratexts (walkthroughs, forums, etc.) (Benson & Chik, 2011), some games are specifically designed for place-based language learning. Augmented reality (AR) applications are particularly interesting in relation to space, for their use of location-aware (GPS-enabled) mobile devices and reliance on players' mobility and engagement with space. In place-based AR mobile games, players are guided towards physical spaces, on campus or in a local neighbourhood, where their interactions with objects in the environment are augmented by textual information on the gaming application. Language learning applications also include quest or wayfinding tasks that encourage collaborative use of the target language (Holden & Sykes, 2011; Hellermann *et al.*, 2019; Zheng *et al.*, 2018). The especially interesting characteristic of AR applications for spatially oriented approaches to language teaching is their capacity to provide technology-enhanced 'socio-environmental infrastructures' that direct learners towards 'embodied and experiential in-the-world' engagement with language resources in the environment (Hellermann *et al.*, 2019: 193; Reinhardt & Thorne, 2020: 421). As Zheng *et al.* (2018: 55) argue, the experience of physical place in AR activities is 'critical for learners to break away from institutional norms and previous thinking patterns in order to develop skilled linguistic action in actual events that lead to prospective actions'.

Materiality and environmental engagement

From the objects-*as*-space perspective that I have adopted in this book, two issues are particularly important in SLA research: first, an understanding of the roles of the non-human components of language learning environments and, second, an understanding of the nature of learners' engagements with human and non-human environmental resources. The first point connects to recent work on material culture and multilingualism by Larissa Aronin and the materialities of the classroom by Kelleen Toohey and their colleagues (Aronin *et al.*, 2018; Aronin & Ó Laoire, 2013; Smythe *et al.*, 2017; Toohey *et al.*, 2015). Writing from the perspective of 'new materialities' theory, Toohey *et al.* (2015: 465) call for school-based language learning research to recognise 'the importance of the nonhuman in human action' and see 'both the human and the nonhuman as coparticipants in shifting flows of activity'. This involves, they argue, viewing classroom activities as 'sociomaterial assemblages' in which human bodies, the physical setup and furniture of the classroom, discourses on teaching and learning, the curriculum and so on are 'entangled' with one another (Toohey *et al.*, 2015: 466).

Aronin and Ó Laoire (2013) make the point that multilingualism studies have conceptualised the environment 'mostly… in terms of people, i.e. community, family, school populations'. They argue, instead, for 'a deliberate focus on the study of materialities (artefacts, objects and spaces) (Aronin & Ó Laoire, 2013: 225). Their paper includes an interesting discussion of what counts as a multilingual artefact and their definition of a 'language-defined object' as 'a meaningful wholeness of material and verbal components' (Aronin & Ó Laoire, 2013: 230) has much in common with my understanding of a language-bearing assemblage. For Aronin and Ó Laoire (2013: 232), such objects differ from other cultural objects in their inclusion of the linguistic component, which 'not only adds to the quality of the object, but it also transforms and defines its nature'. In their book-length study of the material culture of multilingualism, Aronin *et al.* (2018) aim to expose the ties between language, cognition, identity and the material world both in everyday language practices and language teaching in a number of settings. Of particular interest here, however, are the ways in which, in the context of global mobility, the multilingual character of language-bearing objects is transforming everyday living environments into spaces for language learning.

Søren Eskildsen and Guðrún Theodórsdóttir have made interesting use of conversation analysis in studies of language learning interactions beyond the classroom. Eskildsen and Theodórsdóttir (2015) compare recordings of spoken interactions from two large corpora gathered from language classrooms and informal learning situations. Their focus is on how participant talk co-constructs learning spaces and how the two contexts call on different resources. The paper compares two extracts from their out-of-class and in-class corpora, but here I want to focus on their discussion of an out-of-class interaction in which Anna, a learner of Icelandic in her second month in Reykjavik, orders food at a hot dog stand. Anna's recordings of herself speaking Icelandic over a three-year period document the learning strategies that she used in her everyday interactions with locals, friends and service personnel. As conversation analysts, Eskildsen and Theodórsdóttir include a detailed analysis of a fine-grained transcript of the hot dog stand interaction in the paper, which is not reflected in my summary.

In brief, Anna begins by asking the sales assistant, in Icelandic, if she can speak a little Icelandic and he agrees. Anna then has some difficulty in placing her order in grammatically correct Icelandic and the sales assistant corrects her. She then places the order correctly (one hot dog and one coke) and the sales assistant responds by asking, 'with everything?', to which Anna responds accurately. Before closing the transaction, the sales assistant begins a comment in English and Anna interrupts with 'tala Islensku' (speak Icelandic). The sales assistant then says, in Icelandic, that if she is really thirsty, she should drink club soda, rather than coke. This comment is delivered over four turns, with repetitions, as Anna acknowledges her understanding turn-by-turn with 'yes' tokens. The authors' interest in this interaction is in the way that Anna 'has built a context in which, apart from doing her business in the L2, she can co-create opportunities with her expert co-participant' (Eskildsen & Theodórsdóttir, 2015: 149). At the outset, she transforms the service encounter into a language learning situation and, as she does so, the sales assistant willingly takes on the role of language teacher. A point that emerges from the comparison with classroom data is that the classroom provides more time, space and tools for language learning interactions in which there is less at stake. Outside the classroom, Anna has to work harder and take more risks, but 'when the L2 user has insisted on building a room for learning in the wild, the space widens, and an interactional focus on language becomes possible' (Eskildsen & Theodórsdóttir, 2015: 159). Eskildsen and Theodórsdóttir's work is particularly interesting to me as it explores the kinds of interactional work that goes into transforming everyday interactional spaces into settings for language learning.

Language Learning Environments: An Autobiographical View

I have long been interested in narrative inquiry and the idea that the sequential form of the story provides an alternative to conventional paradigmatic argumentation in academic work (Bruner, 1986). For this reason, I want to present some of my own work on spatial aspects of language learning in the form of an autobiographical account of the emergence of the idea of language learning environments in my work. My involvement with SLA research grew out of experiences of teaching English as an second language in Africa, the Middle East and Asia.

More importantly, perhaps, my interest in second language learning was coloured by my own experiences as a self-directed language learner. I studied French and German at school, and as an adult I learned Spanish, Italian and Portuguese by self-instruction. French is the only second language that I speak well, but I read fluently in other European languages and have a limited speaking competence in Cantonese and Japanese. For this reason, I recognise myself in the recent literature on the 'multilingual turn' in SLA (May, 2014). Concepts such as 'multicompetence' (Cook, 1992) and 'truncated multilingualism' (Blommaert, 2010) speak to my personal experience of language learning, which I have always felt is somehow incomplete, even if it does mostly satisfy my needs.

I first became involved in SLA research in the context of self-access and autonomy in language learning, which connected with my experience as a self-directed language learner. Like many who worked in this area in the 1990s, my interests turned from out-of-class learning to classroom and curriculum applications of autonomy. I also became interested in narrative inquiry as a means of investigating the long-term development of autonomy over language learning 'careers' (Benson, 2011b; Benson & Nunan, 2005). Over the past decade or so, I have renewed my interest in language learning beyond the classroom, in the context of what Murray and Lamb (2018: 249) call 'the global shift in focus from classroom-based to out-of-class learning'. With Hayo Reinders, I published what I believe to be the first collection of papers on language learning beyond the classroom (Benson & Reinders, 2011). Subsequently, I have pursued this interest mainly in online settings (Benson, 2017b; Benson & Chan, 2010; Benson & Chik, 2011) and in study abroad and international education (Benson, 2012, 2017a; Benson *et al.*, 2013, 2018; Chappell *et al.*, 2018; Chik & Benson, 2008; Kashiwa & Benson, 2018; Umino & Benson, 2016, 2019).

Out-of-class learning

In the 1990s, research on out-of-class learning was largely confined to self-access and other, mainly computer-based, institutionally organised initiatives. The papers in Benson and Reinders (2011) confirmed our suspicion that there was a vast range of settings in which languages are learned not only beyond the classroom, but also outside language teaching institutions and on the initiative of learners themselves. At that time, I did not think of these settings in terms of space and environment, but instead attempted to draw up a framework for describing and analysing them as settings (Benson, 2011a). This framework identified four dimensions that could be used to describe and differentiate settings for language learning beyond the classroom – location, formality, pedagogy and locus of control – corresponding to the terms out-of-class, informal, non-instructed and self-directed learning. Reinders and Benson (2017) added several more dimensions: trajectory, referring to the development of a learner's engagement with a setting as they grew older or more experienced (Chik, 2014); variety of activities and the degree to which they are form or meaning focused (Lai *et al.*, 2015); mediation, sociality and modality; and a linguistic dimension concerning the skills and levels of competence in focus. This clearly went beyond the description of settings and was now approaching a comprehensive toolkit for analysing any language learning situation beyond or in the classroom. Useful as such a toolkit might be, however, I began to feel that there was a risk of failing to see the wood for the trees.

Two papers, in particular, helped me to make the transition from a focus on the analysis of settings for language learning (the trees) to the idea of language learning environments (the wood). Martin Lamb (2004) conducted an ethnographic investigation of the English language learning of junior high school students in a provincial city in Indonesia. At that time, one might have supposed that Indonesian students learned English exclusively in the classroom. However, Lamb found that they actually did much of their language learning in after-school lessons at school and in private institutions, and by using resources in everyday settings outside school. He found that much of what they learned was learned outside school, but that they nevertheless valued lessons at school, not so much for their content, as for the relationships they established with teachers. Using an ecology of learning perspective, Lai (2015) investigated attitudes to in-class and out-of-class learning among Hong Kong university undergraduates studying a variety of second languages. She found that these students engaged in a variety of out-of-class activities, but valued both in-class and out-of-class learning. She also found that they tended to rely on language classes for form-focused learning, using out-of-class activities mainly for meaning-focused learning. The insight that I gained from these papers was that language learners were increasingly becoming explorers who charted their own routes through a proliferation of online and offline settings and resources. There was both the wider language learning environment that the learners were exploring and the unique language learning environments that each individual put together in the course of their learning journeys.

Language learner biographies

The idea of individual language learning environments as configurations of settings (Chapter 5) first arose in the context of a large-scale narrative inquiry project on Hong Kong students studying English overseas. This study focused on identity in language learning and its main finding was that significant learning in study abroad often involved the development of second language identities (Benson *et al.*, 2013). I also became interested in the case of one female student whose semester at an Australian university was marked by experiences of sexual and racial harassment, but nevertheless turned out to be relatively successful in her estimation (Benson, 2012). The student was one of a group of Hong Kong female students studying at the same university. The point that I made in this study was that each member of the group constructed her own context (I would now say mapped out her individual environment) for language learning from the raw material of a shared study abroad setting (I would now say areal environment). An additional point concerns the process of writing up the study. The interview data that we had in hand were replete with references to place and travel – commuting between home and university, visits to the local shopping mall, weekend excursions and a longer trip to Melbourne and Tasmania – but these were difficult to put together in a narrative account, partly because I was unfamiliar with the geography of the Australian city in which the student studied. Using a street map of the city, I asked her to show me where she had lived, studied and spent her spare time, and where various events had happened. After around half-an-hour, I had a much clearer understanding of the sense of her story. I understood more about the character of the places she had mentioned and how they were interwoven in her experience. She had also added one more important place to the story – a church that she sometimes visited as she passed through the city centre. Although it may not have come across in the published paper, which emphasised context over environment, I had begun to understand that space matters.

A second important insight came from working with Mayumi Kashima as a postgraduate student in Sydney. Kashiwa and Benson (2018) was an outcome of Mayumi's Master of Research thesis, and she later completed a doctoral thesis (Kashiwa, 2019). Having read some of my work on study abroad and Lai's (2015) work on the ecology of in-class and out-of-class learning, Kashiwa became interested in the ecological transitions that international students underwent when they came to Sydney to study English, especially how they came to terms with changed relationships between in-class and out-of-class experiences in their learning. What emerged from her research was the idea that these international students had to reconceptualise and reconstruct their language learning environments. This involved finding new settings for out-of-class learning as well as reconceptualising the relationship between in-class and out-of-class learning. These tasks proved more difficult for some students than it did for others. Kashiwa's research decisively shifted the focus of my attention from 'context' to 'environment', a concept that I was beginning to see in vaguely spatial terms.

One insight that I added to Kashiwa and Benson (2018) concerned the relationship between environments and language learning careers. In my work on language learning (auto)biographies, I have used the idea of a language learning 'career' to capture the entire period over which a person learns a language or languages. A language learning (auto)biography, or history, might cover the whole of a language learning career or a longer or shorter portion of it (Benson, 2011b). I have used the word 'phase' to refer to any well-defined period within a language learning career in which learning is characterised by a more or less stable set of processes or activities. I have also observed that phases in a language learning career are separated from each other by 'critical events', which require 'modifications of self-identity to enable the person to adjust to changed circumstances' (Layder, 2004: 139). I now understood that such transitions often involved a change in the spatial settings for learning and the reconstruction of the learner's learning environment. My contribution to Kashiwa and Benson (2018) was the idea that the transition from an 'at home' environment to a 'study abroad' environment was a sequential shift from one phase of a learning career to another. It has subsequently become clear to me, however, that this implies that an individual language learning environment is both a spatial and a temporal construct: temporal in the sense that a configuration of settings is constructed and modified over time within a phase of a learning career, but also fundamentally spatial in the sense that transitions between phases often involve a radical change in the spatial raw materials from which individual learning environments are constructed.

My most recent work, with Phil Chappell and Lynda Yates, has addressed issues of space more directly, focusing on the ways in which language and learning are intertwined with international students' daily routines in Sydney (Benson *et al.*, 2018; Chappell *et al.*, 2018). This work is partly a response to the gap between the efforts of the local English language teaching (ELT) industry to market Sydney as a friendly and relaxed city in which to learn English and mingle with native speakers and concerns that many international students have limited access to opportunities to use English outside the classroom. We are also interested in the dynamics of language use among students learning the dominant language of a multilingual city. We estimate that the number of international students who study in Sydney each year is equivalent to around 8% of the population of the city, and the demographics of the city mean that these students tend to live in highly multilingual neighbourhoods. Our research confirmed that many live in shared houses with other international students, have part-time jobs in multilingual workplaces and make little contact with native speakers of English beyond school and service encounters. The aim of our studies, however, has been to go beyond social networks to try to understand how English language learning for these students involves broader engagements with language learning resources in spatially distributed environments.

In the first study that we conducted, students were interviewed on their everyday experiences of using and learning English outside the classroom. The following vignette gives a flavour of the kinds of experience we discovered.

> J has come to Sydney from Vietnam to study English in order to enrol on a Masters degree. Her long-term goal is to get a job in Australia and bring her parents over to join her. At present, she studies five days a week at a language college in the CBD and commutes from a shared house in the suburbs. J's parents support her financially, but rent and transport are expensive, so she works weekends at a local shopping mall to make ends meet. In the little free time that she has, she makes opportunities to use and learn English. In her job, she interacts with customers in English and Vietnamese, though using English can be stressful. She speaks English with her Chinese and Indian housemates, but the three women are often tired when they get home and do not have much to say. J uses her time at home to do homework and to watch TV (the housemates enjoy watching lifestyle shows together). At school she makes opportunities to talk to teachers out of class. To save money, she cooks Vietnamese dishes at home, and brings them to school to share with other students and a favourite teacher who eats lunch in the classroom. Although she meets fewer native speakers of English than she would like, J is satisfied with her life in Sydney and feels she is progressing toward her goals.

A point worth noting is that J exemplifies a new generation of transient migrants in Australia (Gomes, 2015; Robertson, 2013), whose experiences as international students in multilingual cities intersect with experiences of work and pathways to migration. Her experience in Australia up to this point was only a slice from an as yet unfinished spatio-temporal journey. Like other students we interviewed, J was resourceful in mapping out an individual language learning environment in Sydney that was also shaped by factors in her daily life including financial constraints and limitations on her free time. The main findings from this study were that (i) individual language learning environments are mapped out within everyday routines that typically involve triangles in which they move between home, school and a place of work; (ii) they are constrained by finance, time and purpose – international students tend to be short of money and time-poor, and they often prioritise formal study to pass language tests or gain academic qualification over out-of-class learning; (iii) but students are also highly resourceful in using their agency to access a range of resources to improve their language skills within these constraints (Chappell *et al.*, 2018).

One observation that followed this first study was that the interview data we had gathered were often spatially inexplicit and gave us only an approximate picture of students' uses of the space of the city. For example, we knew a good deal about J's life, but we did not know where she lived, where she worked, how she travelled from place to place or what she did on her journeys. For this reason, we decided to incorporate a free mobile GPS-enabled diary application – Diaro (http://diaroapp.com) – into our next study, in which we asked students to keep a daily record of where they went and who they met, what they did and which languages they used at each location. For both ethical and technical reasons, we did not collect and analyse these data directly, but instead asked the participants to consult the data during a follow-up interview in which the interviewer guided them through an account of their activities day-by-day over the course of the previous week. These interviews proved to be a rich source of data, documenting how students accessed human, non-human and technological resources in the spaces and interspaces of their everyday lives.

The richness of these data can be sampled in the long narrative account of one student's week that was included in Benson *et al.* (2018). The student chosen for this case study was extraordinarily active and creative in her use of settings and resources and expansive in her use of the spaces of the city. Some participants were much less so. This second study confirmed the idea that international students in Sydney mapped out their language learning environments within the constraints of spatial triangles of home–school–work. What it added to this observation was a sense of the varied shapes and sizes of these triangles, participants' capacities and willingness to break free of them and the influence of these spatial factors on their uses of languages and learning of English. It was through this study, in particular, that I recognised the value of beginning investigations of second language learning with the question of *where* the learning takes place, and of taking research, a little like Stephen Dedalus took Dublin's Sandymount Strand, 'a stride at a time' (Joyce, 1986: 31). The writing of this book has, in a sense, been a pause in which I have attempted to explore theoretical sources relevant to a framework for answering that question.

Research Agendas

Bronfenbrenner (1979: 12) argued that further advance in the scientific understanding of human development requires 'investigation in the actual environments, both immediate and remote, in which human beings live'. Building on Bronfenbrenner's work, Barron (2010: 114) proposed that research should focus on 'how learners initiate and sustain engagement in activities that advance their learning in particular domains' and 'how engagement develops across different settings, timescales, and networks of support'. In contrast to research that focuses on 'near-term knowledge acquisition', she advocated research that views 'learning as a process of becoming that takes place across longer scales of time and within and across the multiple life spaces that a learner inhabits'. These comments point to four main routes along which SLA research on language learning environments might proceed: areal studies of settings and environments, studies of individuals learning in settings, studies of the construction of individual learning environments and design-based studies involving pedagogical innovation.

Settings and environments

One of the most pressing needs in research on language learning environments is for a better understanding of the multiplicity of settings and environments in which languages are learned. By areal studies, I mean studies that approach settings and environments as areas or places and elucidate their spatial characteristics and the affordances for learning they offer. This would include a revival of classroom research that focuses on the spatiality of classrooms and, in particular, the ways in which classroom resources make language available to learners. Equally important are the myriad out-of-class settings for language learning, including designed spaces in educational institutions and transient non-institutional settings that are assembled by learners 'on the fly'. There are two risks in studies of settings: first, that the setting is generalised to a point where it lacks spatial specificity and, second, that it is taken out of the context of the wider institutional, urban/rural/remote, regional, national and global environment. Among the key questions that need to be asked of any setting, therefore, are how language learning resources get into the setting; how the spatiality of the setting is scaled in relation to the wider environment; and how it is produced as a space within the wider production of urban, national and global space. Studies of particular settings may also be scaled up to studies of, say, urban language learning environments. From studies of this kind, we are likely to learn more about inequities in opportunities for language learning, which are ultimately related to imbalances in the distribution of language resources and access to settings.

Much out-of-class language learning research is conducted in schools and universities and involves custom-designed facilities such as self-access centres, computer laboratories and other kinds of learning spaces. Although the design of these spaces deserves more attention, there is also a need for SLA research to spread out into a much wider variety of settings. Within educational institutions, these might include libraries, extracurricular clubs, open spaces and 'schoolscapes' (Laihonen & Szabó, 2018). In the world beyond formal education there is a particular need for more research on informal language learning in home and workplace settings, transactional situations and public meeting spaces; and on language learning on the move, while walking or using public transport. Although there is a great deal of research on multilingualism online and online language learning, very little of this research focuses on the nature of online resources as virtual settings for language learning, especially online and mobile language teaching services such as Duolingo, Buusu and Memrise and social media platforms such as YouTube, TikTok and Instagram. There is a need for a better understanding not only of the spatiality of online resources, but also of the ways in which their use intersects with the terrestrial settings in which they are used, especially the use of resources such as maps, text messages and mobile phone calls to organise language learning on the move.

Individuals in settings

There is also a pressing need for more studies that focus on the interactions of individual learners with the spaces and resources of settings. From a spatial perspective, this aspect of the *where* of language learning is the key to understanding how languages are actually learned. However, interaction in this context has to be understood as more than spoken interaction among *people*, which is, I believe, overemphasised in SLA research. Interaction *with* setting is too often reduced to interaction with other people *in* settings at the expense of understanding the fully embodied encounter between the learner and the spatial resources of the setting, which may or may not include speaking humans. From this perspective, spoken interaction with humans is one kind of interaction with the spatial resources of settings: an important one in the context of language learning, to be sure, but by no means the only important one.

Individual environments

Research on individual learning environments is a matter of studying how individuals put settings and their resources together in space and time, or how they make practical sense of what is available to them within the spatial and temporal constraints of everyday lives. This may involve the reconceptualisation of language learning careers as involving both temporal and spatial development, as well as the reconceptualisation of notions such as language learning strategies, motivation and autonomy, which all entail orientations towards uses of space. Similarly, multilingual identities might be reconceptualised as not only being formed within particular configurations of language and space, but also as being constituted by the learner's position in the language-saturated spaces of their daily lives. SLA research participants are most often learners of English or learners of well-established European languages. In order to gain a better overall understanding of the varied spatial circumstances under which second languages are learned, more languages need to be added to the list, which also implies more types of language learning, including heritage languages, minority languages and dialects, situations – frequent in Africa and Asia – in which people learn several additional languages, dead languages, artificial languages and language learning for recreational purposes.

Design-based research

Recommendations on the pedagogical implications of a spatial perspective on SLA are beyond the scope of this book, and would require a quite different kind of treatment. However, it is clear that, in so far as this perspective arises from awareness of the complexities of language education under globalisation and, especially, in intensely multilingual urban environments (Kramsch, 2014), there are a number of general implications that are likely to lead to new kinds of spatially oriented pedagogy. These offer opportunities for design-based research in which researchers develop and experiment with innovative pedagogies and collect and analyse observational data (Barab & Squire, 2004). One possible future may be forms of second language education in which learners acquire skills in a specific language alongside a broader awareness of languages and multilingualism in local and global environments (Thorne, 2013). This might also be a kind of language education that attaches more value to partial knowledge and varied competences in multiple languages, as well as the skills and practices involved in translanguaging (Ollerhead, 2019). There is also considerable scope for pedagogical initiatives that connect in-class and out-of-class worlds, raise awareness of language learning settings and environments, and help students develop strategies for creating opportunities to learn beyond the classroom.

Research Methods

It could be argued that any research method could be used in research on language learning environments. What matters is not so much the methods that are used, as the inclusion of spatial dimensions in the research design. Are spatial data gathered in the project and do they survive the analysis of data and the writing up of the project? Narrative inquiry methods are a case in point. These are especially suited to capturing, retrospectively, events in the past, sequences of events or processes that are difficult to observe directly. But in my experience, they are less well suited to gathering data on uses of space, and this is largely because both researchers and research participants tend to take space for granted, treating it as a backdrop, and not constitutive of the events narrated (Baynham, 2015). In narrative interviews, interviewees tend to be inexplicit about where things happen, and interviewers do not push them to fill in the detail. As our interviews with international students in Sydney show, it takes a deliberate effort to gather spatial data in narrative interviews. Our use of a GPS-enabled diary as an interview prompt was mainly intended to raise the interviewees' and interviewers' awareness of issues of space and to ensure that space was brought to the foreground of interviews (Benson *et al.*, 2018). Although there is no restriction on the research methods that can be used to study language learning environments, I want to conclude with a brief discussion of three less-used methods that may be particularly apt: direct observation, visual methods and walking methods.

Observation

Observation is the foundational method in scientific research and it also has a place in most second language research manuals. However, its use in second language learning research tends to be limited to classroom observation studies (which are very few) and a subsidiary role in the suites of methods that make up ethnographic research (where observational data often go unreported). Sussman (2016) and Ng (2016: 30) provide useful guides to observational techniques in the context of environmental psychology, where they are used to record 'where people are, what they actually do, and how their behaviours are distributed in space'. Direct observation involves the researcher experiencing places and behaviour with the 'five senses' (Sussman, 2016), but it is often replaced by indirect observation, especially participants' self-reports gathered through diaries or interviews. Direct observation is comparatively time-intensive but it has evident advantages where the focus of attention is on settings for learning and their uses. Within direct observation, Ng (2016) makes a distinction between 'behaviour mapping', which is place-centred (e.g. a study of a setting and its uses by multiple learners), and 'behaviour tracking', which is person-centred (e.g. a study of an individual's use of multiple settings). Direct observation appears to be most suited to place-centred studies of settings, due to the difficulties of directly observing individuals' activities over long periods of time. Sussman (2016) describes three levels of direct observation. Casual observation is unsystematic and unconstrained, and designed to get a sense of what is happening in a situation; data are not necessarily recorded, but casual observations may be the basis for a more focused study. Passive observation involves systematic procedures and formal data collection, but does not involve intervention or change in the environment. Active observation involves observation of the effects of an intervention or change, and corresponds to what I have described as design-based research in SLA.

Sussman recommends that observations be made by two or more observers who compare notes. He also recommends the use of 'ethograms' (a tool borrowed from ethology, or the study of animal behaviour) as 'a qualitative observation method in which the observer notes all aspects of a situation and behavior without a hypothesis or predetermined idea of what may occur' (Sussman, 2016: 24). Observation may be made at regular intervals of time (time sampled) or when certain events occur (event sampled), and map templates may be used to record spatial distributions of behaviour. In individual behaviour tracking, indirect methods are often used, although these usually entail problems with the accuracy and spatial specificity of data. Self-observation may be an option, or technologies may be used such as GPS-enabled applications, or video or audio-recorders attached to participants bodies, which are voice/movement activated or set to record at regular or random intervals. Choice of observational methods will be guided by the purposes of the study, as well as considerations of feasibility and ethics. However, it should be borne in mind that studies that use audio or video recordings often narrow down interaction with the environment to person-to-person spoken encounters and sideline the learners' interactions with non-human aspects of settings.

Visual methods

The use of visual materials in social science research corresponds to an understanding that 'the visual is central to the cultural construction of social life in contemporary Western societies' (Rose, 2016: 2). Although visual methods are not widely used in SLA research, two recent collections have explored their use as tools to elicit data on various aspects of multilingual lives (Kalaja & Melo-Pfeifer, 2019; Kalaja & Pitkänen-Huhta, 2018). In these collections, visual materials are generated by research participants (typically drawings, but also photographs and physical objects) and either analysed visually or used as interview prompts. Kalaja and Melo-Pfeifer (2019) advocate the elicitation of visual materials as an alternative or complement to verbal accounts, especially in research with young children.

Here, I am particularly interested in how visual data spatialise experiences of language learning and use. In Chik (2019), for example, adult Australians from different migrant backgrounds produced drawings representing their experiences of learning different languages, which were analysed as visual narratives and used as interview prompts. An interesting feature of the drawings was the way in which participants associated languages with particular settings or drew self-portraits representing themselves in different spatial situations. Chik also observed that the drawings represented experiences of learning languages either as specific states in time and space, or as progressions over time. As a classroom activity intended to foster reflection on language and mobility, Molinié (2019: 79) asked international students studying in France to draw 'their pathway and project of international mobility' and explain their drawings. Again, the drawings are interesting for the way in which narratives of experience are spatialised on the page, often with the use of sketch maps.

Visual methods have a particular potential to elicit representations of language learning environments. In her doctoral research, Kashiwa (2019) asked English language teachers of international students in Sydney to draw mind maps of what they thought was an ideal language learning environment for their students. Students were asked to draw similar maps, and the teachers redrew their maps after seeing the students' maps and the results of a student survey. The mind maps proved to be a valuable source of data on how the teachers conceptualised their students' activities in and out of school and how they reconceptualised them when informed of students' views. Umino and Benson (2016, 2019) drew on a different kind of visual data, photographs taken by two international students, from Indonesia and China, over several years of study in Japan. Each of the participants made several thousand photographs available to the first researcher and helped her sort and categorise them. The photographs were analysed in terms of the students' evolving participation in communities of practice. While the photographs generated insights into events and co-participants, they were also revealing in regard to the changing ways in which the students constructed images of themselves in the spaces of their lives. What interests me most about visual methods, then, is the potential of visualisation – an inherently spatialising technology – to foreground issues of space that might otherwise be neglected in research.

Walking methods

Walking methods are a relatively new addition to the toolkit of social science research (Ingold & Vergunst, 2008; O'Neill & Roberts, 2020). Participants are typically interviewed on the move, while walking with the researcher on a route that is relevant to the focus of the research. To the best of my knowledge, walking methods have not yet been used in second language learning research, but I believe they have great potential in research on language learning environments. Walking methods speak to the ways in which space and the environment are experienced on the move (Neisser, 1976; Urry, 2007) and the influence of environmental features encountered while walking on the content of talk (Evans & Jones, 2011). O'Neill and Roberts (2020: 7) use walking methods in biographical research and suggest that they respond to two questions: 'What are our imaginary spaces, our sensory scapes?' and 'How biographically do we relate to our "present", our immediate environment, our past(s) and future(s)?'. Walking interviews view individuals 'as evolving and moving in time and place' and address 'mobile ways of knowing' (O'Neill & Roberts, 2020: 8). They also suggest that the value of walking interviews is not just that interviewees are in motion, but rather that 'they are involved subjectively in "passing" through social and material circumstances' (O'Neill & Roberts, 2020: 17). Walking interviews are 'embedded in the daily life of individuals' and have the potential to capture 'how they "put together" experiences and understandings across settings', how they 'consciously "move" between settings, their reflections, evaluations, adjustments and plans in daily practice' (O'Neill & Roberts, 2020: 20). The wording here, reflects my view of individual language learning environments as configurations of settings that are put together within the routines of everyday life. In this respect, I see great potential in the use of walking interviews and observations – which could equally well be carried on public transport or in a car as circumstances dictate – as a means of capturing how language environments are assembled in both space and time.

Coda

Although I began working on this book in early 2018, much of it was written in Sydney, Australia, during the global coronavirus pandemic of 2020. As I am revising the manuscript, it is now late October and the future remains uncertain, locally but, especially, globally. The impact of globalisation on second language learning is a main theme of the book. In particular, I believe that we must think seriously about the statistics cited in Chapter 4, which show that most indicators of globalisation have doubled or more than doubled over the past two decades (World Bank, 2020). We are living in a new world of SLA research in which space matters more than ever before. Yet, almost without noticing it, I find that this is now a very different world. One of the major themes of this book, the acceleration of globalisation, appears to have been halted by another, the agency of non-human objects.

In Australia, international air travel has all but disappeared and very few migrants, international students or visitors are entering the country. Those international students who have stayed are living in very different language learning environments to those they were living in only a few months ago. They are making much less use of the spaces of the city and spending much more time at home and online. Many are living under very difficult personal and financial circumstances. A doctoral student who was planning to conduct walking interviews with international students as they made their way around Australian cities has now been obliged to move her research online. We have all become remarkably adept at using videoconferencing tools to maintain both distant and local, professional and personal relationships. Our uses of space have been regulated as never before, by lockdowns, curfews, international border controls and domestic travel bans. Meanwhile, there is a new awakening, awareness and appreciation of local and immediate physical environments. We now know the five kilometre radii around our homes better than ever before. For many, the pandemic has been an experience of heartbreak and loss. For all of us, it has been a sharp reminder of just how much space matters.

References

Allwright, D. and Bailey, K.M. (1991) *Focus on the Language Classroom*. Cambridge: Cambridge University Press.
Amin, A. and Thrift, N. (2002) *Cities: Re-imagining the Urban*. Oxford: Wiley.
Amin, A. and Thrift, N. (2016) *Seeing Like a City*. Oxford: Polity.
Appadurai, A. (1996) *Modernity at Large: Cultural Dimensions of Globalisation*. Minneapolis, MN: University of Minnesota Press.
Arnauld, A. and Nicole, P. (1662) *La Logique ou l'Art de Penser*. Paris: Guignart, Savreux and de Lavnay.
Arnauld, A. and Lancelot, P. (1780) *Grammaire Générale et Raisonée* (4th edn; first published 1660). Paris: Durand.
Aronin, L. and Ó Laoire, M. (2013) The material culture of multilingualism: Moving beyond the linguistic landscape. *International Journal of Multilingualism* 10 (3), 225–235.
Aronin, L., Hornsby, M. and Kiliańska-Przybyło, G. (2018) *The Material Culture of Multilingualism*. Bern: Springer.
Bachelard, G. (2014) *The Poetics of Space* (trans. M. Jolas; first published in French, 1958). New York: Penguin.
Bailey, K.M. (2006) Looking back down the road: A recent history of language classroom research. *The China Review of Applied Linguistics* 1, 6–47.
Ballard, K. (2016) *The Stories of Linguistics: An Introduction to Language Study Past and Present*. London: Palgrave.
Barab, S. and Squire, K. (2004) Design-based research: Putting a stake in the ground. *Journal of the Learning Sciences* 13 (1), 1–14.
Barad, K. (2007) *Meeting the Universe Halfway: Quantum Physics and the Entanglement of Matter and Meaning*. Durham, NC: Duke University Press.
Barkhuizen, G., Benson, P. and Chik, A. (2014) *Narrative Inquiry in Language Teaching and Learning Research*. New York: Routledge.
Barron, B. (2004) Learning ecologies for technological fluency in a technology-rich community. *Journal of Educational Computing Research* 31 (1), 1–36.
Barron, B. (2006) Interest and self-sustained learning as catalysts of development: A learning ecology perspective. *Human Development* 49, 193–224.
Barron, B. (2010) Conceptualizing and tracing learning pathways over time and setting. *National Society for the Study of Education* 109 (1), 113–127.
Bauman, Z. (1998) *Globalization: The Human Consequences*. Cambridge: Polity.
Baynham, M. (2003) Narrative in space and time: Beyond 'backdrop' accounts of narrative orientation. *Narrative Inquiry* 13 (2), 347–366.
Baynham, M.J. (2009) 'Just one day like today': Scale and the analysis of space/time orientation in narratives of displacement. In J. Collins, S. Slembrouck and M. Baynham (eds) *Globalization and Language in Contact: Scale, Migration and Communicative Practices* (pp. 130–147). London: Continuum.

Baynham, M. (2015) Narrative and space/time. In A. De Fina and A. Georgakopolou (eds) *The Handbook of Narrative Analysis* (pp. 119–139). Oxford: John Wiley and Sons.

Baynham, M. and Simpson, J. (2010) Onwards and upwards: Space, placement, and liminality in adult TESOL classes. *TESOL Quarterly* 44 (3), 420–440.

Beck, U. (2000) *What is Globalization?* Cambridge: Polity.

Béjoint, H. (1994) *Tradition an Innovation in Modern English Dictionaries*. Oxford: Clarendon Press.

Bennett, J. (2010) *Vibrant Matter: A Political Ecology of Things*. Durham, NC: Duke University Press.

Benson, P. (2001) *Ethnocentrism and the English Dictionary*. London: Routledge.

Benson, P. (2011a) Language learning and teaching beyond the classroom: An introduction to the field. In P. Benson and H. Reinders (eds) *Beyond the Language Classroom* (pp. 7–16). Basingstoke: Palgrave Macmillan.

Benson, P. (2011b) Language learning careers as an object of narrative research in TESOL. *TESOL Quarterly* 45 (3), 545–553.

Benson, P. (2012) Individual difference and context in study abroad. In W.M. Chan, K.N. Chin, S.K. Bhatt and I. Walker (eds) *Perspectives on Individual Characteristics and Foreign Language Education* (pp. 221–238). Berlin: Mouton de Gruyter.

Benson, P. (2017a) Sleeping with strangers: Dreams and nightmares in experiences of homestay. *Study Abroad Research in Second Language Acquisition and International Education* 3 (1), 1–20.

Benson, P. (2017b) *The Discourse of YouTube: Multimodal Text in a Global Context*. London: Routledge.

Benson, P. and Nunan, D. (eds) (2005) *Learners' Stories: Difference and Diversity in Language Learning*. Cambridge: Cambridge University Press.

Benson, P. and Chan, N. (2010) TESOL after YouTube: Fansubbing and informal language learning. *Taiwan Journal of TESOL* 7 (2), 1–23.

Benson, P. and Chik, A. (2011) Towards a more naturalistic CALL: Video-gaming and language learning. *International Journal of Computer-assisted Language Learning* 1 (3), 1–13.

Benson, P. and Reinders, H. (eds) (2011) *Beyond the Language Classroom*. Basingstoke: Palgrave Macmillan.

Benson, P. and Hatoss, A. (2019) Multilingual Sydney: A city report. In A. Chik, P. Benson and R. Moloney (eds) *Multilingual Sydney* (pp. 13–25). London: Routledge.

Benson, P., Chappell, P. and Yates, L. (2018) A day in the life: Mapping international students' language learning environments in multilingual Sydney. *Australian Journal of Applied Linguistics* 1 (1), 20–32.

Benson, P., Barkhuizen, G., Bodycott, P. and Brown, J. (2013) *Second Language Identity in Narratives of Study Abroad*. Basingstoke: Palgrave.

Berger, J. (1974) *The Look of Things*. New York: Viking Press.

Bhardwaj, P. (2018) Fibre optic wires, servers, and more than 550,000 miles of underwater cables: Here's what the internet actually looks like. *Business Insider Australia*, 10 June. See https://www.businessinsider.com.au/how-internet-works-infrastructure-photos-2018-5 (accessed 19 February 2021).

Bielsa, E. (2005) Globalization and translation: A theoretical approach. *Language and Intercultural Communication* 5 (2), 131–144.

Block, D. (1996) Not so fast: Some thoughts on theory culling, relativism, accepted findings and the heart and soul of SLA. *Applied Linguistics* 17 (1), 63–83.

Block, D. (2003) *The Social Turn in Second Language Acquisition*. Edinburgh: Edinburgh University Press.

Block, D. (2006) *Multilingual Identities in a Global City: London Stories*. London: Palgrave Macmillan.

Block, D. (2010) Globalization and language teaching. In N. Coupland (ed.) *The Handbook of Language and Globalization* (pp. 287–303). Oxford: Blackwell.

Block, D. (2014a) Moving beyond 'lingualism': Multilingual embodiment and multimodality in SLA. In S. May (ed.) *The Multilingual Turn: Implications for SLA, TESOL, and Bilingual Education* (pp. 54–77). London: Routledge.
Block, D. (2014b) *Social Class in Applied Linguistics.* London: Routledge.
Block, D., Gray, J. and Holborow, M. (2012) *Neoliberalism and Applied Linguistics.* London: Routledge.
Blommaert, J. (2010) *The Sociolinguistics of Globalization.* Cambridge: Cambridge University Press.
Bloomfield, L. (1924) Review of F. De Saussure, *Cours de la Linguistique Générale. The Modern Language Journal* 8 (5), 317–319.
Bloomfield, L. (1933) *Language.* New York: Henry Holt.
Bloomfield, L. (1936) Language or ideas? *Language* 12 (2), 89–95.
Bodenhamer, D.J., Corrigan, J. and Harris, T.M. (eds) (2010) *The Spatial Humanities: GIS and the Future of Humanities.* Bloomington, IN: Indiana University Press.
Bogost, I. (2012) *Alien Phenomenology: Or What it is Like to Be a Thing.* Minneapolis, MN: University of Minneapolis Press.
Boix-Fuster, E. (ed.) (2015) *Urban Diversities and Language Policies in Medium-Sized Linguistic Communities.* Bristol: Multilingual Matters.
Bourdieu, P. (1985) The social space and the genesis of groups. *Social Science Information* 24 (2), 195–220.
Bouzée, P. (1767) *Grammaire Générale, ou Exposition Raisonnée des Eléments Nécessaires du Langage, pour Servir de Fondement a L'étude de Toutes les Langues.* Paris: J. Barbou.
Braudel, F. (1982) *The Wheels of Commerce.* New York: Harper Row.
Brenner, N. (2011) The urban question and the scale question: Some conceptual clarifications. In A. Glick-Schiller and A. Caglar (eds) *Locating Migration: Rescaling Cities and Migrants* (pp. 23–41). Ithaca, NY: Cornell University Press.
Brenner, N. and Schmid, C. (2014) The 'urban age' in question. *International Journal of Urban and Regional Research* 38 (3), 731–755.
Brenner, N. and Schmid, C. (2015) Towards a new epistemology of the urban. *City* 19 (2–3), 151–182.
Bronfenbrenner, U. (1979) *The Ecology of Human Development*: Experiments by Nature and Design. Cambridge, MA: Harvard University Press.
Bronfenbrenner, U. (1999) Environments in developmental perspective: Theoretical and operational models. In S.L. Friedman and T.D. Wachs (eds) *Measuring Environment across the Lifespan: Emerging Methods and Concepts* (pp. 3–28). Washington, DC: American Psychological Association.
Bruner, J. (1986) *Actual Minds: Possible Worlds.* Cambridge, MA: Harvard University Press.
Bryant, L.R. (2011) *The Democracy of Objects.* Ann Arbor, MI: Open Humanities Press.
Bryant, L.R., Srnicek, N. and Harman, G. (eds) (2011) *The Speculative Turn: Continental Materialism and Realism.* Melbourne: re.press.
Cameron, D. (2006) Ideology and language. *Journal of Political Ideologies* 11 (2), 141–152.
Canagarajah, S. (ed.) (2017) *The Routledge Handbook of Migration and Language.* London: Routledge.
Canagarajah, S. (2018) Translingual practice as spatial repertoires: Expanding the paradigm beyond structuralist orientations. *Applied Linguistics* 39 (1), 31–54.
Canagarajah, S. and De Costa, P. (2016) Introduction: Scales analysis, and its uses and prospects in educational linguistics. *Linguistics and Education* 34, 1–10.
Carter, E., Donald, J. and Squires, J. (1993) *Space and Place: Theories of Identity and Location.* London: Lawrence and Wishart.
Casey, E. (1998) *The Fate of Place: A Philosophical History.* Berkeley, CA: University of California Press.
Cerruti, M. and Tsiplakou, S. (eds) (2020) *Intermediate Language Varieties: Koinai and Regional Standards in Europe.* Amsterdam: John Benjamins.

Chappell, P., Benson, P. and Yates, L. (2018) ELICOS students' out-of-class language learning experiences: An emerging research agenda. *English Australia Journal* 33 (2), 43–48.

Chik, A. (2014) Digital gaming and language learning: Autonomy and community. *Language Learning and Technology* 18 (2), 85–100.

Chik, A. (2016) Creativity and technology in in second-language learning and teaching. In R. Jones and J.C. Richards (eds) *Creativity in Language Teaching: Perspectives From Research and Practice* (pp. 180–195). London: Routledge.

Chik, A. (2019) Becoming and being multilingual in Australia. In P. Kalaja and S. Melo-Pfeifer (eds) *Visualising Multilingual Lives: More than Words* (pp. 15–32). Bristol: Multilingual Matters.

Chik, A. (2020) Humorous interaction, language learning, and social media. *World Englishes* 39 (1), 22–35.

Chik, A. and Benson, P. (2008) Frequent flyer: A narrative of overseas study in English. In P. Kalaja, V. Menezes and A.M. Barcelos (eds) *Narratives of Learning and Teaching EFL* (pp. 155–170). London: Palgrave.

Chik, A. and Besser, S. (2011) International language test taking among young learners. *Language Assessment Quarterly* 8 (1), 73–91.

Chik, A., Benson, P. and Moloney, R. (eds) (2019) *Multilingual Sydney*. London: Routledge.

Chomsky, N. (1957) *Syntactic Structures*. The Hague: Mouton.

Chomsky, N. (1966) *Cartesian Linguistics: A Chapter in the History of Rationalist Thought*. Lanham, MD: University of America Press.

Chomsky, N. (1975) *Reflections on Language*. New York: Pantheon Books.

Chomsky, N. (1980) *Rules and Representations*. Oxford: Blackwell.

Chomsky, N. (2006) *Language and Mind*. Cambridge: Cambridge University Press.

Ciolfi, L. (2015) Space and place in digital technology research: A theoretical overview. In S. Price, C. Jewitt and B. Brown (eds) *The SAGE Handbook of Digital Technology Research* (pp. 159–173). London: Sage.

Cole, J. and Vanderplank, R. (2016) Comparing autonomous and class-based learners in Brazil: Evidence for the present-day advantages of informal out-of-class learning. *System* 61, 31–42.

Cook, V.J. (1992) Evidence of multicompetence. *Language Learning* 42 (4), 557–591.

Coulmas, F. (2013) *Writing and Society: An Introduction*. Cambridge: Cambridge University Press.

Cresswell, T. (2015) *Place: An Introduction* (2nd edn; first published, 2004). Malden, MA: Blackwell.

Cronin, M. (2003) *Translation and Globalization*. London: Routledge.

Cunliffe, D. and Herring, S.C. (2005) Introduction to minority languages, multimedia and the web. *New Review of Hypermedia and Multimedia* 11 (2), 131–137.

Danet, B. and Herring, S.C. (2007) *The Multilingual Internet: Language, Culture and Communication Online*. Oxford: Oxford University Press.

Dear, M. (1997) Postmodern bloodlines. In G. Benko and U. Strohmayer (eds) *Space and Social Theory: Interpreting Modernity and Postmodernity* (pp. 49–71). Oxford: Blackwell.

Dear, M., Ketchum, J., Luria, S. and Richardson, D. (eds) (2011) *Geohumanities: Art, History, Text and the Edge of Place*. London: Routledge.

De Certeau, M. (1984) *The Practice of Everyday Life* (trans. Steven Rendall; first published in French, 1980). Berkeley, CA: University of California Press.

DeLanda, M. (2006) *A New Philosophy of Society*. London: Continuum.

DeLanda, M. (2015) *Philosophy and Simulation: The Emergence of Synthetic Reason*. London: Bloomsbury.

DeLanda, M. (2016) *Assemblage Theory*. Edinburgh: Edinburgh University Press.

DeLanda, M. and Harman, G. (2017) *The Rise of Realism*. Cambridge: Polity.

Deleuze, G. and Guattari, F. (2013) *A Thousand Plateaus* (trans. Brian Massumi; first published in French, 1980). London: Bloomsbury.

Descartes, R. (1850) *Discourse on the Method of Rightly Conducting One's Reason and of Seeking Truth in the Sciences* (trans. John Veitch; first published in French, 1637). Edinburgh: Sutherland and Knox.

Dong, J. and Blommaert, J. (2016) Global informal learning environments and the making of Chinese middle class. *Linguistics and Education* 34, 33–46.

Douglas Fir Group (2016) A transdisciplinary framework for SLA in a multilingual world. *The Modern Language Journal* 100 (Supplement), 19–47.

Duarte, J. and Gogolin, I. (eds) (2013) *Linguistic Superdiversity in Urban Areas: Research Approaches*. Amsterdam: John Benjamins.

Duchêne, A. and Heller, M. (eds) (2012) *Language in Late Capitalism: Pride and Profit*. London: Routledge.

Duchêne, A., Moyer, M. and Roberts, C. (eds) (2013) *Language, Migration and Social Inequalities: A Critical Sociolinguistic Perspective on Institutions and Work*. Bristol: Multilingual Matters.

Eco, U. (1995) *The Search for the Perfect Language*. Oxford: Blackwell.

Egbert, J. and Hanson-Smith, E. (eds) (1999) *CALL Environments: Research, Practice and Critical Issues*. Alexandria, VA: TESOL.

Eskildsen, S. and Theodórsdóttir, G. (2015) Constructing L2 learning spaces: Ways to achieve learning inside and outside the classroom. *Applied Linguistics* 38 (2), 143–164.

Evans, J. and Jones, P. (2011) The walking interview: Methodology, mobility and place. *Applied Geography* 31 (2), 849–858.

Ferrante, E. (2019) *Incidental Inventions*. New York: Europa Editions.

Firth, A. and Wagner, J. (1997) On discourse, communication and (some) fundamental concepts in SLA research. *The Modern Language Journal* 81 (3), 285–300.

Foucault, M. (1980) Questions on geography (trans. C. Gordon; first published in French, 1967). In C. Gordon (ed.) *Power/Knowledge: Selected Interviews and Other Writings 1972–1977* (pp. 63–77). Brighton: The Harvester Press.

Foucault, M. (1986) Of other spaces. *Diacritics* 16, 22–27.

Fowler, C.A. and Hodge, B.H. (2011) Dynamics and languaging: Toward an ecology of language. *Ecological Psychology* 23 (3), 147–156.

Friginal, E. (2009) Threats to the sustainability of the call center industry in the Philippines: Implications for language policy. *Language Policy* 8, 51–68.

Fromkin, V., Rodman, R., Hyams, N., Amberber, M., Cox, F. and Thornton, R. (2018) *An Introduction to Language* (Australia and New Zealand 9th edn). Melbourne: Cengage.

Gamble, C., Gowlett, J. and Dunbar, R. (2014) *Thinking Big: How the Evolution of Social Life Shaped the Human Mind*. London: Thames and Hudson.

Gao, S. and Park, J.S. (2015) Space and language learning under the neoliberal economy. *L2 Journal* 7 (3), 78–96.

Garcia, T. (2014) *Form and Object: A Treatise on Things*. Edinburgh: Edinburgh University Press.

García, O. and Fishman, J. (eds) (2002) *The Multilingual Apple: Languages in New York*. Berlin: de Gruyter.

Gardner, D. and Miller, L. (1999) *Establishing Self-Access: From Theory to Practice*. Cambridge: Cambridge University Press.

Garrido, M.R. and Sabaté-Dalmau, M. (2020) Transnational trajectories of multilingual workers: Sociolinguistic approaches to emergent entrepreneurial selves. *International Journal of Multilingualism* 17 (1), 1–10.

Gibson, J.J. (1979) *The Ecological Approach to Visual Perception*. Boston, MA: Houghton Mifflin Company.

Giddens, A. (1985) Time, space and regionalisation. In D. Gregory and J. Urry (eds) *Social Relations and Spatial Structures* (pp. 265–295). Basingstoke: Macmillan.

Gieseking, J.J., Mangold, W., Katz, C., Low, S. and Saegert, S. (eds) (2014) *The People, Place, and Space Reader*. New York: Routledge.

Glück, H. (2014) The history of German as a foreign language in Europe. *Language and History* 57 (1), 44–58.
Goethals, P. (2015) Travelling through languages: Reports on language experiences in tourists' travel blogs. *Multilingua* 34 (3), 347–372.
Golledge, R.G. (1999) Human wayfinding and cognitive maps. In R.G. Golledge (ed.) *Wayfinding Behavior: Cognitive Mapping and Other Spatial Processes* (pp. 5–45). Baltimore, MD: John Hopkins University Press.
Gomes, C. (2015) Negotiating everyday life in Australia: Unpacking the parallel society inhabited by Asian international students through their social networks and entertainment media use. *Journal of Youth Studies* 18 (4), 515–536.
Graham, S. (1998) The end of geography or the explosion of place? Conceptualizing space, place and information technology. *Progress in Human Geography* 22 (2), 165–185.
Gramling, D. (2016) *The Invention of Monolingualism*. London: Bloomsbury.
Gregory, D. (1978) *Ideology, Science and Human Geography*. London: Hutchinson.
Gregory, D. and Urry, J. (eds) (1985) *Social Relations and Spatial Structures*. Basingstoke: Macmillan.
Hägerstrand, T. (1973) The domain of human geography. In R.J. Chorley (ed.) *Directions in Geography* (pp. 67–87). London: Methuen.
Hall, E.T. (1966) *The Hidden Dimension*. Garden City, NY: Doubleday.
Halliday, M.A.K. (1970) Language structure and language function. In J. Lyons (ed.) *New Horizons in Linguistics* (pp. 140–165). London: Penguin.
Halliday, M.A.K. (1978) *Language as Social Semiotic*. London: Edward Arnold.
Halliday, M.A.K. (2003) Introduction: On the 'architecture' of human language. In J. Webster (ed.) *The Collected Works of M.A.K. Halliday. Volume 3: On Language and Linguistics* (pp. 1–30). London: Continuum.
Harman, G. (2016) *Immaterialism*. Oxford: Polity.
Harman, G. (2018) *Object-Oriented Ontology: The New Theory of Everything*. London: Pelican.
Harris, R. (1990) On redefining linguistics. In H.G. Davis and T.J. Taylor (eds) *Redefining Linguistics* (pp. 18–52). London: Routledge.
Harris, Z. (1981) *A Theory of Language and Information: A Mathematical Approach*. Oxford: Clarendon Press.
Harvey, D. (1969) *Explanation in Geography*. London: Edward Arnold.
Harvey, D. (1973) *Social Justice and the City*. Athens, GA: University of Georgia Press.
Harvey, D. (1975) The geography of capitalist accumulation: A reconstruction of the Marxian theory. *Antipode* 7 (2), 9–21.
Harvey, D. (1978) The urban process under capitalism: A framework for analysis. *International Journal of Urban and Regional Research* 2 (1–3), 101–131.
Harvey, D. (1982) *The Limits to Capital*. Oxford: Blackwell.
Harvey, D. (1989) *The Condition of Postmodernity*. Oxford: Blackwell.
Harvey, D. (2006) *Spaces of Global Capitalism: A Theory of Uneven Geographical Development*. London: Routledge.
Heidegger, M. (1977) Being, dwelling, thinking. In M. Heidegger (ed.) *Poetry, Language, Thought* (pp. 145–162). New York: Harper Row.
Held, D., McGrew, A., Goldblatt, D. and Perraton, J. (1999) *Global Transformations. Politics, Economics, Culture*. Cambridge: Polity.
Hellermann, J., Thorne, S.L. and Haley, J. (2019) Building socio-environmental infrastructures for learning in the wild. In J. Hellermann, S. Eskildsen, S. Pekarek-Doehler and A. Piirainen-Marsh (eds) *Conversation Analytic Research on Learning-in-Action: The Complex Ecology of Second Language Interaction 'in the Wild'* (pp. 193–218). Cham: Springer.
Higgins, C. (2015) Intersecting scapes and new millennium identities in language learning. *Language Teaching* 48 (3), 373–389.

Higgins, C. (2017) Space, place, and language. In S. Canagarajah (ed.) *The Routledge Handbook of Migration and Language* (pp. 102–116). London: Routledge.

Higgins, C. (2019) Place-based narratives among new speakers of 'Ōlelo Hawai'i. In R. Piazza (ed.) *Discourses of Identity in Liminal Places and Spaces* (pp. 193–216). New York: Routledge.

Higgins, C. and Ikeda, M. (2019) The materialization of language in tourism networks. *Applied Linguistics Review* 12 (1), 123–152. https://doi.org/10.1515/applirev-2019-0100

Hjelmslev, L. (1961) *Prologomena to a Theory of Language* (trans. F.J. Whitfield; first published in Danish, 1943). Madison, WI: University of Wisconsin Press.

Hobbs, M. and Dofs, K. (2018) Spaced out of zoned in? An exploratory study of spaces enabling autonomous learning in two New Zealand tertiary learning institutions. In G. Murray and T. Lamb (eds) *Space, Place and Autonomy in Language Learning* (pp. 201–208). London: Routledge.

Hobsbawm, E. (1990) *Nations and Nationalism since 1780: Programmes, Myths, Reality*. Cambridge: Cambridge University Press.

Hogan-Brun, G., Mar-Molinero, C. and Stevenson, P. (eds) (2009) *Discourses on Language and Integration: Critical Perspectives on Language Testing Regimes in Europe*. Amsterdam: John Benjamins.

Holden, C.L. and Sykes, J.M. (2011) Leveraging mobile games for place-based language learning. *International Journal of Game-based Learning* 1 (2), 1–18.

Howatt, A.P.R. (1984) *A History of English Language Teaching*. Oxford: Oxford University Press.

Hu, G. (2005) Contextual influences on instructional practices: A Chinese case for an ecological approach to ELT. *TESOL Quarterly* 39 (4), 635–660.

Hubbard, P., Kitchin, R. and Valentine, G. (eds) (2004) *Key Thinkers on Space and Place*. London: Sage.

IELTS (2012) Demand for IELTS increases around the world. See https://www.ielts.org/news/2012/demand-for-ielts-increases-around-the-world (accessed 19 February 2021).

IELTS (2017) IELTS numbers rise to three million. See https://www.ielts.org/news/2017/ielts-numbers-rise-to-three-million-a-year (accessed 19 February 2021).

Ingold, T. (2011) *The Perception of the Environment: Essays on Livelihood, Dwelling and Skill* (reissue; first published 2001). London: Routledge.

Ingold, T. and Vergunst, J.L. (eds) (2008) *Ways of Walking: Ethnography and Practice on Foot*. London: Routledge.

International Organisation for Migration (2019) *World Migration Report 2020*. Geneva: IOM.

Jacquemet, M. (2012) Language, media and digital landscapes. In P. Auer, A. Stukenbrock, B. Szmrecsanyi and M. Hilpert (eds) *Space in Language and Linguistics* (pp. 473–493). Berlin: Walter de Gruyter.

Jakobson, R. and Halle, M. (1956) *Fundamentals of Language*. The Hague: Mouton.

Jameson, F. (1984) Postmodernism, or the cultural logic of late capitalism. *New Left Review* 146, 53–92.

Janta, H., Lugosi, P., Brown, L. and Ladkin, A. (2012) Migrant networks, language learning and tourism employment. *Tourism Management* 33 (2), 431–439.

Johnson, S. (1755) *A Dictionary of the English Language*. London: W. Strahan.

Johnston, R. (2009) Spatial science. In R. Kitchin and N.J. Thrift (eds) *International Encyclopedia of Social Science* (pp. 384–395). Amsterdam: Elsevier Science.

Joseph-Lester, J., King, S., Blier-Carruthers, A. and Botazzi, R. (2020) *Walking Cities: London*. London: Routledge.

Joyce, J. (1986) *Ulysses* (first published, 1922). London: Bodley Head.

Kalaja, P. and Pitkänen-Huhta, A. (eds) (2018) Visual methods in applied language studies. Special issue of *Applied Linguistics Review* 9 (2–3), 157–473.

Kalaja, P. and Melo-Pfeifer, S. (eds) (2019) *Visualising Multilingual Lives: More than Words*. Bristol: Multilingual Matters.

Kandinsky, W. (1946) *On the Spiritual in Art* (edited by H. Rebay). New York: Solomon Guggenheim Foundation.

Kashiwa, M. (2019) Ecologies of language learning and teaching: Teacher cognition of language learning environments beyond the classroom. Unpublished PhD thesis, Macquarie University.

Kashiwa, M. and Benson, P. (2018) A road and a forest: Conceptions of the relationship between in-class and out-of-class learning at home and abroad. *TESOL Quarterly* 52 (4), 725–747.

Keil, R. (2017) *Suburban Planet: Making the World Urban from the Outside in*. Cambridge: Polity.

Kelly, L.G. (1969) *25 Centuries of Language Teaching*. Rowley, MA: Newbury House.

Kilroy, P. (2016) Discovery, settlement or invasion? The power of language in Australia's historical narrative. *The Conversation* April 1, 2016.

King, L. and Carson, L. (eds) (2016) *The Multilingual City: Vitality, Conflict and Change*. Bristol: Multilingual Matters.

Kinginger, C. (2009) *Language Learning and Study Abroad: A Critical Reading of Research*. New York: Palgrave Macmillan.

Kramsch, C. (ed.) (2002) *Language Acquisition and Language Socialization: Ecological Perspectives*. London: Continuum.

Kramsch, C. (2008) Ecological perspectives on foreign language education. *Language Teaching* 41 (3), 389–408.

Kramsch, C. (2014) Teaching foreign languages in an era of globalization: An introduction. *Modern Language Journal* 98 (1), 296–311.

Kulstad, M. and Carlin, L. (2013) Leibniz's philosophy of mind. In E.N. Zalta (ed.) *The Stanford Encyclopedia of Philosophy* (Winter 2013 Edition). See https://plato.stanford.edu/archives/win2013/entries/leibniz-mind/ (accessed 19 February 2021).

Kuper, H. (1972) The language of sites in the politics of space. *American Anthropologist* 74 (3), 411–440.

Kuure, L. (2011) Places for learning: Technology-mediated language learning practices beyond the classroom. In P. Benson and H. Reinders (eds) *Beyond the Language Classroom* (pp. 35–46). Basingstoke: Palgrave Macmillan.

Lai, C. (2015) Perceiving and traversing in- class and out-of- class learning: Accounts from foreign language learners in Hong Kong. *Innovation in Language Learning and Teaching* 9 (3), 265–284.

Lai, C. (2017) *Autonomous Language Learning with Technology beyond the Classroom*. London: Bloomsbury.

Lai, C., Zhu, W. and Gong, G. (2015) Understanding the quality of out-of-class English learning. *TESOL Quarterly* 49 (2), 278–308.

Laihonen, P. and Szabó, T.P. (2018) Studying the visual and material dimensions of education and learning. *Linguistics and Education* 44, 1–3.

Lakoff, G. (2013) Neural social science. In D.D. Franks and J.H. Turner (eds) *Handbook of Neurosociology* (pp. 9–26). Dordrecht: Springer.

Lamb, M. (2004) 'It depends on the students themselves': Independent language learning at an Indonesian state school. *Language, Culture and Curriculum* 17 (3), 229–245.

Lamb, T. (2015) Towards a plurilingual habitus: Engendering interlinguality in urban spaces. *International Journal of Pedagogies and Learning* 10 (2), 151–165.

Lamb, T. and Vodicka, G. (2018) Collective autonomy and multilingual spaces in super-diverse urban contexts: Interdisciplinary perspectives. In G. Murray and T. Lamb (eds) *Space, Place and Autonomy in Language Learning* (pp. 9–28). London: Routledge.

Lantolf, J.P. (1996) SLA theory-building: 'Letting all the flowers bloom!' *Language Learning* 46 (4), 713–749.

Larsen-Freeman, D. (2001) Individual cognitive/affective learner contributions and differential success in SLA. In M.P. Breen (ed.) *Learner Contributions to Language Learning: New Directions in Research* (pp. 12–24). London: Longman.
Larsen-Freeman, D. and Cameron, L. (2008) *Complex Systems and Applied Linguistics*. Oxford: Oxford University Press.
Latour, B. (2005) *Reassembling the Social: An Introduction to Actor-Network Theory*. Cambridge: Cambridge University Press.
Lawrence, D.H. (1921) *Sea and Sardinia*. New York: Thomas Seltzer.
Layder, D. (2004) *Social and Personal Identity: Understanding your Self*. London: Sage.
Lee, C. (2017) *Multilingualism Online*. London: Routledge.
Lefebvre, H. (1976) *The Survival of Capitalism: Reproduction of the Relations of Production*. New York: St Martin's Press.
Lefebvre, H. (1977) *De l'État*. Paris: Union Générale d'Éditions.
Lefebvre, H. (1991) *The Production of Space* (trans. D. Nicholson-Smith). Oxford: Blackwell.
Leibniz, G.W. (1896) *New Essays Concerning Human Understanding* (trans. A.G. Langley; first published in Latin, 1664). London: Macmillan.
Lévi-Strauss, C. (1963) *Structural Anthropology*. New York: Basic Books.
Lewis, M. (1993) *The Lexical Approach: The State of ELT and a Way Forward*. Hove: Language Teaching Publications.
Lewis, R. (2012) *Language, Mind and Nature: Artificial Languages in England from Bacon to Locke*. Cambridge: Cambridge University Press.
Li, W. (2018) Translanguaging as a practical theory of language. *Applied Linguistics* 39 (1), 9–30.
Lightfoot, D. (2006) *How New Languages Emerge*. Cambridge: Cambridge University Press.
Little, D. (2015) University language centres, self-access learning and learner autonomy. *Cahiers d'APLIUT* 34 (1), 1–13.
Locke, J. (1690) *An Essay Concerning Human Understanding*. London: Thomas Basset.
Lorente, B.P. (2018) *Scripts of Servitude: Language, Labor Migration and Transnational Domestic Work*. Bristol: Multilingual Matters.
Low, S. (2016) *Spatializing Culture: The Ethnography of Space and Place*. New York: Routledge.
Macfarlane, R. (2003) *Mountains of the Mind: A History of a Fascination*. London: Granta Books.
Maingueneau, D. (2009) *Aborder la Linguistique*. Paris: Points.
Mandel, E. (1975) *Late Capitalism*. London: Verso.
Marx, K. (1967) *Capital: A Critique of Political Economy* (3 vols). New York: International Books.
Marx, K. (1973) *Grundrisse*. London: Penguin/New Left Review.
Marx, K. and Engels, F. (1970) *The German Ideology*. New York: International Publishers.
Massey, D. (1985) New directions in space. In D. Gregory and J. Urry (eds) *Social Relations and Spatial Structures* (pp. 1–8). Basingstoke: Macmillan.
Massey, D. (1991) Flexible sexism. *Environment and Planning D: Society and Space* 9 (1), 31–57.
Massey, D. (1994) *Space, Class, and Gender*. Cambridge: Polity.
Massey, D. (2005) *For Space*. London: Sage.
Matras, Y. (2009) *Language Contact*. Cambridge: Cambridge University Press.
Matras, Y. and Robertson, A. (2015) Multilingualism in a post-industrial city: Policy and practice in Manchester. *Current Issues in Language Planning* 16 (3), 296–314.
May, S. (ed.) (2014) *The Multilingual Turn: Implications for SLA, TESOL and Bilingual Education*. London: Routledge.
Mazereanu, E. (2019) Market size of the global language services industry, 2009–2021. See statista.com/statistics/257656/size-of-the-global-language-services-market (accessed 19 February 2021).

Mercer, S. (2016) The contexts within me: L2 self as a complex dynamic system. In J. King (ed.) *The Dynamic Interplay between Context and the Language Learner* (pp. 11–28). Basingstoke: Palgrave Macmillan.

Merleau-Ponty, M. (2012) *Phenomenology of Perception*. London: Routledge.

Meskill, C. and Guan, S. (2012) Learning languages in cyberspace. In Z. Yan (ed.) *Encyclopedia of Cyber Behavior* (pp. 1136–1144). Hershey, PA: IGI Global.

Miéville, C. (2009) *The City and the City*. London: Macmillan.

Milton, J. (1644) *Of Education: To Samuel Hartlib*. London: T. Underhill and T. Johnson.

Molinié, M. (2019) From the migration experience to its visual narration in international mobility. In P. Kalaja and S. Melo-Pfeifer (eds) *Visualising Multilingual Lives: More than Words* (pp. 73–94). Bristol: Multilingual Matters.

Moore, A. (2008) Rethinking scale as geographical category: From analysis to practice. *Progress in Human Geography* 32 (2), 203–225.

Moores, S. (2012) *Media, Place and Mobility*. Basingstoke: Palgrave Macmillan.

Morton, T. (2013) *Realist Magic: Objects, Ontology, Causality*. Ann Arbor, MI: Open Humanities Press.

Müller, M. (1864) *Lectures on the Science of Language*. London: Longman.

Murray, G. (2018) Researching the spatial dimension of learner autonomy. In A. Chik, N. Aoki and R. Smith (eds) *Autonomy in Language Learning and Teaching: New Research Agendas* (pp. 93–113). London: Palgrave Macmillan.

Murray, G. and Lamb, T. (eds) (2018) *Space, Place and Autonomy in Language Learning*. London: Routledge.

Murray, G., Fujishima, N. and Uzuki, M. (2014) The semiotics of place: Autonomy and space. In G. Murray (ed.) *Social Dimensions of Autonomy in Language Learning* (pp. 81–99). Basingstoke: Palgrave Macmillan.

Mynard, J. and Edlin, C. (2016) Virtual and other learning spaces: Introduction to the special issue. *Studies in Self-Access Learning Journal* 7(2), 110–114.

Neisser, U. (1976) *Cognition and Reality*. San Francisco, CA: Freeman.

Newgarden, K. and Zheng, D. (2016) Recurrent languaging activities in World of Warcraft: Skilled linguistic action meets the Common European Framework of Reference. *ReCALL* 28 (3), 274–304.

Newton, I.S. (1962) *Mathematical Principles of Natural Philosophy* (trans. A. Motte, 1729; revised F. Cajori; first published in Latin, 1687). Berkeley, CA: University of California Press.

Ng, C.F. (2016) Behavioral mapping and tracking. In R. Gifford (ed.) *Research Methods for Environmental Psychology* (pp. 29–52). Oxford: Wiley Blackwell.

Nunan, D. (2003) The impact of English as a global language on educational policies and practices in the Asia-Pacific region. *TESOL Quarterly* 37 (4), 589–613.

Nunan, D. and Richards, J.C. (eds) (2015) *Language Learning beyond the Classroom*. London: Routledge.

Ochs, E. (2012) Experiencing language. *Anthropological Theory* 12 (2), 142–160.

Ollerhead, S. (2019) Teaching across semiotic modes with multilingual learners: Translanguaging in an Australian classroom. *Language and Education* 33 (2), 106–122.

O'Neill, M. and Roberts, B. (2020) *Walking Methods: Research on the Move*. London: Routledge.

O'Rourke, B. and Pujolar, J. (2015) New speakers and processes of new speakerness across time and space. *Applied Linguistics Review* 6 (2), 145–150.

Ortega, L. (2014) Ways forward for a bi/multilingual turn. In S. May (ed.) *The Multilingual Turn: Implications for SLA, TESOL and Bilingual Education* (pp. 32–53). London: Routledge.

Palfreyman, D. (2014) The ecology of learner autonomy. In G. Murray (ed.) *Social Dimensions of Autonomy in Language Learning* (pp. 175–191). Basingstoke: Palgrave Macmillan.

Panofsky, E. (1957) *Gothic Architecture and Scholasticism.* Cleveland, OH: The World Publishing Company.
Pascoe, B. (2018) *Dark Emu: Aboriginal Australia and the Birth of Agriculture.* Broome: Magabala Press.
Patel, R. and Moore, S. (2018) *A History of the World in Seven Cheap Things: A Guide to Capitalism, Nature, and the Future of the Planet.* Oakland, CA: University of California Press.
Peake, L., Patrick, D., Reddy, R.N., Tanyildiz, G.S., Ruddick, S. and Tchoukaleyska, R. (2018) Placing planetary urbanization in other fields of vision. Introduction to a special issue of *Environment and Planning D: Society and Space,* 36 (3) 374–386.
Pennycook, A. (2007) *Global Englishes and Transcultural Flows.* London: Routledge.
Pennycook, A. (2012) *Language and Mobility: Unexpected Places.* Bristol: Multilingual Matters.
Pennycook, A. (2018) Posthumanist applied linguistics. *Applied Linguistics* 39 (4), 445–461.
Pennycook, A. and Otsuji, E. (2015) *Metrolingualism: Language in the City.* London: Routledge.
Peterson, M. (2016) The use of massively multiplayer online role-playing games in CALL: An analysis of research. *Computer Assisted Language Learning* 29 (7), 1181–1194.
Phipps, A. (2007) *Learning the Arts of Linguistic Survival: Languaging, Tourism, Life.* Clevedon: Channel View Publications.
Piller, I. (2016) *Linguistic Diversity and Social Justice: An Introduction to Applied Sociolinguistics.* Oxford: Oxford University Press.
Poulantzas, N. (1978) *State, Power and Socialism.* London: Verso.
Pred, A. (1977) The choreography of existence: Comments on Hägerstrand's time-geography and its usefulness. *Economic Geography* 53 (2), 207–221.
Prigogine, I. and Stengers, I. (1984) *Order Out of Chaos: Man's New Dialogue with Nature.* London: Verso.
Rampton, B. (1997) Retuning in applied linguistics. *International Journal of Applied Linguistics* 7 (1), 3–25.
Reinders, H. and Benson, P. (2017) Language learning beyond the classroom: A research agenda. *Language Teaching* 50 (4), 561–578.
Reinhardt, J. and Thorne, S.L. (2020) Digital games as language-learning environments. In J. Plass, R. Mayer and B. Homer (eds) *Handbook of Game-Based Learning* (pp. 409–435). Cambridge, MA: MIT Press.
Richardson, M. (1982) Being-in-the-market versus being-in-the-plaza: Material culture and the construction of social reality. *American Ethnologist* 9 (2), 421–436.
Roberts, S. (2010) Listening to (and saving) the world's languages. *The New York Times,* 29 April. See https://www.nytimes.com/2010/04/29/nyregion/29lost.html (accessed 19 February 2021).
Robertson, S. (2013) *Transnational Student-Migrants and the State: The Education-Migration Nexus.* Basingstoke: Palgrave Macmillan.
Rodman, M. (1992) Empowering place: Multilocality and multivocality. *American Anthropologist* 94 (3), 640–656.
Rojo, L.M. and Del Percio, L. (eds) (2020) *Language and Neoliberal Governmentality.* London: Routledge.
Rose, G. (1993) *Feminism and Geography: The Limits of Geographical Knowledge.* Minneapolis, MN: University of Minnesota Press.
Rose, G. (2016) *Visual Methodologies: An Introduction to Researching with Visual Materials* (4th edn; first published, 2001). London: Sage.
Sánchez, A. (2014) Spanish as a foreign language in Europe: Six centuries of language teaching materials. *Language and History* 57 (1), 59–74.
Sassen, S. (1991) *The Global City: New York, London and Tokyo.* Princeton, NJ: Princeton University Press.

Saussure, F. de (1983) *Course in General Linguistics* (trans. R. Harris; first published in French, 1916). London: Duckworth.
Scollon, R. (2001) *Mediated Discourse: The Nexus of Practice*. London: Routledge.
Sebald, W.G. (2002) *The Rings of Saturn*. London: Vintage.
Shields, R. (2006) Knowing space. *Theory, Culture and Society* 23 (2–3), 147–149.
Simmel, G. (1997) The metropolis and mental life (first published in German, 1903). In D. Frisby and M. Featherstone (eds) *Simmel on Culture: Selected Writings* (pp. 174–185). London: Sage.
Singleton, D. and Aronin, L. (2007) Multiple language learning in the light of the theory of affordances. *Innovation in Language Learning and Teaching* 1 (1), 83–96.
Smakman, P. and Heinrich, D. (eds) (2018) *Urban Sociolinguistics: The City as a Linguistic Process and Experience*. London: Routledge.
Smith, N. (1991) *Uneven Development: Nature, Capital and the Production of Space*. Oxford: Blackwell.
Smythe, S., Hill, C., MacDonald, M., Dagenais, D., Sinclair, N. and Toohey, K. (2017) Materiality and language learning in classrooms. In S. Smythe, C. Hill, M. MacDonald, D. Dagenais, N. Sinclair and K. Toohey (eds) *Disrupting Boundaries in Education and Research* (pp. 34–58). Cambridge: Cambridge University Press.
Sockett, G. (2014) *The Online Informal Learning of English*. Basingstoke: Palgrave Macmillan.
Soja, E. (1989) *Postmodern Geographies: The Reassertion of Space in Critical Social Theory*. London: Verso.
Soja, E. (2009) Taking space personally. In B. Wharf and S. Arias (eds) *The Spatial Turn: Interdisciplinary Perspectives* (pp. 11–35). London: Routledge.
Stanek, L. (2008) Space as a concrete abstraction: Hegel, Marx and modern urbanism in Henri Lefebvre. In K. Goonewardena, S. Kipfer, R. Milgrom and C. Schmid (eds) *Space, Difference, and Everyday Life: Henri Lefebvre and Radical Politics* (pp. 62–79). New York: Routledge.
Stauffer, R.C. (1957) Haeckel, Darwin, and ecology. *The Quarterly Review of Biology* 32 (2), 138–144.
Sussman, R. (2016) Observational methods: The first step in science. In R. Gifford (ed.) *Research Methods for Environmental Psychology* (pp. 9–28). Oxford: Wiley Blackwell.
Thibault, P. (2011) First-order languaging dynamics and second-order language: The distributed language view. *Ecological Psychology* 23 (3), 210–245.
Thorne, S.L. (2008) Transcultural communication in open internet environments and massively multiplayer online games. In S. Magnan (ed.) *Mediating Discourse Online* (pp. 305–327). Amsterdam: John Benjamins.
Thorne, S. (2013) Language learning, ecological validity, and innovation under conditions of superdiversity. *Bellaterra Journal of Teaching and Learning Language and Literature* 6 (2), 1–27.
Toffoli, D. (2020) *Informal Learning and Institution-Wide Language Provision: University Language Learners in the 21st Century*. Basingstoke: Palgrave Macmillan.
Toohey, K., Dagenais, D., Fodor, A., Hof, L., Nunez, O. and Singh, A. (2015) 'That sounds so coool': Digital tools and literacy practices. *TESOL Quarterly* 49 (3), 461–485.
Trudgill, P. (2017) The spread of English. In M. Filppula, J. Klemola and D. Sharma (eds) *The Oxford Handbook of World Englishes* (pp. 14–34). Oxford: Oxford University Press.
Tuan, Y. (1977) *Space and Place. The Perspective of Experience*. Minneapolis, MN: University of Minnesota Press.
Tudor, I. (2003) Learning to live with complexity: Towards an ecological perspective on language teaching. *System* 31 (1), 1–12.
Tupas, A. (ed.) (2015) *Unequal Englishes: The Politics of English Today*. Basingstoke: Palgrave Macmillan.
Umino, T. and Benson, P. (2016) Communities of practice in study abroad: A four-year study of an Indonesian student's experience in Japan. *The Modern Language Journal* 100 (4), 1–18.

Umino, T. and Benson, P. (2019) Study abroad in pictures: Photographs as data in life-story research. In P. Kalaja and S. Melo-Pfeifer (eds) *Visualising Multilingual Lives: More than Words* (pp. 173–193). Bristol: Multilingual Matters.

United Nations (2018) 68% of the world population projected to live in urban areas by 2050, says UN. *United Nations Department of Economic and Social Affairs News*, 16 May. See https://www.un.org/development/desa/en/news/population/2018-revision-of-world-urbanization-prospects.html (accessed 19 February 2021).

Urry, J. (2007) *Mobilities*. Cambridge: Polity.

Ushioda, E. (2015) Context and complex dynamic systems theory. In Z. Dörnyei, P.D. MacIntyre and A. Henry (eds) *Motivational Dynamics in Language Learning* (pp. 47–54). Bristol: Multilingual Matters.

Van Lier, L. (1988) *The Classroom and the Language Learner: Ethnography and Second Language Classroom Research*. London: Longman.

Van Lier, L. (2000) From input to affordance: Social-interactive learning from an ecological perspective. In J.P. Lantolf (ed.) *Sociocultural Theory and Second Language Learning* (pp. 245–259). Oxford: Oxford University Press.

Van Lier, L. (2002) An ecological-semiotic perspective on language and linguistics. In C. Kramsch (ed.) *Language Acquisition and Language Socialization: Ecological Perspectives* (pp. 140–164). London: Continuum.

Van Lier, L. (2004) *The Ecology and Semiotics of Language Learning: A Sociocultural Perspective*. Boston, MA: Kluwer Academic Publishers.

Virilio, P. (1994) *The Vision Machine*. Bloomington, IN: Indiana University Press.

Vygotsky, L.S. (1994) The problem of the environment. In R. van der Veer and J. Valsiner (eds) *The Vygotsky Reader* (pp. 338–354). Oxford: Blackwell.

Wharf, B. and Arias, S. (eds) (2009) *The Spatial Turn: Interdisciplinary Perspectives*. London: Routledge.

White, C. and Bown, J. (2018) Emotion in the construction of space, place and autonomous learning opportunities. In G. Murray and T. Lamb (eds) *Space, Place and Autonomy in Language Learning* (pp. 29–43). London: Routledge.

White, S.H. and Siegel, A.W. (1984) Cognitive development in time and space. In B. Rogoff and J. Lave (eds) *Everyday Cognition: Its Development and Social Context* (pp. 238–277). Cambridge, MA: Harvard University Press.

Whitney, W.D. (1875) *The Life and Growth of Language: An Outline of Linguistic Science*. New York: D. Appleton.

Whorf, B. (1956) *Language, Thought and Reality: Selected Writings*. Cambridge, MA: MIT Press.

Wilken, R. and Goggin, G. (2012) *Mobile Technology and Place*. London: Routledge.

Wilkins, J. (1668) *An Essay towards a Real Character and a Philosophical Language*. London: Gellybrand and Martin.

Wilton, A. and Ludwig, C. (2018) Multilingual linguistic landscapes as a site for developing learner autonomy. In G. Murray and T. Lamb (eds) *Space, Place and Autonomy in Language Learning* (pp. 76–94). London: Routledge.

World Bank (2020) *World Bank Open Data*. See http://data.worldbank.org (accessed 19 February 2021).

Wray, A. (2008) *Formulaic Language and the Lexicon*. Cambridge: Cambridge University Press.

Wyld, H.C. (1907) *The Historical Study of the Mother Tongue: An Introduction to Philological Method*. London: John Murray.

Zheng, D., Liu, Y., Lambert, A., Lua, A., Tomei, J. and Holden, D. (2018) An ecological community becoming: Language learning as first-order experiencing with place and mobile technologies. *Linguistics and Education* 44, 45–57.

Index

abstraction, 29
   concrete abstraction, 29, 39
actor-network theory, 31, 121
affordance, 95
agency, 94, 112
applied linguistics, 8
assemblage, 69
   language-bearing assemblage, 6, 9, 65–89, 101; definition, 75; mobilities of, 81–85, 115–116, 119
   social assemblage, 6–7, 78–79, 83–84, 99, 101
assemblage theory, 6, 66–71
   detachability of components, 69–70, 76
   downward causality, 70, 76, 84
augmented reality, 125

context, 1
   and space, 1
   context vs. environment, 7
conversation analysis, 126–127

design-based research, 136
diary, online GPS-enabled, 133, 136
dictionaries, 57–62, 85
digital games, 125

ecology,
   ecology of language learning, 7, 94–98
   ecology of learning, 7, 92–94
   ecology of visual perception, 22–23
environment, 22–23, 31, 94
   environment vs. context, 7, 9
   person and environment, 33
   vs. setting, 9
environmental psychology, 14, 32, 137–138

globalisation, 16, 140
   of biography, 114
   and mobilities of language, 81–85
   and second language learning, 1–3, 85–88, 114–117
   of SLA research, 4
grammar books, 43–46, 57–62, 84

interaction
   among human and non-human objects, 30–31, 97–98

language,
   as abstract object, 43
   artificial languages, 46
   as assemblage, 74
   and nation state, 84–85
   as object or process, 72
   as physical or non-physical object, 9, 66–7, 70–71, 71–72, 73
   and reason, 44–45
   spatiality of language, 38, 42–56, 61, 66
   and speech, 76, 78–79
   standardisation of, 59, 60–62, 84–85
   systemic views, 41, 50, 60
   and thought, 76–78
language classroom research, 3, 122
language learning environment, 7, 91–117
   areal, 7, 99, 100–111, 134

individual, 7, 99, 111–114, 135; as assemblage, 112–113; as configuration of settings, 113
of international students, 106, 131–133
learners relation to, 96, 114
environmental resources, 97–98, 101–104
online resources in, 108–111
second and first language learning environment, 96–97
transitions between environments, 113, 130–131
language testing, 87
linguistics, 5, 37–63
Chomskyan linguistics, 38, 44–45, 54–57, 62
comparative philology, 47–49, 84–85
computational linguistics, 62
Hallidayan linguistics, 54–57, 62
history of linguistics, 42–56
integrated approaches, 38
Saussurean linguistics, 37, 49–53
structuralism, 53
twentieth-century linguistics, 54–56
localisation, 87

mobilities, 2, 79–88
of digital information, 83, 109
of language-bearing assemblages, 6–7, 81–88, 115–116, 119
mobility systems, 80–81
mobilities theory, 6
mobility of people, 86–87,
monolingualism, 59–60, 100
multilingual cities, 2, 88, 104–108, 112, 121
multilingualism, 2, 92, 100, 121, 121, 128

narrative inquiry, 121–122, 136
neoliberalism, 30

object
definition, 8
human and non-human, 30–31; non-human objects in language learning, 126
observation, 137–138

ontology
flat ontology, 68, 92
object-oriented ontology, 6, 8, 67–71
spatial ontology, 66

place
place vs. space, 32–33
Port Royal Grammar, 43–46

scale, 24, 79, 83–84, 99, 101, 122–123
second language acquisition (SLA), 1
complex and dynamic systems theory, 95
conception of language in, 63, 65
definition, 8
social turn in, 1, 11
sociocultural theory, 95
space in SLA research, 119–140
transdisciplinarity in, 11
second language learning, 65, 91–117
definition, 8
inequities in, 7, 114–117
and language policy, 101
objects-*in*-space and objects-*as*-space views, 92
out-of-class language learning, 3, 128–129
study abroad, 129–133
second language teaching, 57–58, 87, 116–117
setting, 93, 98
for language learning, 101–14, 135; definition, 102; and environment, 113
social learning space, 124
social sciences, 40–41
sociolinguistics, 41
and SLA research, 120–124
sociolinguistics of globalisation, 12, 81–82
space
disciplinary space, 39–42; in social sciences, 40; in linguistics, 41
empty space, Newtonian conception of, 18–19, 20–21, 39, 40, 45, 53, 55
empty space, production of, 27–29, 60

fragmentation of space, 27, 30–31, 42, 104–105
mental space, 40
online space, 108–111
in SLA research, 119–140; research agendas, 133–136; research methods, 136–140
spatial metaphors, 21–22, 23, 62, 86, 109–110; in Saussure 51–52; in Chomsky and Halliday, 55–56
objects-*in*-space vs. objects-*as*-space view, 4–5, 11, 20, 22, 34, 53, 65–66
physicality of space, 18–23
relational space, 22
spatial theory, 4, 11–35
critical spatial theory, 11–12
in geography, 12
Marxist spatial theory, 12, 17, 24–27, 30
postmodern spatial theory, 12–13, 17, 30
social construction of place, 5, 14, 31–34
social production of space, 5, 11, 24–29, 115–116
spatial science, 12

time geography, 31
translation, 87, 115–116

urbanisation, 26–27
planetary urbanisation, 26

visual research methods, 138–139

walking research methods, 139–140
writing, 57, 61, 76, 78–79

For Product Safety Concerns and Information please contact our EU Authorised Representative:

Easy Access System Europe

Mustamäe tee 50

10621 Tallinn

Estonia

gpsr.requests@easproject.com

www.ingramcontent.com/pod-product-compliance
Ingram Content Group UK Ltd.
Pitfield, Milton Keynes, MK11 3LW, UK
UKHW020241200525